WAR WITHOUT END

IN

NIGERIA

LANDMINES, BOMBS & EXPLOSIVE REMNANTS OF WAR
(THE LAW, TREATY, CONVENTIONS, PRACTICE AND
PROCEDURE IN ECOWAS COURT)

NOEL AGWUOCHA CHUKWUKADIBIA

Published by: **Cleanbills Publishers**

Copyright © 2014 **NOEL AGWUOCHA CHUKWUKADIBIA**

ISBN: 9781502834867

All rights reserved. This book is copyright and no part of it may be re-printed, stored in a retrieval system, or transmitted in any form or by any means, electronic, mechanical, electrostatic, magnetic tape, photocopying, recording or otherwise, without the written permission of the copyright owner.

Printed by: **Charleston, SC, United States of America**

DEDICATION

To **Dr. Goodluck Ebele Jonathan** GCFR (Nigeria), **Barak Hussein Obama** (USA), **Xi Jinping** (China) and **Francois Hollande** (France) for their fight against global violence and terrorism. And i*n honour of:*

The Hon. Justice Mahmud Mohammed (GCON, OFR) Chief Justice of Nigeria
The Hon. Justice Walter S. Nkanu Onnoghen (JSC, CON, CFR)
The Hon. Justice Suleiman Galadima (JSC, OFR, CFR)
The Hon. Justice Mary-Peter Odili (JSC, CFR)
Rt. Hon. Emeka Ihedioha CON, KSC
Hon. Justice Ibrahim Auta, Chief Judge, Federal High Court of Nigeria
Hon. Justice Paschal Nnadi, Chief Judge, Imo State
Hon. Justice P.I. Okpara, President, Customary Court of Appeal, Imo State
Hon. Justice Chioma Nwosu-Iheme (JCA)
Hon. Justice Nonye Okoronkwo (JCA)
Hon. Justice Ijeoma Agugua
Hon. Justice Goddy Anunihu
Hon. Justice Florence Duru-Oha Igwe
Hon. Justice P.C. Ikpeama
Hon. Justice Ononeze Madu
Hon. Justice Ogadinma Agada
Hon. Justice K.A. Ojiako
Hon. Justice S.M. Shuaibu
Hon. Justice F.C. Abosi
Hon. Justice V.U. Okorie
Hon. Justice Matthew Njoku
Mr. Lucius Nwosu SAN
Chief Arthur Eze
Mr. Sola Omole (DG NTA)
Mallam Ladan Salihu (DG FRCN)
Chief Leo-Stan Eke (MD ZINOX)
Prof. Mrs. Theresa Udenwa
Mr. Julius Nwagwu (Commander)
Mr. Ken Ojiri
Chief Tony Chukwu
And in memory of: Dappa Sogbere Ph.D and Miss Nkechi Osuji

TABLE OF CONTENTS
***** ***** *****

Dedication
Table of Contents
Cases Cited
List of Statutes
List of Abbreviations
Preface
Acknowledgment
Foreword
Introduction

Chapter One:	The War	1
Chapter Two:	Civil War Diary Of A Civilian	10
Chapter Three:	Mine Ban Treaty	34
Chapter Four:	After The War	52
Chapter Five:	Landmines And Explosive Remnants Of War	64
Chapter Six:	MBT and Road-Map In Selected Countries	78
Chapter Seven:	Victims Assistance	89
Chapter Eight:	Pleas In Law	94
Chapter Nine:	Nigeria's Response To Mine Ban Treaty	103
Chapter Ten:	Access To Ecowas Court	125
Chapter Eleven:	Victims And Human Rights	133
Chapter Twelve:	Locus Standi Of Landmines Victims To Sue State Parties To Mine Ban Treaty (MBT)	138
Chapter Thirteen:	Bombs	153
Appendix I		173
Appendix II		176
Appendix III		178
Appendix IV		183
References		219
Periodicals		219
Journals		219
Index		220

CASES CITED

ABACHA & ORS V. FAWEHINMI (2000) LEPLR – 14 (SC) PP 31 – 32; PARAS F – G
ADEPOJU V. OKE (1990) 3 NWLR (PT. 594) 154 at 169
AEGEAN SEA CONTINENTAL SHELF (GREECE V. TURKEY) ICJ Report 1976 at 15 – 16
AKOKHIA V. C.O.P. (1984) 5 NCLR 836
ATTORNEY GENERAL OF CROSS RIVER STATE & 2 ORS V. CHIEF OKON (2007) FWWB (EPT. 395) 370
BALARD V. GOMLINSON (1885) 29 Ch.D 115
C.A. SAVAGE & 2 ORS V. M.O. UWAECHUE (1972) 3 SC. 214
COOK V. GILL (1973) L.R. 8 C.P 107
DR. BASIL UKAEGBU V. ATTORNEY-GENERAL OF IMO STATE (1985) 1 S.C.N.L 212
EZEADUKWA V. MADUKA & ANOR (1997) LPELR – 8062 (CA) Pages 45 – 46; Para F – A
EZEUGO V. STATE (2013) LPELR–19984 (CA) Page 116; Para D –F
GANI FAWEHINMI V. ABACHA (1996) 9 NWLR, Part 475; P. 710
GBEMERE V. SHELL PET. DEV. COMPANY NIG. & ORS. In Suit No: FHC/CS/13/153/2005 (Unreported Decision) of 14 Nov. 2008
IBRAHIM V. OSIM (1987) 4 NWLR (PT. 67) at 365
JALLCO LTD V. OWONI BOYS TECH. SERVICES LTD (1995) 4 NWLR (PT. 391) 534; Para E – G
KUSADA V. SOKOTO NATIVE AUTHORITY DC 131/68 delivered on 13th December, 1968
MOSES V. KENROW NIG LTD (1992) 9 NWLR (PT. 264) 207 at 224
MOHAMMED VS OLAWUNMI (1990) NWLR (PT. 133) 458
MRS. YETUNDE ZAINAB TOLANI VS KWARA STATE JSC & ORS (2009) LPELF CA/IL/2/2008
NAFIU RABIU VS STATE (1981) 2 NCLR 293,
NASIRU BELLO & ORS VS. A.G OYO STATE (1986) 5 NWLR (PT. 45) 828.
OKPARA V. SHELL PET. DEV. COMPANY NIG LTD. SUIT N: FHC/PH/CS/518. Unreported Decision of federal High Court, Port Harcourt Division of 29 September, 2006
OSAWE V. REGISTRAR OF TRADE UNIONS (1983) 4 NCLR 556, H.C. Bendel State.
OSHEVIRE V. BRITISH CALEDONIAN AIRWAYS LTD (1990) 7 NWLR (PT. 163) PP 489 – 507 R.2
PAKUM INDUSTRIES LTD V. NIGER SHOE LTD (1985) 5 NWLR

(PT 93) at 134
PAULINUS NWAELE V. ENUGU STATE COMMISSIONER OF POLICE & ORS (2001) CHR 445
READ V. BROWN (1988) 22. Q.B.D. 128 (CA)
RINCO CONSTRUCTION CO. V. VEEPEE INDUSTRIES LTD (2008) 9 NWLR (PT. 929) 85; Pages 96 – 97; Para E – A
TAIWO V. TAIWO (1958) 3 FSC 80 at 182
THE REGISTERED TRUSTEES OF THE SOCIO-ECONOMIC RIGHTS AND ACCOUNTABILITY PROJECT (SERAC) VS PRESIDENT FEDERAL REPUBLIC OF NIGERIA 7 ORS
TIMOTHY VS. OFOKA (2008)9 NWLR (PT. 109) PG 204
UZOUKWU & ORS V. EZEONU II & ORS (1991) 6 NWLR (PT. 200) 708 at 759 – 760

LIST OF STATUTES

Convention on Certain Weapons (CCW) 1980
Harmful Waste (Special Criminal Provision etc.) ACT. Cap F10 LFN, 2004
Mine Action and effective coordination: the United Nations Policy A/56/448/Add 2 dated Sept. 1998
MINE ACTION PORTFOLIO 2010 - 2011
MINE BAN TREATY, 1997
NESREA ACT
PRACTICE DIRECTION IN ECOWAS COURT (2014)
PROTOCOL ON EXPLOSIVE REMNANTS OF WAR (Protocol V to the 1980 Convention), 28 November, 2003.
PROTOCOL ON EXPLOSIVE REMNANTS OF WAR (Protocol V to the 1980 Convention) 28 November, 2003
SUPPLEMENTARY PROTOCOL (A/SP.1/01/05) of ECONOMIC COMMUNITY OF WEST AFRICAN STATES
Terrorisim (Prevention) Act 2011, (LFN)

LIST OF ABBREVIATIONS

AC	-	Ammonium Chlorate
AFCARD	-	Armed Forced Convalescence and
AFRC	-	Armed Forced Convalescence and
AG	-	Action Group
AN	-	Ammonium Nitrate
AP	-	Anti Personnel
APM	-	Anti-Personnel Mine
ATM	-	Anti-Tank Mine
AU	-	African Union
AXO	-	Abandoned Explosives Ordnance
BAC	-	Battle Area Clearance
BLS	-	Base Line Survey
CCTV	-	Close Circuits Television
CCW	-	Convention on Certain Weapons
CPA	-	Comprehensive Peace Agreement
DRC	-	Democratic Republic of Congo
ECOWAS	-	Economic Community of West African State
EDD	-	Explosive Detection Dogs
ELIS	-	Ethiopian Landmine Impact Survey
EMAO	-	Ethiopian Mine Action Office
EOD	-	Explosive Ordnance Disposal
ERW	-	Explosive Remnants of War
HE	-	High Explosive
ICBL	-	International Campaign to Ban Landmines
ICJ	-	International Court of Justice
IED	-	Improvised Explosive Devices
IM	-	Information Management
ISU	-	Implementation Support Unit
KPC	-	Kosovo Protection Corps
LE	-	Low Explosives
LFN	-	Laws of the Federation of Nigeria
LGCCSB	-	Local Government and Customary Courts
LIS	-	Land Impact Survey

M.R.E	-	Mine Risk Educations
MBT	-	Mine Ban Treaty
MMC	-	Mechanicals Mine Clearance
MOD	-	Mine Detection Dogs
MOD	-	Ministry of Defence
NAP	-	Nairobi Action Plan
NATO	-	North Atlantic Treaty Organization
NGO	-	Non-governmental Organization
NPC	-	Northern Peoples Congress
OAS	-	Organization of American States
OPC	-	Odua Peoples' Congress
		Rehabilitation Department
		Rehabilitation Department Centre
		Service Boards
SHA	-	Suspected Hazardous Areas
TAB	-	Tajik-Afghan Border
TIA	-	Task Impact Assessment
TUB	-	Tajik Uzbek Border
U.N	-	United Nations
UNMAP	-	The United Nations Mine Action Programme
UPGA	-	United Progressives Grand Alliance
UXO	-	Unexploded Ordnance
WCC	-	World Council of Churches

PREFACE
*** *** ***

This book does not prophesy any doom or impending doom in Nigeria. It is not also suggestive of war or war situation. It is just a reminder to the Nation of Nigeria to wake up from a long-drawn slumber over the plight of the people of former Eastern Nigeria who are constantly traumatized by ugly reminders of echoes of war through abandoned and unregulated Landmines and explosive remnants of war. These landmines, Unexploded Ordnance and abandoned explosives Ordnance have not failed to be at war with unsuspecting Civilian population who regularly come in contact with them in their various locations where they patiently wait for their victims. Nigeria did not clear the war affected areas (states) of such contaminations since the civil war ended-and many have lived with the impression that there is no remedy.

The book has provided a gamut of remedies to affected landmines and explosive remnants of war victims as well as the forum where such grievances may be ventilated.

It has therefore, become imperative to finally put to end the events of the unfortunate War behind us as a country. Once the war affected areas are cleared of contaminants and available lands declared fit for Agricultural purposes, that civil war would have ended completely as their would be no more endemic reminders of the war. That would include the payment of compensation to thousands of landmines victims/survivors majority of whose mothers were not even born during that war. A good number of them die every year for want of care; and just before the publication of this book Miss Nkechi Osuji – a landmine victim and an orphan died in a road transport accident on Aba – Owerri road when she was going to collect some help from a politician. She, alongside others had taken the Nigerian Government to ECOWAS Court for an order of court to compel the Nigerian Government to clear was affected areas of South-East of Landmines and other explosive remnants of war. The book is the missing link to forgotten events of the Nigeria Civil War.

It is a conscious effort by the Author – a legal practitioner of note within regional courts and international tribunals to open up new vistas of legal practice to many Lawyers whose practice had been restrictive and limited to the provinces. I encourage Lawyers, Lecturers and students of legal studies to make this book a must read. This would even assist the Bench.

Chief Barr. Uzoma Onyeike (KSC)
Owerri, Imo State, Nigeria

ACKNOWLEDGEMENT
**** **** ****

An acknowledgement to a work of this nature cannot certainly be a true mirror of the gratitude owed the countless number of people whose direct and indirect contributions congealed the concept into this permanent shape and form. And not all with the short memory of man chain. None will the inadequate of words in the hands of a pupil be able to capture!

I express my gratitude to Mrs. Pauline Ijeoma Ufom, Dr. Mrs. Ada Madu (Ada Ikeduru), Dr. Emeka Uhegbu, Dr. Bala Yakubu, Jude Ujunwa Egbe, Vin. Agu, Nkechi Osuji, Joseph Egbujuo-Dike Ukwu and all my clients who are Victims of Mine Action. Interactions with all these people ignited my interest to research into this uncommon issue of Landmines and other explosive remnants of war contaminations in the former Eastern region.

I also place on record my vast gratitude to Chief Barr. Uzoma Onyeike, Barr. Alex Williams, Barr. Ike C. Ibe, Barr. Naths Epelle, Barr. Loveday Njoku, Barr. Emeka Nnadi, Barr. Nick Arikaibe, Amb. Moses Emeanuru, Etuk Essien John Esq, Prince Charles Ozuzu, Hon. Isaac Anyim, Hon. Nnanna Ugo, Augustine Nwachukwu, Emeka Izuka, Onyeze Kalu, Emeka Ugochukwu, my Secretary Justina Eluwe, Miss Ifunnaya Opara, Miss Ugomma Ibeto, Miss Ihuaku Onyeonoro, Sam Delight Uzoma, Obed Njoku, Chinedu Ike, Chike Ezenwilo, Barr. Charles Abiahu, Mrs. Chika Odom and Pat. Odom. I am, in addition thankful to my dear wife Ijeoma Stella Chukwukadibia, our children Ezinne, Chiziterem, Palispalis, Somachi, Chimeremeze and Bishop Chiemela for their prayerful support and forbearance. Let me acknowledge the contribution of Dr. Dappa Sogbere – a Chief Superintendent of Police and Author of "A Hand Book of Instructions on Explosives Ordnance Disposal (EOD) in the Nigeria Police" in granting me the permission to use and rely on chapter 6 and 7 of his book as He transited without sighting this book.

The support of the following persons who read through the manuscript and work is acknowledged - Prof Uba Nnabue, Prof Nnamdi Obiaraeri, Barr. Chris Okewulonu, Barr. Charles Onyeagbako, Dr. Tony Oha, Mr. Emma Ogu and Barr. Eugene Okolie, Barr. Frank Ezuma, Barr. Mrs. Uchenna Njoku, Barr. Godfrey I. Ijeoma and Barr. Elias Nwankwo Nwafor. For whatever error that are left or that are found in the book, I plead guilty!

Rt. Hon. Noel Agwuocha Chukwukadibia, KSC

FOREWORD
*** *** ***

War is actually not a tea party. Often, war takes place where communication breaks down or where there is insincerity, dishonesty and where ego leads the way of conscience. When this takes place, people or nations go to battle without taking into account thoroughly the consequences of such outing.

Going through this book reveals a conscious effort by the Author to expose the nonchalance of the Nigerian Authorities to the predicament of the people from the war affected communities of the Nigeria Civil War in the old Eastern Nigeria (now South-East and parts of South-South zones). Those people who did not die or who couldn't be killed in the cross fire of combatant soldiers during the Civil War upto the time of cessation of hostilities in 1970 became even more vulnerable to decimation by Landmines Actions as well as explosive remnants of war. What the Author seems to have reminded the Nigerian Authorities is to properly ensure that these forgotten parts of the Nigeria Civil War which entails the clearing of war affected communities of deadly ordnance contaminants should be revisited with speed as even those whose were not even born by the time the Civil War ended have since fallen victims of Landmines, Bombs, UXO's, AXO's abandoned by parties to the conflict.

In the absence of any thorough post civil war National Mine Action Plan, in the absence of a formal clearing and treatment of War Affected areas making the land free from contamination for Agricultural production, it does appear there is a suble contamination of the Nigeria Civil War.

The Author's argument about the latent consequences of abandonement of Mine Actions Victims as well as his concern to understand the social dynamics attendant to it, provide an historic context within which to consider the need to clear the war affected areas of the on-going environmental degradation, contamination and to completely demilitarize the affected zone. As it is now, Nigeria has not made peace with violence in so far as the sores of the war remain endemic. An all round peace package is needed in this country.

Prof. Francis Ukaigwe
Nkwere, Imo State, Nigeria

INTRODUCTION
**** **** ****

The initial intention at the commencement of this book was no more than to frank my pleadings in a human rights suit initiated by my clients who are landmines victims/survivors against the Federal Republic of Nigeria at the Community Court of Justice (ECOWAS). It was difficult and quite laborious to start as it seemed recondite because it was going to be the first time Mine Action Victims in any part of the globe would be taking a National Government or State Party to Court for the enforcement of their Fundamental Human Rights.

The discussion in this book is limited to remedies available to Victims of Landmines and other explosive remnants of war victims. It concerns particularly the rights of victims who neither participated in the Nigeria Civil War but were injured at the conation of conflicts. This group involves, those victims whose mothers may not even have been born during the period of any armed conflict, but who unfortunately became injured by well-laid but abandoned Landmines. This book is designed to be a guide in approaching the court on humanitarian issues under International Humanitarian Laws that abundantly dove-tail into guaranteed Fundamental Human Rights and jurisprudence.

This work is a conscious effort to engage the attention of Nigeria - a State Party to Mine Ban Treaty to the continuing and on-going discrimination against Mine Action Victims of the Nigerian Civil War. It is in addition an attempt to draw the attention of the Nigerian Government as well as the International Community to the fact of on-going and continuous contamination and degradation of war affected Communities of the Nigeria Civil War by the massive presence of Landmines, Bombs and other Explosive Remnants of War.

The case of the Nigerian Mine Action Victim is most pathetic. He is not known at the Local Government level not to talk about the State and Federal levels. Whether or not there are Landmine victims in the former Eastern Nigeria commands the least mention in the Nigeria media. I recall the moving question posed by Demining Consultant Dr. Bala Yakubu: "In a War we spent one million dollars daily to prosecute, can't we afford care center for victims of War?" We have soon forgotten those who died during the war, or the victims who have died since the end of the war from dangerous Ordnance and other Explosive Remnants of War left behind by the actors of that unfortunate war. We hasten to bring to the front burner Innocent Nigerian citizens who have suffered severe injuries after the war from huge explosive ordnance left behind by the military in their farms and environments. The only thing that Federal Government of Nigeria did immediately after the civil war with respect to War Victims who were mostly combatants was the establishment of a Rehabilitation programme; but this was strictly for Convalescence only and did not include skills acquisition before disengagement of Mine Victims who lost legs and hands.

Midway into the War in 1969, the Gowon's administration established the Armed Forces Convalescence and Rehabilitation Department (AFCARD). But immediately after the War, the Armed Forces Convalescence and Rehabilitation Department was upgraded to Armed Forces Convalescence and Rehabilitation Center (AFRC) to carter for the large number of victims of the war. But as soon as the Government settled from the War, it commenced the process of pruning down the large size of the Armed Forces especially from 250,000 to about 85,000 fighting soldiers. The first to go were victims of Landmines and other victims of the War. This set of victims were adequately compensated by the Ministry of Defence which worked out the basis and yardstick for such assistance.

The soldiers of the Nigerian Army were paid based on their disability status. However, an entirely different yardstick was used in respect of those numbers of the Nigerian Army coming from the Biafran side. Priority was given to those who were members of the Nigerian Army and Nigeria Police before the declaration of secession. They were to be re-absorbed into the Nigerian army and secondly examined by a medical Board; and considered based on the status of their injuries as their Nigerian army counterparts. Unfortunately the injured soldiers who were recruited by the defunct Biafra Authority were abandoned and left on their own, as a result of which most of them began to hiberanate around the River Niger Head Bridge and at various roundabouts as well as other big cities in the East.

The defunct Oji River Rehabilitation center was established by the Government of East Central State under Ajie Dr. Ukpabi Asika. The center in a short-while catered for injured Biafran War Soldiers. These ex-Biafran Soldiers faced the problem of non-categorization of disabilities and so could not be availed the benefit enjoyed by those absorbed by the Federal Government. It was this group of people that accounted for the large number of landmines and other explosive Remnants of War Victims. Following the creation of more States out from the defunct East Central State, victims of Landmines and other ERW's moved out of the Rehabilitation Center to their new States of Origin only to be forgotten as no such facility was on ground to accomodate them. These states did not set up Mine Victims peer-to-peer Group support programme. There ought to have been Camps or settlement centers established for the Mine Victims donor Agencies, as well as other humanitarian Agencies to know how and where to locate them. This did not take place and has not happened!

This is as it affects soldiers who sustained Mine Action Injuries during the Nigeria-Biafra War. The present work is concerned with Civilian populace who neither participated in the civil war nor fought on the sides of the Combatants/Parties to the conflict, but who were injured by landmines and other ERS's after the end of the Civil War on the 15th January, 1970. The victims' in their numbers and coming mostly from Civil War affected areas. All the farms fall within the territory now in firm control of the Federal Government of Nigeria. Nigeria ought to have embarked on Mine risk, education, or mine reduction exercises after the War but did nothing, and that failure of duty resulted to a large number of persons injured by landmines and other ERW's. These victims have since been abandoned, forgotten and in most cases not even known, only to have their succour within the cockpit of Fundamental Human Rights.

Noel Agwuocha Chukwukadibia
E-mail: nobus_nobus@yahoo.com
Website: www.noelagwuochachukwukadibia.com
Eziama Oparanadim, Ahiazu-Mbaise, Imo State, Nigeria.

"I believe in Nigeria, I love Nigeria and we all must work for Nigeria; that is everybody, the Government and the opposition, in order to make Nigeria great. That is my wish. Nigeria will survive beyond 2015" - *Gen. Yakubu Gowon (Rtd)Former Head of State of Nigeria, Daily Sun, Thursday October 2nd 2014 (44 YEARS AFTER THE CIVIL WAR)*

CHAPTER ONE

THE WAR

Historic Declaration of Biafra by Lt. Col. Chukwuemeka Odumegwu-Ojukwu, on May 30, 1967

"Fellow countrymen and women, you, the people of Eastern Nigeria;

Conscious of the supreme authority of Almighty God over all mankind, of your duty to yourselves and posterity;

Aware that you can no longer be protected in your lives and in your property by any Government based outside Eastern Nigeria;

Believing that you are born free and have certain inalienable rights which can best be preserved by yourselves;

Unwilling to be unfree partners in any association of a political or economic nature; Rejecting the authority of any person or persons other than the Military Government of Eastern Nigeria to make any imposition of whatever kind or nature upon you;

Determined to dissolve all political and other ties between you and the former Federal Republic of Nigeria; Prepared to enter into such association, treaty or alliance with any sovereign state within the former Federal Republic of Nigeria and elsewhere on such terms and conditions as best to serve your common good;

Affirming your trust and confidence in me; having mandated me to proclaim on your behalf, and in your name that Eastern Nigeria be a sovereign independent Republic. Now therefore, I, Lieutenant-Colonel Chukwuemeka Odumegwu-Ojukwu, Military Governor of Eastern Nigeria, by virtue of the authority, and pursuant to the principles recited above, do hereby solemnly proclaim that the territory and region known as and called Eastern Nigeria together with her continental shelf and territorial waters shall henceforth be an independent sovereign state of the name and title of The Republic of Biafra. And I Do Declare That:

(i)   All political ties between us and the Federal Republic of Nigeria are hereby totally dissolved.

(ii)   All subsisting contractual obligations entered into by the

(iii) Government of the Federal Republic of Nigeria or by any person, authority, organization or government acting on its behalf, with any person, authority or organization operating, or relating to any matter or thing, within the Republic of Biafra, shall henceforth be deemed to be entered into with the Military Governor of the Republic of Biafra for and on behalf of the Government and people of the Republic of Biafra, and the covenants thereof shall, subject to this Declaration, be performed by the parties according to their tenor;

(iii) All subsisting international treaties and obligations made on behalf of Eastern Nigeria by the Government of the Federal Republic of Nigeria shall be honoured and respected;

(iv) Eastern Nigeria's due share of all subsisting international debts and obligations entered into by the Government of the Federal Republic of Nigeria shall be honoured and respected.

(v) Steps will be taken to open discussions on the question of Eastern Nigeria's due share of the assets of the Federation of Nigeria and personal properties of the citizens of Biafra throughout the Federation of Nigeria.

(vi) The right, privileges, pensions, etc., of all personnel of the Public Services, the Armed Forces and the Police now serving in any capacity within the Republic of Biafra are hereby guaranteed;

(vii) We shall keep the door open for association with, and would welcome, any sovereign unit or units in the former Federation of Nigeria or any other parts of Africa desirous of association with us for the purposes of running a common services organization and for the establishment of economic ties;

(viii) We shall protect the lives and property of all foreigners in Biafra, we shall extend the hand of friendship to those nations who respect our sovereignty, and shall repel any interference in our internal affairs;

(ix) We shall faithfully adhere to the charter of the Organization of African Unity and the United Nations organization;

(x) It is our intention to remain a member of the British Commonwealth of Nations in our right as a sovereign, independent nation. Long live the Republic of Biafra! And may God protect all those who live in her."

"The Civil War is over"
Broadcast by (Biafran) Major-General Philip Effiong on Monday, January 12, 1970

"Fellow Countrymen, as you know, I was asked to be the officer administering the government of this Republic on the 10th of January, 1970. Since then, I know that some of you have been waiting to hear a statement from me. I have had extensive consultations with the leaders of the community, both military and civil, and I am now encouraged and hasten to make this statement to you by the mandate of the armed forces and the people of this country. I have assumed the leadership of the government.

Throughout history, injured people have had to resort to arms in their self-defense where peaceful negotiations fail. We are no exception. We took up arms because of the sense of insecurity generated in our people by the events of 1966. We have fought in defense of that cause. I take this opportunity to congratulate officers and men of our armed forces for their gallantry and bravery which had for them the admiration of the whole world. I thank the civil population of their steadfastness and courage in the face of overwhelming odds and starvation. I am convinced now that a stop must be put to the bloodshed which is going on as a result of war. I am also convinced that the suffering of our people must be brought to an immediate end. Our people are now disillusioned and those elements of the old government regime who have made negotiations and reconciliation impossible have voluntarily removed themselves from our midst.

I have therefore instructed an orderly disengagement of troops, I am dispatching emissaries to make contact with Nigeria's field commanders in places like Onitsha, Owerri, Awka, Enugu and Calabar with a view to arranging armistice. I urge General Gowon, in the name of humanity, to order his troops to pause while an armistice is negotiated in order to avoid the mass suffering caused by the movement of population. We have always believed that our differences with Nigeria should be settled by peaceful negotiations. A delegation of our people is there ready to meet representatives of Nigeria Federal Government anywhere to negotiate a peaceful settlement on the basis of OAU resolutions.

The delegation will consist of the Chief Justice, Sir Louis Mbanefo leader, Chief A.E Bassey and Mr. E. Aguma. The delegation will have full authority to negotiate on our behalf. I have appointed a council to advise me on the government of the country. It consists of long live the Chief Justice, Sir Louis Mbanefo, Brigadier P.C Amadi (Army),

Brigadier C.A. Nwawo (Army), Captain W.A. Anuku (Navy), Wing Commander J.I Ezeilo (Air Force), Inspector-General of Police, Chief P.I Okeke, Mr. J.I Emembolu (Attorney-General), Professor Eni Njoku, Dr I. Eke, Chief A.E, Udofia, Chief J. M Echeruo. Any question of government in exile is repudiated by our people.

Civilian population are hereby advised to remain calm and cooperate with the armed forces and the police in the maintenance of law and order. They should remain in their homes and stop mass movements which have increased suffering and loss of lives.

On behalf of our people, I thank those foreign governments and friends who have steadfastly given us support in our cause. We shall continue to count on their continued help and counsel. I also thank His Holiness the Pope, the Joint Church Aid and other relief organizations, for the help they have given for the relief of suffering and starvation. I appeal to all governments to give urgent help for relief and to prevail on the Federal Military Government to order their troops to stop all military operations.

May God help us all!"

Long live the Federal Republic of Nigeria.

****   ****   ****

Statement at Dodan Barracks on January 15, 1970 by Major-General Phillip Effiong (Administrative Officer, Republic of Biafra)

"I, Major-General Philip Efiong, Officer Administrating the Government of the Republic of Biafra, now wish to make the following declaration:

That we affirm that we are loyal Nigerian Citizens and accept the authority of the Federal Military Government of Nigeria. That we accept the existing Administrative and Political Structure of the Federation of Nigeria. That any future constitutional arrangement will be worked out by representatives of the people of Nigeria. That the Republic of Biafra hereby ceases to exist."

"The Dawn of National Reconciliation" – Gowon's Civil War Victory Message to the Nation, 15 January 1970

"Citizens of Nigeria,

It is with a heart full of gratitude to God that I announce to you that today marks the formal end of the Civil War. This afternoon at Dodan Barracks, Lt. Col. Philip Effiong, Lt. Col. David Ogunewe, Lt. Col.

Patrick Anwunah, Lt. Col. Patrick Amadi and Commissioner of Police, Chief Patrick Okeke Formally proclaimed the end of the attempt at secession and accepted the authority of the Federal Military Government of Nigeria. They also formally accepted the present political and administrative structure of the country. This ends thirty months of a grim struggle. Thirty months of sacrifice and national agony. Exactly four years ago on January 15, 1966, a group of young army officers overthrew the Government of the country with violence. The country hoped, however, that the military regime which followed would quickly restore discipline and confidence in the army and introduce a just, honest, patriot and progressive government. The country was disappointed in those hopes, there were further tragic incidents in the army leading to the death of many officers and men in July 1966.

I then assumed the leadership of the Federal Military Government. I gave a solemn pledge to work to reduce tension in the army and the country, to restore the Federal Constitution and to prepare the country for an orderly return to civilian rule as early as possible. Despite my efforts and the co-operation of all other members of the Supreme Military Council, the former Lt. Col. Ojukwu pushed us from one crises to another. This intransigent defiance of Federal Government Authority heightened tensions and led to the much regretted riots in September/October 1966. He subsequently exploited the situation to plunge the former Eastern Region into secession and the nation into a tragic war. The world knows how hard we strove to avoid the civil war. Our objectives in fighting the war to crush Ojukwu's rebellion were always clear. We desired to preserve the territory and unity of Nigeria. For as one country we would be able to maintain lasting peace amongst our various communities; achieve rapid economic development to improve the lot of our people; guarantee a dignified future and respect in the world for our prosperity and contribute to African Unity and modernization. On the other hand, the small successor states in a disintegrated Nigeria would be victims of perpetual war and misery and non-colonialism. Our duty was clear. And we are, today, vindicated.

The so-called "Rising Sun of Biafra" is set for ever. It will be great disservice for anyone to continue to use the word Biafra to refer to any part of the East Central State of Nigeria. The tragic chapter of violence is just ended. We are at the dawn of national reconciliation. Once again, we have an opportunity to build a new nation.

My dear compatriots, we must pay homage to the fallen. To the heroes, who have made the supreme sacrifice that we may be able to build a nation great in justice, fair play, and industry. They will be mourned for ever by a grateful nation. There are also the innocent men, women, and children who perished, not sided of this tragic fratricidal conflicts. Let it be our resolution that all those dead shall have not died in vain. Let the greater nation we shall build be their proud monument forever.

Now, my dear countrymen, we must recommence at once in grater earnest, the task of healing the nation's wounds. We have at various times repeated our desire for reconciliation in full equality, once the secessionist regime abandoned secession. I solemn repeat our guarantees of general amnesty for those misled into rebellion. We guarantee the security of life and property of all citizens in every part of Nigeria and equality in political rights. We also guarantee the right of every Nigerian to reside and work wherever he chooses in the Federation, as equal citizens of one united country. It is only right that freedom, taking into full account the legitimate right and needs of the other man. There is no question of second class citizenship in Nigeria. On our side, we fought the war with great caution, not in anger or hatred, but always in the hope that common sense would prevail. Many times we sought a negotiated settlement, not out of weakness, but in order to minimize the problems of reintegration, reconciliation, and reconstruction. We knew that however the war ended, in the conference room, our brothers fighting under other colours rejoin us and that we must together rebuild the nation anew. Those now freed from the terror and misery of the secessionist enclave are therefore doubly welcome. The nation is relieved. All energies will now be lent to the task of reintegration and reconciliation. They will find, contrary to the civil [thus in press release; but probably 'evil'?] propaganda with which they were fed, that thousands and thousands of Ibos have lived and worked in peace with other ethnic groups in Lagos and elsewhere in the Federation throughout the dark days of the civil war. There is, therefore, no cause for humiliation on the part of any group of the people of this country. The task of reconciliation is truly begun.

The nation will be proud of the fact that the ceremony today at Dodan Barracks of reunion under the banner of the Federal Republic of Nigeria was arranged and conducted by Nigerians amongst ourselves alone. No foreign good officers was involved. That is what we always prayed for. We always prayed that we should resolve our problems by ourselves, free from foreign mentors and go-betweens however well intentioned. Thus, our nation is come of age. And the meeting of today's event must be enshrined in the nation's memory for ever.

There is an urgent task to be done. The Federal Government has mounted a massive relief operation to alleviate the suffering of the people in the newly liberated areas. I have as announced, assigned special responsibility for this to a member of the Federal Executive Council. We are mobilizing adequate resources from the Federal Government to provide food, shelter, and medicines for the affected population. Rehabilitation and reconstruction will follow simultaneously to restore electricity, transport and communications. We must, as a matter of urgency, resettle firms and reopen factories to ensure that normal economic life is resumed by everyone as soon as possible. Special attention will be given to the rehabilitation of women and children in particular, so long denied the comfort of homes, the blessing of education and assurance of a future by Ojukwu's wicked tyranny and falsehood. We must restore at once to them hope and purpose in life.

Federal troops have a special charge to give emergency relief to the people in the areas they have liberated before civilian help can come. They must continue and testify their splendid work this regard. The state administrations are giving emergency relief the first priority. The rehabilitation Commissions and the Voluntary Agencies are extending their efforts. The appropriate agencies of Federal Government will soon make further announcements about additional relief measures.

My government has directed that former civil servants and public corporation officials should be promptly reinstated as they come out of hiding. Detailed arrangements for this exercise have been published. Plans for the rehabilitation of self-employed people will also be announced shortly. The problem of emergency relief is a challenge for the whole nation. We must prove ourselves equal to the task. Our resources, which have enabled us to prosecute the war successfully and without obligations to anyone, are considerable. I appeal to the nation for volunteers to help in the emergency relief operations in the newly liberated areas. Doctors, nurses, engineers, technicians, builders, plumbers, mechanics, and administrators - all skilled hands willing to help are urgently required. The detailed arrangements for recruitment will soon be announced. I am sure that there will be a prompt and good response to this call.

You will have heard that my Government may seek the assistance of friendly foreign governments and bodies, especially in the provision of equipment to supplement our national effort. There are, however, a number of foreign governments and organizations whose so-called assistance will not be welcome. There are the governments and organizations which sustained the rebellion. They are thus guilty of the act of love for humanity. Their purpose was to disintegrate Nigeria and Africa and impose their will estrange us again from one another with their dubious and insulting gifts and their false humanitarianism. Regarding the future, we shall maintain our purpose to work for stability with the existing political structure of a minimum of twelve states. The collision of three giant regions with pretentions to sovereignty created distrust and fear and to the tragic conflict now ending. The multi-state structure will therefore be retained with the minimum of present twelve states. Immediate post-war planning and reconstruction will continue on this basis. Any new constitution will then be the result of discussions by the representative of all the people of Nigeria.

I am happy that despite the war, Nigeria has maintained a strong and expanding economy. Plans also for advance for faster economic modernization. Our enormous material resources and our large dynamic population will make this possible. We pledge to ensure rapid development for the benefit of the Nigerian people themselves. It will be much easier to achieve reconciliation and reintegration in increasing prosperity.

Fellow countrymen, the civil war is truly over. We thank God. But the state of national emergency and emergency regulations remain. Discipline and sacrifice are essential if we are to achieve our goals in the immediate post-war period and lay sound foundation for the future. I demand your patience, resolution, and continued dedication. I demand of the workers and employers continued restraint in industrial relations in keeping with the recent decree. A decree on price control will soon be promulgated. We shall soon review wages and salaries to improve the lot of the ordinary man. The immediate economic problems are challenging and we must behave accordingly. On this occasion, I wish to place on record the nation's gratitude to the Organization of African Unity for its splendid diplomatic and moral support for the Federal cause. I thank particularly the Chairman of the Consultative Committee on Nigeria, His Imperial Majesty Haile Selassie and other members of the committee. I also thank the President of the OAU General Assembly, Presidents Mobutu, Boumedienne, and Ahidjo, who presided over OAU summit discussions of the Nigerian crises. The enemies of Africa were restrained by the demonstration of such solid support. I thank the Secretary General of the United Nations, U Thant, for his understanding attitude towards our country's crises and the specialized agencies for their assistance. I also thank the friendly governments who gave us moral and material support in the darkest hour of our need. The nation will remember them as true friends. It is the desire of my Government that our relations with them should grow stronger. Consistent with our basic policy, we shall maintain correct relations with all foreign governments notwithstanding the anxieties they may have caused us. As we emerge from our greatest trial we shall endeavour to work for peace in the world and for a better economic deal for the less developed countries of the world.

The Armed Forces deserve the greatest praise for their valour in battle, their loyalty and dedication and for their resourcefulness in overcoming the formidable obstacles placed in our way. I praise them for observing strictly the code of conduct issued to them at the beginning of the operations. It is necessary now more than ever when the rebellion is ended for them to maintain the high standard they have attained. The letter and spirit of the code must be obeyed. Their first duty is to protect the lives and property of all surrendering troops and civilians and to give them humane treatment. Stern disciplinary measure will be taken against any who violate the code. I know, however, that I can continue to count on your loyalty and discipline.

I also praise the civilian population everywhere in the country for their patience, sacrifice, loyalty, and steadfast support for the fighting troops and for One Nigeria. We must all be justly proud. All Nigerians share the victory of today. The victory for national unity, victory for hopes of Africans and black people everywhere. We must thank God for His mercies. We mourn the dead heroes. We thank God for sparing us to see this glorious dawn of national reconciliation. We have ordered that Friday, Saturday, and Sunday be national days of prayer. We must seek His guidance to do our duty and to contribute our quota to the building of a great nation, founded on the concerted efforts of all its people and on justice and equality. A nation never to return to the fractious, sterile and selfish debates that led to the tragic conflict just ending. We have overcome a lot over the past four years. I have therefore every confidence that we will become a great nation. So help us God."

CHAPTER TWO
CIVIL WAR DIARY OF A CIVILIAN

Nigeria had her Independence from the British Government on the 1st October, 1960. Some of her political leaders then included:

1. Dr. Nnamdi Azikiwe – President
2. Sir Abubakar Tafawa Balewa – Prime Minister
3. Chief Festus Okotie-Eboh – Federal Minister of finance
4. Dr. Michael I. Okpara – Premier, Eastern Region
5. Sir Ahmadu Bello, the Sadauna of Sokoto – Premier, Northern Region
6. Chief Samuel Ladoke Akintola – Premier, Western Region
7. Chief Dennis Osadebay – Premier, Mid-Western Region

The politicians started very well but after some time, they became very corrupt. Bribery and corruption was very common among them and Civil Servants. Politicians, started to misuse the Nations money. Large sums of money was carried away and saved in the foreign banks by same politicians and top civil servants.

In 1963, when the country had a national census, population figures were inflated in some regions in order to attract the national revenue. This led to disagreement, disaffection and dissatisfaction in different quarters. Finally, the National Census figures were rejected and cancelled by the Federal Government.

In 1964, the National Census was repeated and the result was still not satisfactory. Figures from some Regions were still doubtful. As the exercise involved heavy financial expenditure, the nation could not afford another count and the figures were accepted with considerable doubt.

In 1965, Regional Elections into the Western House of Assembly. Powerful political parties such as Northern Peoples Congress (NPC), United Progressive Grand Alliance (UPGA), Action Group (AG), presented opposing candidates, whose "tugs" became very dangerous and started burning down houses, cars and other property belonging to their opponents. Human beings were burnt alive in the Western Region. The Western Crisis continued for a long time and the Federal Government could not restore peace. There was oppression, discontent, bribery and corruption. The country was in confusion, many people were dissatisfied.

THE NATIONAL CRISIS

15th January, 1966: There was a coup d'état in the night, the Army overthrew the Government and took over from the Civilians. Many of the political leaders were killed including the Prime Minister - Sir Abubakar; the Premier of Western Region - Chief Samuel Akintola; the Premier of Northern Region – Sir Ahmadu Bello, the Federal Minister of Finance – Chief Festus Okotie Eboh. This ended the first Republic of Nigeria. Major General J.T.U. Aguiyi Ironsi, a native of Umuahia, became the first Military Head of State of Nigeria. He made promises and proposals for a better Government and everybody was happy for the Military takeover. The following Military Governors were appointed for the Regions

1. Northern Region – Lt. Col. Hassan Katsina
2. Eastern Region – Lt. Col. Chukwuemeka Odumegwu Ojukwu
3. Western Region – Col. Adekunle Fajuyi
4. Mid-West Region – Lt. Col. David Ejoor

29th July, 1966: The 2nd Military coup de tat by other Army officers. Major General Aguiyi Ironsi and Col. Adekunle Fajuyi his host were killed at Ibadan to the shock of every Nigerian. Many Military Officers from other Regions were also killed, especially officers of Eastern Nigeria (Ibo) origin.

1st August, 1966: General Yakubu Gowon declared himself the Military Head of State of Nigeria. He appointed Brigadier Adebayo as the Governor of Western Region in place of Col. Adekunle Fajuyi. There followed a general massacre of the Ibos in other parts of Nigeria, especially in the Northern Region. The Igbos were killed in thousands in the Northern towns; railway stations, motor stations and aerodromes. People were flown back to Eastern Region in pieces. Hospitals in the Eastern Region were filled to the brim by wounded people from Northern Nigeria. Col. C Odumegwu Ojukwu started calling the Igbos to come home. There was great distress, confusion and agony everywhere in the Eastern Region. The Igbos felt rejected by other Nigerians. Efforts were made by Lt. Col. Odumegwu Ojukwu to restore peace between the people of Eastern Nigeria and other Nigerians, but it was not possible.

4th January, 1967: Officials from Eastern Region under their Military Governor Ojukwu met the Nigerian Officials at Aburi in Ghana to find a solution to the crises. But the Nigerians gave very difficult conditions to the Igbos. Some of the agreements reached at Aburi were rejected by Nigeria, when they came back from Ghana. Trouble then continued in Nigeria.

27th May, 1967: General Yakubu Gowon created the 12 States of Nigeria viz: 1. North Western State; 2. North Central State; 3. North Eastern State; 4. Kano State; 5. Benue Plateau State; 6. Kwara State; 7. Western State; 8. Mid-West State; 9. Lagos State; 10. East Central State; 11. South Eastern State; 12. Rivers State.

30th May, 1967: The Republic of Biafra was declared by Col. Chukwuemeka Odumegwu Ojukwu. There was a great jubilation all over Eastern Region. The Igbos who felt pushed out of Nigeria were happy and prepared to die in defence of Biafra. General Gowon ordered Ojukwu to withdraw the declaration of Biafra. But the Biafrans were behind Ojukwu and promised to fight in defence of Biafra.

THE CIVIL WAR

6th July, 1967: Nigeria declared war against Biafra. They boasted of crushing Biafra in 48 hours. Nigeria imposed sea and air blockade against Biafra. Ships and Aeroplanes were stopped from bringing food, weapons and other foreign materials to Biafra. Life in Biafra became difficult. Young men happily joined the Biafra Army and Air force and was started from the border towns of Nsukka, Calabar, Awgu and Afikpo. Gradually, many of these border towns were deserted by Biafrans. War continued more seriously until Enugu was also taken by the Federal troops. People from Enugu, Nsukka, Calabar ran back to the remaining towns in Biafra.

Many University students from Nigeria and foreign Universities came home and joined the Army in defence of Biafra. But Nigeria, with her greater population, superior weapons and support by Great Britain, Russia and other African Countries proved very superior and more powerful over Biafra. Biafran Engineers and Scientists invented local bombs, grenades, war ships and amoured cars which helped Biafra to withstand Nigeria for some years. The Biafran "Ogbunigwe" popularly known among Nigerian Soldiers as "Ojukwu Bucket" was a terror to Nigerians and it killed them in hundreds.

The Civil War was so serious that almost all the young men and women in Biafra became Soldiers or Militia. Majority of people, especially children, old men and women died of hunger and disease – "Kwashiorkor". Charitable Organizations such as World Council of Churches (W.C.C); The International Red Cross Society; The Caritas

International, started bringing in food e.g. rice, beans, corn meal, tinned fish and meat, salt, stock fish and other food items into Biafra. This helped to save majority of lives in Biafra. As the war raged on with great difficulties and hardship against the Biafrans, many people started to sabotage the efforts of the Biafrans to survive the war. People in the Rivers State, South eastern State and Mid-West State who particularly supported Biafra, turned against Biafra. Even some Igbos including people from Ikwere, Onitsha, Enugu and Nsukka, crossed to the Nigerian side and started to plan and execute the war against Biafra. This resulted in great disappointed and hopelessness among the true Biafrans. Sabotage was one of the evils that greatly demoralized the true Biafran Civilian and army forces, and finally led to the collapse of the glorified Republic of Biafra.

The Biafran Government constructed new and modern Airports at Uli and Uga. This made it possible for friendly Aeroplanes from the above Charitable Organizations and Countries to bring in food materials and light weapons by night into Biafra. Friendly Aeroplanes carrying food and other materials into Biafra came in between 8.00pm and 5.00am. Even then, they were still attacked and often destroyed by the Nigerian war planes. Majority of Biafran Soldiers fought the war without uniforms, majority were almost naked. They had no shoes, no clothes, no food for many days and often no transport. At a stage, very young boys and old men were conscripted into the Biafran Army and with only two days military training, they were carried to the numerous war fronts, from where majority never came back. Yet, true Biafrans were not discouraged. As the Civil War continued in different sectors, many Biafrans towns were evacuated and occupied by the enemy e.g. Nsukka, Enugu and Calabar. The population of Port Harcourt increased as many people from the disturbed areas ran to Port Harcourt and resumed their business. Many young men joined the force.

Early in 1968, I decided to join the Biafran Army. I went for the army selection and was selected. But at night when I woke up and gave the war a serious thought, my conscience or "inner man" warned me never to join the Biafran Army. I took a decision to stay away and remain a civilian and give Biafra the necessary moral and financial support, as long as the war lasted. Port Harcourt became badly threatened by the enemy. There were rumours of many saboteurs in the town. True Biafrans became more vigilant and worried, because nobody wanted to lose the "Garden City" – Port Harcourt to the enemy.

16th May, 1968: Around 6.30am, the enemy or saboteurs started shelling

Port Harcourt to the great surprise of everybody. There was utter confusion in the town as rockets, bombs and shells landed here and there killing and wounding many people. Unfortunately, I had been very sick of serious malaria for the past few days and could not eat any food. I was trying to come down from the third-floor of No. 31 Potts Johnson Street, Port Harcourt where I lived to buy some food from the hotel, when this confusion started. On reaching the street, I saw many people carrying their loads and evacuating Port Harcourt. Many were lying down dead or crying, because of the rocket wounds they received. It was a horrible sight. I managed myself back to my room and through the window, I saw that Port Harcourt was becoming empty. I took up my handbag containing a few clothes, some documents and my certificates. My room was well furnished and everything I had was left in the room. I was too sick and weak to walk, I nearly decided to stay, but I tried to follow others.

On my way towards Diobu, I met a woman and begged her to help me carry my bag. We continued seeing dead bodies and wounded people in pulls of blood, yelling in pains for help, which was not possible. Patients lying in the hospitals ran away in their sick uniform, the very sick ones were abandoned behind to die. With the last breath, I reached mile one Diobu and bought some food. As I was eating, the shelling was directed towards Diobu and we had to move homewards. The road was filled up with men, women, children, cars and bicycles, everybody carrying a heavy load. The Army and Police blocked the road and were beating up people to go back to Port Harcourt. We continued pushing towards home, passing dead bodies of old men, women and children. People who could not walk or small children whose parents could not carry were abandoned on the road. Rockets and bombs continued landing along the road among great crowds of people going home. By 9.00pm, the shelling increased at Diobu, the army and police were helpless and gave way for people to go home. We walked 15 miles that night to Igirita, where we stayed at the motor station till the following morning.

17th May, 1968: I was so weak, with pains all over my legs and body and could not walk anymore. Fortunately, at about 5.30am I saw a friend driver one Mr. Sylvester Ezeukwu of Aro-Egbu Oguta, who was kind enough to take me in his van and brought me home in company of Ijego Regina Odunze his sister-in-law. My parents who were very anxious of the situation of Port Harcourt and my continued stay there, were very happy to see me. The evacuation of Port Harcourt shocked every true Biafran. People began to realize the seriousness of the war and the wickedness of the saboteurs. The Ikwere people who had been jealous of the Ibos, saw an opportunity to kill the Ibos. Majority of people who entered Ikwere Villages for protection were rounded up and massacred by the people who declared that they were not Ibos and that they support Nigeria. They claimed closer relationship with the Rivers people, who actually sabotaged all the Biafran efforts to retain Port Harcourt. Thus, the Ibos lost Port Harcourt and Ikwere people to the Rivers State. On arrival, I warned my people that since Port Harcourt was evacuated, there was no place that could resist the activities of the Nigerian Soldiers. The enemy continued pushing towards Owerri and Aba, but the ill-equipped Biafran forces continued to contain them for a few months. I reported at the Local Government office at Aba and was deployed and sent to Uratta County Council Owerri. The Secretary of the Council Mr. J.P. Inyang of Ikot-Ekpene, picked interest in me and posted me to Ara Umunwoha Court, where I worked on Rate Tickets. For several months in Port Harcourt, teachers were not paid. I was asked to continue under Uratta County Council until our salaries were paid. So I continued working until Owerri was disturbed and I left Owerri without payment.

14th September, 1968: Owerri was seriously threatened by saboteurs. Shelling noise and bomb explosions were heard very close to Owerri. People from Obinze, Oforola, Avu and Umuguma started evacuating their homes, moving towards Irette, Orogwe and other towns away from the vandals.

15th September, 1968: I was at Orogwe where I visited my sister Dorothy, when news came that Irette people were on the run and that the enemy had entered Owerri township. I ran back home meeting our people with their loads coming towards Orogwe. On arrival, I saw my people ready to move away from home. We hurriedly packed a few things and left to Orogwe where we stayed with Dorothy and her husband till the next day.

16th September, 1968: My parents and I came back to Irette, killed one of our goat and as we cooked the meat, shelling started to land at Irette. We took a few other things and the remaining goats and left to Orogwe. Orogwe was equally disturbed that afternoon. We moved to Ogbaku in company of my parents, our grandmother Madam Uchanwa, her son's wives and their children including Mr. G.U Nneji. Dorothy refused to move away from Orogwe. We left Orogwe to Okpala Ogbaku, people were panicking greatly as the enemies were around. I walked back from Ogbaku to Orogwe and persuaded Dorothy to follow us. She delayed our movement, but later followed us back to Okpala Ogbaku. The natives were badly worried as people from different places flocked into their villages.

17th September, 1968: The Ogbaku people were so afraid and started carrying property into the bush. We, the refugees followed them into the bush and made temporary sheds in the bush. We could hear children, goats and fowls crying all over the bush. In the night, a very heavy rain started and continued till morning. Everybody, including our old grandmother and our property was badly beaten by the heavy rain.

18th September, 1968: We were warned by the Biafran Soldiers that it was dangerous to stay in the bush. We sent some people to Obudi Agwa who bought us a cup of salt at £3 or £6.00 We got ready and I took my people to my friends at Obudi Agwa to Mr. Francis Obi's compound, where we stayed until Obudi Agwa was equally disturbed by the Nigerian vandals, despite desperate efforts by the natives to keep off the enemy.

5th October, 1968: Enemy rockets started to land at Obudi-Agwa, despite all efforts to contain the enemy. Everybody was disappointed. Life had already become very difficult. Many bicycles had no tyres. People had to carry heavy loads on their heads. I left with my people from Obudi-Agwa to Izombe on foot. We stayed with our relations at Izombe – Mrs. Ada Ugorji Nwauwa and her grown up sons and daughters. In a few days' time, the enemy reached Izombe, but they were beaten back to Obudi-Agwa. At Izombe, I suffered from frustration and abuse from Dorothy who was so wicked towards my mother and myself. My father equally was very unreasonable and wicked to me. At a stage I decided to avoid both Dorothy and my father as much as possible. I actually was very unhappy at Izombe.

12th October, 1968: My father and his in-law Mr. Silas Mbakwe took our grandmother who was abandoned by Mr. G.U. Nneji and his family at Izombe to Ejemekwuru where they stayed. They left us at Izombe because the family was observed to be too raw and noisy in their behavior. They became uneasy and left to Ejemekwuru Refugee Camp.

2nd November, 1968: Izombe was badly threatened as rockets from both Ogbaku and Obudi-Agwa landed at Izombe. We could not stay at Izombe. In the evening, we packed our things and moved to Mgbele near Nkwesi. I was given sleeping accommodation by the church teacher at Mgbele. In the morning, we entered the Refugee Camp. My father took us to his old friend Court Clerk – Mr. Ozor, who was friendly with us at

Mgbele. At Mgbele Refugee Camp, we stayed with refugees from Ogoni, Egbema, Okuku and other disturbed areas e.g. Agwa.

19th November, 1968: After a serious malaria disease which worried me, I travelled to Oguta to the Divisional Officer Mr. Chukwudolue and told him how I have been suffering since the war and asked him to help me. He was kind to me and appointed me as a security officer in charge of Mgbele Refugee Camp. He told me to bring my reports on my observations every week to his office. I was very grateful to him.

21st November, 1968: I was conscripted in the night by some Biafran Soldiers at Nkwesi. Other officials of the Refugee Camp and some of the Refugees were also conscripted. But I was released in the morning.

25th November, 1968: For several months past, I had only 6d or 5kobo in my pocket and tried to preserve it. My parents and Esther left Mgbele to Lawa in Ogbaku. My father after selling our remaining 3 goats, and some quantity of stock fish given to us, Could give me only £1. Biafran money which was almost valueless. I was surprised and begged him for more, but he refused. My mother was highly worried over my poor condition. Even Mr. Justice Nlemibe who was there with us begged my father to give me more money, but my father refused and left towards home. My mother gave me the only 10s she had, and left in tears.

27th November, 1968: I got my first share of stock fish as an officer in the camp. I sold it and bought garri, while Mrs. Comfort the wife of Mr. Justice Nlemibe started to help in feeding me, some days, I stayed without food.

28th December, 1968: I hired a bicycle from Nkwesi and followed some refugees from Ikwerre to Ohaji farm settlement village to buy garri in the evening we got a small quantity of garri from there and left at about 10:00pm and rode all the night to avoids conscript until we reached Mgbele at 2:30am a distance of about 15 miles.

13th January, 1969: My bicycle spoilt at the farm settlement Ohaji. My companions left me behind. I dragged the bicycle with a heavy load of garri in the night, through the bush path alone from the farm to Mgbele (15 miles) my companions who left me that night, were conscripted that night at Izombe. I suffered terribly.

27th January, 1969: News came to me at Mgbele that our grandmother who left us at Izombe had died in her home town-Umuguma. It was not possible for us to travel to Umuguma because of the war. Which became very serious against Biafra.

10th March, 1969: As I traded on Garri and medicine (tablets) my bag containing my medicines and other important documents was stolen at Izombe market, when I was repairing my bicycle. My trade on medicine at the farm settlement thus stopped.

15th March, 1969: Esther came to Mgbele and told of Theophilus my junior brother, who came back from the war front. She also told me of the death of Regina Eleogu wife of my uncle Geoffrey Okorie. There was heavy conscription along all roads. But I traveled with Esther on foot through Izombe, Akabor, Ejemekwuru, Amakohia-Ubi, Ndegwu to Irette, often through the bush paths to avoid the soldiers. I got home safely. I gave my mother the sum of £50 to keep for me and told her my experiences at Mgbele. I walked back at Mgbele at about 9:00pm the following day.

18th March, 1969: I left for the farm settlement to buy garri, but on the way I was conscripted. I was later released as a well-known person. We slept at the farm. My bicycle was spoilt and I dragged it along with a heavy load of garri throughout the following day. I reached Mgbele at about 4pm, very tired.

21st March, 1969: As a result of a circular letter from the Ministry of Education asking teachers to go back to school, I went to Oguta, reported to the D.O and went to the secretary of Oguta County Council for teaching appointment. The secretary posted me to L.A. School Mgbara – Egbema. I had never been to Egbema before, but I agreed to go in order to get my arrears of salaries from March 1968 to March 1969.

25th March, 1969: My friend Emmanuel Njiole Onwuka of Aro Igirita, who used to trade on garri with me, took me on his bicycle to the farm-settlement, where I spent the night because of heavy conscription. I reached Mgbara Egbema the following day being 26th March. I went to the Councilor Mr. Uwakwe, who received me well and actually became a father to me at Mgbara-Egbema. His yams and cassava were cleared by the Army but whenever he ate, he invited me to eat with him. Some days we stayed without food. I had other friends like Mr. Gabriel Kamalu, Mr. Aloysius Mefor, Gabriel Ugwuoha and Nathiel Chimezie, who helped me to manage life at Egbema. I started to buy cassava land from the natives and with the help of friendly soldiers, I got people who helped me to process the garri. I often hired refugees who harvested and grated the cassava for me. I took active part in the garri processing for the first time I fried garri in my life. I often bought cassava at ₤50 – ₤55 and after selling; I realized between ₤80 - ₤95. Through this method, I started to feed myself.

7th April, 1969: I had a dream which worried me greatly. In it, I met some student, friends at the control Post Owerri. One Mr. Shadrack Njoku of Umuoba Uratta told me to go and look for my wife Justina Ozurumba, whom I promised to marry, but because of the war we were separated for about one year, unable to locate the where-about of each other. Mr. S. Njoku warned me to go and take my wife that she was suffering greatly and waiting patiently for me. I was badly disturbed after this dream.

25th April, 1969: My mother arrived Egbema unexpectedly looking for me, she was brought to Egbema by our relation Mr. Olumba of Amafor Ohaji and I was highly surprised to see her. She brought the good news that they had received a massage from the father of Justy that they were anxious to know about me. I was told that Justy and her parents were at Umuomi-Ikeduru. My mother left after two days with a letter I wrote to Justy telling her of my where-abouts and promised to come and see her. I was very happy with this massage and encouraged to look for money for marriage with Justy.

5th May, 1969: I made a risky journey from Egbema on foot to Irette. I met several teams of conscriptors on the way, but I was able to escape being conscripted into the army. I got home safely. My parents were very happy to see me.

6th May, 1969: I left on foot to Egbu (Owerri) which had become a ghost town as the vandals were recently driven away from Owerri town. At Egbu, I met my mother in-law at the church compound where she went for Relief materials. She was very happy and greatly surprised to see me again. We got ready and set off to Uzagba Ikeduru where she said Justy was working in the treasury at Eziama – Ikeduru. The journey was so far and I was very much exhausted before we arrived there. My meeting with Justy after a very long time was a happy and remarkable one.

8th May, 1969: I traveled from Uzoagba through Amaimo, Ibem, Obolo and Umueze to Umuduru Mbano, to see the Zonal Inspector of Education in charge of Port Harcourt - Mrs. Okorocha to make enquiry about my salary He was surprised to see me and showed sympathy for my terrible suffering. He directed me to the former town clerk of Port Harcourt

Municipal Council, Mr. J.E Nyambi of Calabar, who was then at Etiti. My bicycle was too bad to carry me to Etiti, where conscription was very hot.

16th May, 1969: I took my parents and my uncle Geoffery Okorie to Ebgu to discuss my arrangement on marriage with Justina. I spent heavily that day and we left for Irette with Justy. There was curfew at Owerri town and the Police refused our journey that night to Irette. But after I had spoken so much to them, they were impressed and one of them offered to take us through the town to the control post from Egbu round-about a distance of about 2 miles. We were very grateful to the Police and got to Irette at about 11:00pm.

21st May, 1969: I left Irette for Umuduru-Mbano on bicycle. I was delayed on the way by bad bicycle. Offices were closed before I arrived. I slept at the Police station Umuduru Mbano. The following morning, I left to Etiti, where I met the town Clerk Mr. Nyambi, who gave me a letter asking me to explain my where-about since Port Harcourt was disturbed, before I could be paid my arrears of salaries according to the Local Government regulations. He asked me to make my explanations in triplicates and return them to him at Etiti. I left Etiti and rode back to Umuduru, then to Ikembara-Ikeduru, where I visited the Uratta Country Council Secretary Mr. J.P Inyang, who first developed me at Owerri. He gave me forms for my clearance. I left for home through Amauzari; Ogwa; Orodo; Ogbaku to Irette. My people were happy to see me as everybody was afraid of conscription. On the 24th May, I left home for Egbema, not minding the army conscription.

28th May, 1969: I left Egbema for Irette people and soldiers at Egbema warned me of the serious conscription on the way and concluded that I would not come back, unless as a soldier. I trusted in God and left. At the checkpoint I spoke so much and was permitted to pass on, till I reached Irette.

2nd June, 1969: I left Irette in the morning for Etiti in Okigwe. I repaired my bicycle at Owerri. I repaired my bicycle again at Ibeme-Mbano at ₤1.5s. I reached Etiti at about 7pm. I was stranded and passed the night with some staff of the Port Harcourt Municipal Council in their office.

3rd June, 1969: I met the town clerk who gave me his own letter attached to my written explanation and directed me to the secretary Local Government and Customary Courts Service Board at Isu County Council. Orlu. I rode all the way from Etiti, on the way I met some Army friends, who gave me some food. I reached Isu County Council very late at about 8:30pm and was told that the secretary's office was at Umuna-Orlu, about 5 miles away. I left that night to Umuna 9:30.pm and stayed on the road at the checkpoint with soldiers till morning.

4th June, 1969: I met the secretary of the Local Government and Customary Court Service Board, who after some delay gave me another letter to the Permanent Secretary Security Division Ministry of Defence, State House Enugu (Etiti). I left Umuna that afternoon back to Etiti at the heat of conscription. I reached Etiti at about 7:15pm and slept in the office with some Staff of the Port Harcourt Municipal Council.

5th June, 1969: I left the office early in the morning to Orieagu to meet the permanent Secretary Security Division. On arrival there I was told that he left to Uruala-Orlu the previous day. I was directed to the office of the Ministry of Foreign affairs to look for transport to Uruala. Through personal introduction, I got to know two boys from Irette who were working with the Ministry. Unfortunately, there was no dispatch to Uruala, I was then received by my town boys Mr. Emetom and Mr. Opara of Amaikpu Irette. They gave me breakfast. I could not ride back to Uruala on bicycle I stayed two days at Orieagu partly with the Ministry Police at the office of the Permanent Secretary and partly with the staff of the Ministry of external Affairs waiting for the return of the Permanent Secretary Security Division Ministry of Defence.

7th June, 1969, Saturday: I met the permanent Secretary Security Division at about 9:00am. I felt badly disappointed when the Permanent Secretary after reading the letters I gave him, asked me to come to his head-office at Uruala-Orlu for a letter of clearance. My bicycle was very bad and I was tired of riding after being on the road for several days.

I left to Uruala, and there I saw only old men and women on the road, the rest of the people were soldiers and it was risky to move about as a civilian (young and strong) at okohia in Umuduru. I met my friend Mr. Onukogu an officer in the Boff, who took me to his camp and gave me food and drink and expressed fear about my journey. I repaired bicycle with ₤1. And continued my journey. At Isu St. John's, Orlu, I went in to see my friend Mr. Ernest Ihejirika on seeing me, Mr. Ihejirika was highly surprised and asked how I managed to come all the way from Owerri. After my explanations he was worried and told me that no young man a civilian could come out in their area because of conscription for the past one month. He begged me to stay back with him, or travel back to Owerri because the road to Uruala was too bad. But I was determined to continue my journey. Ernest shed tears as he bade good bye to me. I left Isu, travelled through Abba, Dikenafai, Isiekenesi passing Military Camps and quarters for wounded soldiers.

At Uruala, about a few poles to the office of the Permanent Secretary Security Division of Defence, I was conscripted by a group of angry soldiers who seized my pass book and refused to listen to my explanation. We were taken to a compound where old men and even sick young men conscripted into the Army were kept. We all were made to sit on the floor throughout the night.

8th June, 1969: I was not allowed to speak to the officers of the conscription in the morning, we were marched to the road junction leading to Akokwa, Osina and Orlu township, we were kept there waiting for transport to the Army training camp at Ugiri Mbano. I still had my handbag containing the clothes I retuned with from Port Harcourt my certificates and my bicycle, belonging to Justy my intended wife. In the afternoon, the army got a tipper vehicle, which loaded the conscripted people. I put in my handbag and my bicycle and we left towards Ugiri. I was so unhappy all the time, because I realized that none of people could locate my where about since the 2nd of the month when I left home. At Ugiri, army training camp, I saw a village of people conscripted from different places and brought down for training. I had a wonderful courage and determined never to join the Army. Several officers spoke to us encouraging us to go and fight in Defence of Biafra our father land. We were commanded to run round the large camp then to the training ground. At this point, I took my bicycle, put on my dirty and rumpled shirt and joined the company of the officers who addressed us, I pretended to have come in to see someone. I followed them and encouraged another young man who had told me of how he was conscripted at Orlu, on his way to look for medicine for his father at the point of death.

I followed the officers to the main office and pretended to be looking for someone. Luckily I met an officer, a lieutenant, who asked me what I wanted. I told him that I came to see my brother who was conscripted, and that I wanted somebody to take me out of the large training camp with several strong check points. As God would have it, this young man got a bicycle and told me to follow him. I told my friend to follow me closely under the officer's protection, we were able to cross all the strong checkpoints to Orie-Amaraku, where he bade us good bye. I gave him the only Biafran £1, note I had, and we set off at a top speed towards Owerri. On our way to Owerri, my new friend from Orlu could not believe his eyes at our lucky escape from the military camp. He asked me whether I was a magician or an ordinary human being. On our arrival to Owerri at about 7pm. He could not express his thanks to me. We parted and wished each other greater luck and long-life. On my arrival at Irette, I saw my mother and Justy very miserably planning how and where to look for me. It was a very happy reunion. I told them my experiences for the past six days and my wonderful escape from the Military Service. Everybody was surprised and gave thanks to God.

22ⁿᵈ June, 1969: my stay at Egbema became very difficult because the councilor had nothing left for our feeding. Our appeal to the natives to help in my feeding did not yield any fruit. Therefore I stayed hungry. But a friend Mr. Gabriel Kamalu gave me ₤1. Stock fish with which I made a small soup.

2ⁿᵈ July, 1969: I was staying at Obinikpa near Egwe-Oguta. Very early in the morning the whole town was invaded by a team of soldiers from Umuaka-Orlu who came for conscription. Unfortunately, I was conscripted along with many old men and we were taken to Ozara School, ready to be carried away. Fortunately, there was a team of Air Force Officers and men on training. The Air officer was annoyed with the soldiers who conscripted us and ordered his boys to flog the soldiers. To our surprise, the soldiers were flogged in our presence and we were all released on the spot. I was so happy that day, and on reaching my friend's house, I took my handbag and left to Egbema. On my way back, I visited Mr. Edwin Ukachukwu of Ezi-Orsu Oguta who was happy to see me. I arrived Egbema at about 7pm to the great surprise of the Soldiers and natives who concluded that I must have joined the Army because nobody at that time could travel freely along the roads.

13ᵗʰ July, 1969: life became very difficult, food and salt were not available, and for the first time, I ate without salt.

16ᵗʰ July, 1969: I fried garri for the first time in my life. My Police Customers from Oguta came to Mgbara Egbema and bought all my garri.

17ᵗʰ July, 1969: I left Egbema in a very heavy rain to Irette. I escaped army conscription at Agwa. Amakohia Ubi Ndegwu and Irette. I reached home in that rain and was told that my father was under arrest and in the army guard-room at Mr. Emmanuel Opara's compound, because of a false accusation that my father bought garri from the soldier who was suspected of stealing garri from the army stores. I left at one to the Army officer a captain, who was engineered by some natives to keep my father under arrest. After speaking to him, he released my father at once and everybody was happy and grateful to me.

21st July, 1969: I left from Egbu to Okigwe, but at Amakohia Ikeduru where I met Mr. L.N Akparanta the Zonal Inspector of Education for Owerri/Orlu Divisions. He advised me to go back home and write a letter to Okigwe to the town clerk of the Port Harcourt Municipal Council then at Etiti on my arrears of salaries. He warned me that there was very serious conscription on all the roads and that I should try and go back. He was surprised at my courage to move about. I went back to Egbu, to the surprise of everybody. I went back to Irette on the 24th July. I met my friend B.O.G Awuzie at Owerri for the first time since Sept. 1968. It was a happy meeting. We told stories of our ugly experience of the war.

26th July, 1969: I went back to Egbu, met Justy at Owerri. We visited B.O.G.A and later left for Egbu on the 27th July and we discussed at length on finding a wife for B.O.G.A he was directed to a girl at Mpama Egbu by Justy.

30th July, 1969: I left Egbu to Irette. On my way, I visited my uncle Matthew Ozuzu who was sick at the General Hospital Owerri. His condition was bad.

2nd August, 1969: I met Justy at Owerri we went together to hand over some documents to the Secretary of Uratta County Council. At last we walked back to Irette and walked back to Egbu the following day 3rd August 1969.

13th August, 1969: I got my clearance paper from the State House-Owerri, after going from the C.I.O office to the state house, (Security Division) I was asked to meet the Secretary of Local Government and Customary Courts Service Board then at Mbawsi-Aba, who would give me another latter to the town clerk of the P.H Municipal Council for my arrears of salaries, still at Etiti-Okigwe.

14th August, 1969: I left Irette and travelled back to Egbema, not minding the very serious conscription on the road. On reaching Egbema everybody was surprised that I was not conscripted into the Army. I went mainly to close the school for holidays and collect my things from Egbema.

18th August, 1969: I left Egbema in the morning, walking all the way because my bicycle was spoilt. I reached Irette in the evening escaping the several teams of soldiers on conscription.

21st August, 1969: I left from Egbu on my way to Mbawsi on foot. Justy was worried because the journey was very risky and there was no transport. On the way I met a soldier travelling to Mbawsi. He gave protection on the way. At Ahiara Mbaise the weather became very bad. To my greatest surprise, I heard a voice calling on me from a building by the market. On reaching there, I was surprised to see one girl from the home- Esther Chienyenwa Ashilonu, whom I knew when we were school children. She told me that her father was living there as a tailor for the soldiers and that he had travelled. As we were talking with her, a very heavy rain started. She took us in, gave us food and sleeping accommodation till the next morning being 22nd August, 1969.

22nd August, 1969: I set off with the Soldier (friend) and we walked all the way with great difficulties, because of bad roads and lack of transport. We reached Ubakala near Umuahia, where my friend (soldier) joined an army vehicle and I continued alone. I reached Mbawsi on foot and looked for the office of the Local Government and Customary Court Service Board at many corners of the town. At last I was directed to a town Mbubo, about 6 miles from Mbawsi. I walked along a very lonely and bad road until I reached the office and was received with sympathy after telling them my experience. I was given another letter, asking the town clerk Mr. J.E Nyambi at Etiti to pay me my arrears of salaries from March 1968 to August 1969. I left for home and passed some soldiers at Umunwanwa near Ubakala – Umuahia.

23rd August, 1969: I walked back to Egbu. My wife and her people were very happy to see me I told them of my sufferings and experiences on the way to Mbawsi.

27th August, 1969: I left home and travelled to Etiti in Okigwe. At Orieagu market square, I met the town clerk Mr. I.E Nyambi and gave him the clearance letter I got from Mbubo-Mbawsi. He read the letter and told me that there was no money left with him. He took my address and promised to invite me for my pay anytime money was available. I came back to Umuduru-Mbano and passed the night at the Police Station. I met a School mate Mr. Nnaji Omeji of Obazu Mbieri, who was a police man. He gave me ₤1. Biafra note to buy food.

28th August, 1969: I came back home from Umuduru-Mbano. My wife and my parents were happy to see me again because travelling at that time was very risky. Only women and old men were seen on the roads. Others were soldiers.

30th August, 1969: Justy was at Ikembara-Ikeduru for her friend Helen Opara's wedding which I also attended the wedding ceremony of Mr. and Mrs. Benneth Opara.

30th August, 1969: I reported back to the Secretary of Uratta County Council, who deployed me again as a teacher and posted me to the L.A school Irette. I traveled to Egbu in the evening and met my mother in-law sick. Justy also was sick after travelling to Ubomiri to see the Education Secretary, Mr. Ekeocha on her deployment.

15th September, 1969: I started school at L.A school Irette. The teachers and the pupil were very happy to receive me. We stayed at Mr. James Okenwa's compound-Umungada-Irette, because he was a counselor.

20th September, 1969: I went to Okwu-Ogbaku on behalf of the staff of the L.A school Irette to get our share of relief materials given to teachers in Ogbaku Parish.

11TH October, 1969: I traveled to Naze to ask of my friend Mr. S. Le. Maduagwu. I saw his mother and other relations, who gave me his address. I left from there to Egbu and passed the night at my in-law's place.

17th October, 1969: My uncle Mathew Ozuzu who had been sick in the General Hospital died. His corpse was carried home the following day 18th Oct. 1969 and buried on his compound.

26th October, 1969: I quarreled with our church Agent (teacher) because he refused to sign a letter I wrote to the W.C.C Management Committee of relief materials to the L.A. school pupils Irette. He later signed the letter and started treating me more friendly. At this period, life became very difficult and many people were dying almost every day out of hunger and disease. Between 2nd Nov. and 13th Nov. 1969, the following people died: Our sister Ayozie Njoku, Ononiwu Monye, Anyanwu Nlemadim, Orikanjuru Amadi wife of our brother Mr. J.O Amadi and Aginwa Ogu of Umunwanlo died.

8th November, 1969: I went to Owerri for salt and got $1^{1/2}$ cups of salt from the Secretary of Uratta County Council Mr. J.P. Inyang.

14th November, 1969: I spent a nice time with Mr. B.O.G Awuzie at Owerri and later traveled to Egbu. Justy and her people were happy to see me.

21st November, 1969: I left home to Owerri in the evening for the wake keeping in honour of late Mrs. Augusta Inyang wife of the Secretary of Oratta Country Council. In the morning, we attended the Requiem Mass at St. Pauls' church Owerri. After a brief entertainment I visited B.O.G Awuzie and later traveled home.

27th November, 1969: My friend Mr. J.P Inyang gave me one stock fish after explaining my difficulties and lack of payment to him.

30th November, 1969: The letters of advice which I wrote to parents and citizens of Irette on the importance of sending their children back to school without minding the hardships were read in the three churches at Irette. St. Paul's church, St Helen's Church and St. Peter's church. I left with my wife to Egbu and we reached Egbu at night.

3rd December, 1969: I gathered Umuoyo men and spoke to them on the importance of good behaviour, the attendance to important meetings, fighting against evil, planting of cassava and the use of conscription to eliminate enemies; recommending the remaining young men for conscription into the Army. Their relationship with the soldiers who were using some of them as agents against their brothers. The importance of sending their children back to school without minding the hardships caused by the war. Everybody was happy and grateful to me for the address.

5th December, 1969: Our relation, Major R. Ogbonna of Avu came to Irette to inform us that our cousin Victor Nneji a 2nd Lieutenant had been killed in the Ikot-Ekpene Sector of the war. Everybody wept bitterly. The war situation became very bad there were bad news of death and great suffering in the small area left for Biafra. I started to consider my condition as a civilian and decided to join the Army under special arrangement with some officials as a last resort.

27th December, 1969: I walked all the way with my wife from Egbu to Umuguma to attend the wedding ceremony of Mr. and Mrs. Bethram Mbanu. At the end of the ceremony, we walked to Irette, where we spent a few days. The war situation was very bad in all the sectors, conscription was at its highest peak and men were no longer seen along the roads. The condition of soldiers became terribly bad as majority of them stayed without food and moved about almost naked, which led to their great wickedness to the civilians both men and women.

8th January, 1970: The Nigerian soldiers over ran the remaining parts of Biafra. Owerri was disturbed for the second time and very unexpectedly. People ran away to different sections of Biafra. As I was at Egbu, immediately the shelling and rockets landed between Egbu and Naze, everybody was set packing. There was great panic everywhere, our soldiers also were set moving away from their camps. This happened in the night at about 9.00pm. We carried our loads as much as we could and with my parent's in-law and my wife, we left Egbu that night to Umuoba. I came back to Egbu with my father in-law and collected a few other things, while my wife and her mother waited anxiously for us at Umuoba.

9th January, 1970: We left Umuoba Church compound where we slept and moved to Umuorii Uratta where we spent two nights. The enemy soldiers moved very close and we left to Ikeduru.

12th January, 1970: With very heavy loads on bicycles we travelled on foot to Ikembara – Ikeduru where Mrs. Helen Opara was married. On the way we saw my Biafran Soldier disarmed and frightened. We learnt that the Nigerian Soldiers had entered everywhere and had asked for a total surrender from both Civilians and Soldiers in Biafra. As all the Biafran soldiers were disarmed, nobody could disobey the Nigerian Soldiers. I found it very difficult and terrifying to see the Nigerian Soldiers. I went into the bush with my wife to avoid the Soldiers who were seizing our girls and women from their parents and husbands. They were also killing people who tried to resist their orders. People were asked or ordered to shout "One Nigeria!" we managed the night at Uzagba sleeping on the floor with only a cloth.

13th January, 1970: We started coming back to Egbu. We took bush paths dragging heavy loads on bicycles mainly to avoid the Nigerian Soldiers from seizing the young girls and valuable property from us. Luckily, we reached Egbu safely. Two young Nigerian Soldiers opened and searched our boxes but did not remove anything from us. We entered the house and remained indoors, because the vandals continued taking girls and property from their owners.

14th January, 1970: I left Egbu to Irette, to check up whether my parents and brothers had returned. At home, I met Theophilus Benedict and Agabus, who came back from different sectors. We remained hungry at home, waiting anxiously for our parents to return. We had nothing to eat at home. People continued coming back from different places.

15th January, 1970: Shadrack came home and joined us to stay waiting for our parents. We heard officially that the Nigerian Civil War had ended. Nigerian Soldiers were all over our place with their arms. They continued seizing valuable property and girls from their owners.

16th January, 1970: Our Parents came back from Awomama, where they suffered terrible hardship and loss of their valuable property. My father told us his ugly experiences and his sufferings in dragging a spoilt bicycle with very heavy loads in the great heat of the sun. But they were particularly very happy to see all of us, because many people especially Soldiers of the Biafran Army were shot dead in hundreds by the Nigerian Soldiers. People from Orogwe, Ogbaku and Ohii looted all the property belonging to Bishop Lasbrey College Irette. These included, beds, boxes; book and other valuable goods.

17th January, 1970: I left Irette for Egbu. At Owerri, I met my friend Mr. Manasseh Ogolo of Obodo who was going home with his family. He gave me a pant and asked me to check him up at Aba. On my arrival to Egbu, Justy and her parents were happy to receive me. I told them about the safe return of my parents and brothers who were in the Biafran Army. People flocked into Owerri to get relief materials: rice, beans, garri, corn meal, milk and other items from the Red Cross Offices or Relief Centres. These were shared by the Nigerian Soldiers who were not happy to see any young man as a Biafran. They were very cruel to the Biafran. I started coming to Owerri every day, lining up among many people most of them sick, dirty and old, but staying in the lines not minding the cruelty of the Soldiers. I was always there in order to get food for my parents at home. My junior brothers Shadrack and Theophilus refused to go to Owerri and struggle for relief. My parents and I were not happy with them. My father became very sick after his sufferings at Awomama. His condition was very bad and his legs started to swell. He sent me to our relation at Owerri Mr. Igbo who brought him some medicine.

29th January, 1970: I travelled on foot to Ulakwo Obubu to see Monica and her husband and to report to them of my father's bad health and ask them for money to help treat my father. I actually saw Monica and her husband, but they had no money or any other thing to offer as a help to our father. I walked back through Emii where I visited Rev. Godwin Nwaneri and John-bull. I reached Egbu late in the evening.

5th February, 1970: I went to Owerri and registered under the Local Government Staff for reabsorption. Many people especially Civil Servants reported to Owerri and registered for re-employment.

9th February, 1970: I came to Owerri with Justy for registration as teachers. There were no forms for Voluntary Agency teachers' registration. I registered as a staff of the Local Government. We met many friends who also survived the war. People were selling their valuable property at give away prices just to get money and buy food materials.

10th February, 1970: I was attacked by about 20 Nigerian Soldiers at Egbu, who were jealous of my stay with Justy, who was dealing on palm wine in their compound and they wanted to take her from me. My father-in-law abused some of their servants who after buying garri from Mrs. Adaku Jones Ozurumba wanted to take back their money after several hours. These boys went and reported to their masters, who came to the compound to make trouble. As soon as they saw me, they all attacked me. I did my best to defend myself from them. I ran to their Officer, who stopped them from beating me. By this time, I had got serious injuries on my head and my terrilene short was torn to pieces. The Officer took me to their M.R.S for the First Aid treatment. At night, a greater number of the vandals came back to my in-laws compound to attack us. My wife and I stayed in the bush behind the compound throughout the night to avoid greater trouble with the vandals.

11th February, Wednesday, 1970: My mother-in-law took Justy and myself to her relation at Ihitte Uratta, where I stayed taking treatment for the injuries I received during the fight with the vandals. We spent 4 days at Ihitte and my health improved considerably.

15th February, Sunday, 1970: News reached us that the Nigerian vandals then at Egbu had left to another place. We came back from Ihitte to Egbu where I continued treating the wound on my head.

Culled from the Nigeria Civil War Diary of: *Prince Chukwuemeka Charles Ozuzu A retired School Principal   Irete, Owerri-West LGA Imo State, Nigeria*

SUMMARY OF FACTS ON CESSATION OF HOSTILITIES 1967 - 1970

The fact that there was a fratricidal War in Nigeria between 1967 and 1970 – called Nigerian Civil War or Nigeria – Biafra War.

The fact that there were four regions in Nigeria up to 1967 May, namely Eastern Region, Western Region, Northern Region and Mid-West Region.

The fact that Hostilities/conflict broke out following the problem in the North which resulted in the massacre of Easterners.

Fact of declaration of Hostilities between Nigeria and Biafra in which more than 3 Million people died on both sides to the conflict.

Fact that Nigeria Army used more and superior Munitions, Conventional anti-personnel and anti-vehicle landmines to fight those on the Biafran side in the Nigerian Civil War.

Fact that Nigerian Army laid landmines and used many of the landmines as nuisance mines. The Army also kept no records of mined Areas, Mine fields and such other Areas and locations where it used mines or abandoned Bombs and Explosive Remnants of War.

Fact of Nigeria using weapons of Mass destruction in the War many of which weapons it abandoned at various Areas, fields and Bushes where battles were fought or where soldiers used as make-shift Military Camps.

Fact that the Federal Republic of Nigeria took effective, charge, control and possession of all the territories situate in the War affected Areas immediately after the War.

Fact that there are Landmines, Bombs, Explosive Remnants of War, still scattered in War affected Areas in some States of Nigeria but more particularly in South-East, and South-South zones of Nigeria.

Fact of Nigeria failing/neglecting to undertake the clearing/removal of Mines, ERW's from War contaminated or affected Areas/communities immediately after the Civil War.

Fact that Nigeria owes a duty of care to keep contaminated/war affected Areas safe for physical, mental development.

Fact that Nigeria did not take proper care or pay proper attention to Citizens, families, communities living with ERW's, AXO's, UXO's resulting in the injuries to the Citizens and the death of thousands of people.

Fact of Nigeria not embarking on mine risk education of people living in and around contaminated and War affected Areas resulting in the Citizens injuries.

Fact of Nigeria not rehabilitating and providing some assistance to the Mine Victims who indeed did not participate in the War, many of the victims were not even born after the Nigeria Civil War.

Fact that Nigeria is now in control and has so been in control of all those areas that were affected by the Civil War.

Fact that not less than 178,000 Square kilometers of lands have not been cleared in war affected areas.

Fact that these weapons are still in the bushes and war contaminated Areas and are still threatening the Civilian population.

Fact that Nigeria has abandoned the Victims, who are Nigerian citizens of Igbo extraction, Ikwerre; Efiks to die with the Bombs just because they fought the Civil War. This it did by ordering the contractors to stop work of clearing and removing of Bombs and ERWs.

Fact that out of all the contaminated Areas, Imo State alone has 45% uncleared.

Fact that the Civil War is subtly continuing and there is gross abuse of Victims Fundamental Human Rights.

Fact that Nigeria did not tell the truth to the UN when she declared complete compliance with Article 5 of Ottawa Convention.

Fact that Agricultural activities are hampered in the former Eastern Region of Nigeria – now South-East and South-South by lack of lands for cultivation and other Agricultural purposes because of massive contamination. This has made the people of South-East and South-South largely dependent on food supplies from the North. This seems like a deliberate policy to strike a balance of dependence on oil and food between the North and South. That was one battle too many, too costly and tortuous on the psyche of Nigerians. It looks like the war is yet to end!

Some years after, there was the Maitasine religious crisis in Borno State during the time of Alhaji Shehu Shagari's reign as president. In the west, there was the reign of terror unleashed by the Odua Peoples Congress (OPC).

There was also a series of Kano uprisings leading to reprisals and counter-offensive. Then came real militancy in the creeks of Niger Delta. This was followed by a corresponding kidnapping of foreigners and oil workers. Kidnapping soon spread to Igboland and anchored there for a long period. As this was going on there were the Odi and Zakibiam incidences. Shortly after this episode, came the Fulani herdsmen who laid siege on the people of Plateau State. It wasn't long those masquerading as Fulani Herdsmen metamorphosed into full blast insurgents in the name of "Boko Haram." Their initial grouse was against western education and all that it stands for. But these were all excuses to launch a full scale war against Nigeria's sovereignty. The "Boko Haram" insurgents pitched their battles in the North East zone of Nigeria and more particularly in Borno, Gombe, Adamawa and Yobe States fighting Nigerian Soldiers with equally very sophisticated weapons. Depending on the vagaries of battle and firing power, both sides had occasions to retreat, re-group and fight back. At each turn, very many and large cache of munitions are abandoned in the forests, military cells and camps. The Boko Haram insurgents somehow adopted non-conventional methods to conceal their ammunitions ranging from burying them in the ground to hiding some of these weapons in the churches as well as in mosques.

The Konduga Battle in Borno State was embarked upon to repel Boko Haram Sect's advance to Maiduguri. At the same time Nigeria Military intensified air strikes on Bama, Gwoza and Madagali axis, including some vulnerable parts of Adamawa State in hot pursuit of the insurgents. "Troops have also launched intense strikes on all known cells and camps of the insurgents in that axis. Jet fighters are taking charge in Madagali, Gulak and other vulnerable towns and villages. The Insurgents relocated to Gwoza because Sambisa Forest is no longer habitable leaving behind a large cache of arms." By the time the final battle is won against insurgents, a duty would have been created on the Nigeria State to not only to demilitarize all the known theatres of war but also to clear all the areas where munitions were abandoned or emplaced during conflict situation to prevent explosions years after the war. If this is not done all those people who ran away when insurgents took over their communities would return to meet deaths waiting for them.

The above represents the picture of how the Nigerian Civil War was fought and how Landmines, Uxo's, Axo's and Other Explosive Remnants of War came to be scattered in the civil war affected and contaminated areas in the South-South and South-East zones of Nigeria parts of the former Eastern region and yet when the civil war ended, Nigerian Government now in control of all the territories where the war was fought but they did not go back to pick-up, remove and clear the Explosive Remnants of War leading to a subtle continuation of the Civil War in the former Eastern Region by reason of sporadic explosions in farmlands and fields. The need therefore has arisen for a theory to clear these Explosive Remnants of war to actually end the Civil War indeed and in fact. Beyond this Nigeria needs to investigate some of the happenstances that led to the Nigeria Civil War and some issues Gideon Orkars Coup. It is important to find out whether the blood of women, children and some people of the then Eastern Region of Nigeria violently killed in the senseless pogrom that took place in the North in the 60's is still speaking through the Boko Haram insurgency. *Source: The Nation on Sunday – September 14, 2014; Page 3*

CHAPTER THREE

MINE BAN TREATY (MBT)

The 1997 Mine Ban Treaty formally known as the, "Convention on the Prohibition of the Use, Stockpiling, Production and Transfer of Antipersonnel Mines and on Their Destruction" opened for signature in Ottawa, Canada on 3 December, 1997. The Treaty is the most comprehensive international instrument for ridding the world of the scourge of landmines. Today there are 158 states party to the Mine Ban Treaty – more than 80% of all the countries in the world. States parties are governments that have ratified or acceded to the treaty. It is sometimes referred to as the Ottawa Convention. The treaty is a legally-binding international agreement that bans the use, production, manufacture and transfer of anti-personnel mines. Although 80% of the world's nations have joined the treaty, and an overwhelming global stigmatization of use of this weapon has been achieved, there remains a lot of work to be done. More than a third of the worlds – 72 states – are still contaminated by landmines. Globally, hundreds of thousands of landmine survivors thirst to see their rights respected and their needs met. It requires States Parties to:

- Never use antipersonnel mines nor "develop, produce, otherwise acquire, stockpile, retain or transfer" them;
- Destroy mines in their stockpiles within four years;
- Clear mines in suspected or known mined areas in their territory within 10 years;
- In mine-affected countries, conduct risk education and ensure that mine survivors, their families and communities receive comprehensive assistance;
- Offer assistance to other States Parties, for example in providing for survivors or contributing to clearance programs; and
- Adopt national implementation measures (such as national legislation) in order to ensure that the term of the treaty are upheld in their territory.

So its disarmament and humanitarian achievements are unique:

- Vast tracts of land have been cleared and put back into productive use.
- There are fewer new mine victims and in fewer countries each year. There were 4,191 new landmines/UXO casualties in 2010 compared to 7,987 recorded in 2001;

- The trade in antipersonnel mines has virtually stopped and the number of producing countries is down to only a handful, not all of which are producing actively;
- Over 45 million antipersonnel mines have been removed from arsenals and destroyed and are now out of circulation forever;
- The new international norm – where used anywhere by anyone is considered abhorrent – is gathering strength. This is true with state parties but does not regulate insurgents and terrorist gangs. More and more states are joining the treaty and working hard to implement it. Even non-member states are responding to international pressure and abiding by the spirit of the agreement.

However, this is still a "success in progress" in Nigeria and much remains to be done. Although the annual rate of injuries and deaths caused by antipersonnel mines diminishes, the absolute number of mine survivors keeps growing each year and many of their needs are not being met. Besides, Nigeria, as a state party still harbours a large cache of landmines in its holding which she claims are for instruction and teaching at the Nigerian Defence Academy and Military Schools. MBT provides for regular inventory of mines in the kitty of the country but this has not been done in the past seven years. Besides, it is not certain where they use these anti-personnel mines for instructions and teaching. It is equally worrisome about the communities or environment where such is put in use within Nigeria.

Mine Ban Treaty (Ottawa Convention) 18 September 1997
"Convention on the Prohibition of the Use, Stockpiling, Production and Transfer of Anti-Personnel Mines and on Their Destruction"
Preamble:
The States Parties,
Determined to put an end to the suffering and causalities caused by anti-personnel mines, that kill or maim hundreds of people every week, mostly innocent and defenceless civilians and especially children, obstruct economic development and reconstruction, inhabit the repatriation of refugees and internally displaced persons, and have other severe consequences for years after emplacement,

Believing it necessary to do their utmost to contribute in an efficient and coordinated manner to face the challenge of removing anti-personnel mines placed throughout the world, and to assure their destruction,

Wishing to do their utmost in providing assistance for the care and rehabilitation, including the social and economic reintegration of mine victims,

Recognizing that a total ban of anti-personnel mines would also be an important confidence-building measure,

Welcoming the adoption of the protocol on Prohibitions and Restrictions on the Use of Mines, Booby-Traps and Other Devices, as amended On 3 May 1996, annexed to the Convention on Prohibitions or Restrictions on the Use of Certain Conventional Weapons Which May Be Deemed to Be Excessively Injurious or to Have Indiscriminate Effects, and calling for the early ratification of this protocol by all States which have not yet done so,

Welcoming also United Nations General Assembly Resolution 51/45 S of 10 December 1996 urging all States to pursue vigorously an effective, legally-binding international agreement to ban the use, stockpiling, production and transfer of anti-personnel landmines,

Welcoming furthermore the measures taken over the past years, both unilaterally and multilaterally, aiming at prohibiting, restricting or suspending the use, stockpiling, production and transfer of anti-personnel mines,

Stressing the role of public conscience in furthering the principles of humanity as evidenced by the call for a total ban of anti-personnel mines and recognizing the efforts to that end undertaken by the International Red Cross and Red Crescent Movement, the International Campaign to Ban Landmines and numerous other non-governmental organizations around the world,

Recalling the Ottawa Declaration of 5 October 1996 and the Brussels Declaration of 27 June 1997 urging the international community to negotiate an international and legally binding agreement prohibiting the use, stockpiling, production and transfer of anti-personnel mines,

Emphasizing the desirability of attracting the adherence of all States to this Convention, and determined to work strenuously towards the promotion of its universalization in all relevant fora including, inter alia, the United Nations, the Conference on Disarmament, regional organizations, and groupings, and review conferences of the Convention on Prohibitions or Restrictions on the Use of Certain Conventional Weapons which May Be Deemed to Be Excessively Injurious or to Have Indiscriminate Effects,

Basing themselves on the principle of International humanitarian law that the right of the parties to an armed conflict to choose methods or means of warfare is not unlimited, on the principle that prohibits the employment in armed conflicts of weapons, projectiles and materials and methods of warfare of a nature to cause superfluous injury or unnecessary suffering and on the principle that a distinction must be made between civilians and combatants,

Have agreed as follows:

Article 1: General obligations

1. Each State Party undertakes never under any circumstance:

    a) To use anti-personnel mines;

    b) To develop, produce, otherwise acquire, stockpile, retain or transfer to anyone, directly or indirectly, anti-personnel mines;

    c) To assist, encourage or induce, in any way, anyone to engage in any activity prohibited to a State Party under this Convention.

2. Each State Party undertakes to destroy or ensure the destruction of all anti-personnel mines in accordance with the provisions of this Convention.

Article 2: Definitions

1. "Anti-personnel mine" means a mine designed to be exploded by the presence, proximity or contact of a person and that will incapacitate, injure or kill one or more persons. Mines designed to be detonated by the presence, proximity or contact of a vehicle as opposed to a person, that are equipped with anti-handling devices, are not considered anti-personnel mines as a result of being so equipped.

2. "Mine" means a munition designed to be placed under, on or near the ground or other surface areas and to be exploded by the presence, proximity or contact of a person or a vehicle.

3. "Anti-handling device" means a device intended to protect a mine and which is part of, linked to, attached to or placed under the mine and which activates when an attempt is made to tamper with or otherwise intentionally disturb the mine.

4. "Transfer" involves, in addition to the physical movement of

anti-personnel mines into or from national territory, the transfer of title to and control over the mines, but does not involve the transfer of territory containing emplaced anti-personnel mines.

5. "Mined area" means an area which is dangerous due to the presence or suspected presence of mines.

Article 3: Exceptions

1. Notwithstanding the general obligations under Article 1, the retention or transfer of a number of anti-personnel mines for the development of and training in mine detection, mine clearance, or mine destruction techniques is permitted. The amount of such mines shall not exceed the minimum number absolutely necessary for the above-mentioned purposes.

2. The transfer of anti-personnel mines for the purpose of destruction is permitted.

Article 4: Destruction of stockpiling anti-personnel mines

Except as provided for in Article 3, each State Party undertakes to destroy or ensure the destruction of all stockpiled anti-personnel mines it owns or possesses, or that are under its jurisdiction or control, as soon as possible but not later than four years after the entry into force of this Convention for that State Party.

Article 5: Destruction of anti-personnel mines in mined areas

1. Each State Party undertakes to destroy or ensure the destruction of all anti-personnel mines in mind areas under its jurisdiction or control, as soon as possible but not later than ten years after the entry into force of this Convention for that State Party.

2. Each State Party shall make every effort to identify all areas under its jurisdiction or control in which anti-personnel mines are known or suspected to be emplaced and shall ensure as soon as possible that all anti-personnel mines in mind area under its jurisdiction or control are perimeter-marked, monitored and protected by fencing or other means, to ensure the effective exclusion of civilians, until all anti-personnel mines contained therein have been destroyed. The marking shall at least be to the standards set out in the Protocol on Prohibitions or Restrictions on the Use of Mines, Booby-Traps and Other Devices, as amended on 3 May 1996, annexed to the Convention on Prohibitions or Restrictions on the Use of Certain Conventional Weapons Which May Be Deemed to Be Excessively Injurious or to Have Indiscriminate Effects.

3. If a State Party believes that it will be unable to destroy or ensure the destruction of all anti-personnel mines referred to in paragraph 1 within that time period, it may submit a request to a Meeting of the Sates Parties or for completing the destruction of such anti-personnel mines, for a period of up to ten years.

4. Each request shall contain:
   a) The duration of the proposed extension;
   b) A detailed explanation of the reasons for the proposed extension, including:
   (i) The preparation and status of work conducted under national demining programs;
   (ii) The financial and technical means available to the State Party for the destruction of all the anti-personnel mines; and
   (iii) Circumstances which impede the ability of the State Party to destroy all the anti-personnel mines in mined areas;
   c) The humanitarian, social, economic, and environmental implications of the extension; and
   d) Any other information relevant to the request for the proposal.

5. The meeting of the States Parties or the Review Conference shall, taking into consideration the factors contained in paragraph 4, assess the request and decide by a majority of votes of States Parties present and voting whether to grant the request for an extension period.

6. Such an extension may be renewed upon the submission of a new request in accordance with paragraphs 3, 4 and 5 of this Article. In requesting a further extension period a State Party shall submit relevant additional information on what has been undertaken in the previous extension period pursuant to this Article.

Article 6: International co-operation and assistance

1. In fulfilling its obligations under this Convention each State Party has the right to seek and receive assistance, where feasible, from other State Parties to the extent possible.

2. Each State Party undertakes to facilitate and shall have the right to participate in the fullest possible exchange of equipment, material

and scientific and technological information concerning the implementation of this Convention. The States Parties shall not impose undue restrictions on the provision of mine clearance equipment and related technological information for humanitarian purpose.

3. Each State Party in a position to do so shall provide assistance for the care and rehabilitation, and social and economic reintegration, of the mine victims and for mine awareness programs. Such assistance may be provided, inter alia, through the United Nations system, international, regional or national organizations or institutions, the International Committee of the Red Cross, national Red Cross and Red Crescent societies and their International Federation, non-governmental organizations, or on a bilateral basis.

4. Each State Party in a position to do so shall provide assistance for mine clearance and related activities. Such assistance may be provided, inter alia, through the United Nations system, international or regional organizations or institutions, or on a bilateral basis, or by contributing to the United Nations Voluntary Trust Fund for Assistance in Mine Clearance, or other regional funds that deal with demining.

5. Each State Party in a position to do so shall provide assistance for the destruction of stockpiled anti-personnel mines.

6. Each State Party undertakes to provide information to the database on mine clearance established within the United Nations system, especially information concerning various means and technologies of mine clearance, and lists of expert agencies or national points of contact on mine clearance.

7. State Parties may request the United Nations, regional organizations, other State Parties or other competent intergovernmental or non-governmental fora to assist its authorities in the elaboration of a national demining program to determine, inter alia:

   a) The extent and scope of the anti-personnel mine problem;

   b) The financial, technological and human resources that are required for the implementation of the program;

   c) The estimation number of years necessary to destroy all anti-personnel mines in mind areas under the jurisdiction or control of the concerned State Party;

d) Mine awareness activities to reduce the incidence of mine-related injuries or deaths;

e) Assistance to mine victims;

f) The relationship between the Government of the concerned State Party and the relevant governmental entities that will work in the implementation of the program.

8. Each State Party giving and receiving assistance under the provisions of this Article shall cooperate with a view to ensuring the full and prompt implementation of agreed assistance program.

Article 7: Transparency measures

1. Each State Party shall report to the Secretary-General of the United Nations as soon as practicable, and in any event not later than 180 days after the entry into force of this Convention for that State Party on:

a) The national implementation measures referred to in Article 9;

b) The total of all stockpiled anti-personnel mines owned or possessed by it, or under its jurisdiction or control, to include a breakdown of the type, quantity and, if possible lot numbers of each type of anti-personnel mine stockpiled;

c) The extent possible, the location of all mined areas that contain, or are suspected to contain, anti-personnel mines under its jurisdiction or control, to include as much detail as possible regarding the type and quantity of each type of anti-personnel mine in each mined area and when they were emplaced;

d) The types, quantities and, if possible, lot numbers of all anti-personnel mines retained or transferred for the development of and training in mine detection, mine clearance or mine destruction, as well as the institutions authorized by a State Party to retain or transfer anti-personnel mines, in accordance with Article 3;

e) The status of programs for the conversion or decommissioning of anti-personnel mine production facilities;

f) The status of programs for the destruction of anti-personnel mines in accordance with Article 4 and 5, including details of the methods which will be used in destruction, the location sites and the applicable safety and environmental standards to be observed;

g) The types and quantities of all anti-personnel mines destroyed after the entry into force of this Convention for that State Party, to include a breakdown of the quantity of each type of anti-personnel mine destroyed, in accordance with Article 4 and 5, respectively, along with, if possible, the lot numbers of each type of anti-personnel mine in the case of destruction in accordance with Article 4;

h) The technical characteristics of each type of anti-personnel mines produced, to the extent known, and those currently owned or possessed by a State Party, giving, where reasonable possible, such categories of information as may facilitate identification and clearance of anti-personnel mines; at a minimum, this information shall include the dimensions, fusing, explosive content, metallic content, colour photographs and other information which may facilitate mine clearance; and

i) The measures taken to provide an immediate and effective warning to the population in relation to all areas identified under paragraph 2 of Article 5.

2. The information provided in accordance with this Article shall be updated by the States Parties annually, covering the last calendar year, and reported to the Secretary-General of the United Nations not later than 30 April of each year.

3. The Secretary-General of the United Nations shall transmit all such reports received to the States Parties.

Article 8: Facilitation and clarification of compliance

1. The states parties agree to consult and cooperate with each other regarding the implementation of the provision of this Convention, and to work together in a spirit of cooperation to facilitate compliance by States Parties with their obligations under this Convention.

2. If one or more States Parties wish to clarify and seek to resolve questions relating to compliance with the provisions of this Convention by another State Party, it may submit, through the Secretary-General of the United Nations, a Request for

Clarification of that matter to the State Party. Such a request shall be accompanied by all appropriate information. Each State Party shall refrain from unfounded Requests for Clarification, care being taken to avoid abuse. A State Party that receives a Request for Clarification shall provide, through the Secretary-General of the United Nations, within 28 days to the requesting State Party all information which would assist in clarifying this matter.

3. If the requesting State Party does not receive a response through the Secretary-General of the United Nations within that time period, or deems the response to the Request for Clarification to the unsatisfactory, it may submit the matter through the Secretary-General of the United Nations to the next Meeting of the States Parties. The Secretary-General of the United Nations shall transmit the submission, accompanied by all appropriate information pertaining to the Request for Clarification, to all States Parties. All such information shall be presented to the requested State Party which shall have the right to responds.

4. Pending the convening of any meeting of the States Parties, any of the States Parties concerned may request the Secretary-General of the United Nations to exercise his or her good offices to facilitate the clarification requested.

5. The requesting State Party may propose through the Secretary-General of the United Nations the convening of a Special Meeting of the States Parties to consider the matter. The Secretary-General of the United Nations shall thereupon communicate this proposal and all information submitted by the States Parties concerned, to all States Parties with request that they indicate whether the favour a Special Meeting of the States Parties, for the purpose of considering the matter. In the event that within 14 days from the date of such communication, at least one-third of the States Parties favours such a Special Meeting, the Secretary-General of the United Nations shall convene this Special Meeting of the States Parties within a further 14 days. A quorum for this Meeting shall consist of States Parties.

6. The Meeting of the States Parties or the Special Meeting of the States Parties, as the case may be, shall first determine whether to consider the matter further, taking into account all information submitted by the States Parties concerned. The Meeting of the States Parties or the Special Meeting of the States Parties shall

make every effort to reach a decision by consensus. If despite all efforts to that end no agreement has been reached, it shall take decision by a majority of States Parties present and voting.

7. All States Parties shall cooperate fully with the Meeting of the States Parties or the Special Meeting of the States Parties in the fulfilment of its review of the matter, including any fact-finding missions that are authorized in accordance with paragraph 8.

8. If further clarification is required, the Meeting of the States Parties or the Special Meeting of the States Parties shall authorize a fact-finding mission and decide on its mandate by a majority of the States Parties present and voting. At any time the requested State Party may invite a fact-finding mission to its territory. Such a mission shall take place without a decision by a Meeting of the States Parties or a Special Meeting of the States Parties to authorize such a mission. The mission, consisting of up to 9 and 10, may collect additional information on the spot or in other places directly related to the alleged compliance issue under the jurisdiction or control of the requested State Party.

9. The Secretary-General of the United Nations shall prepare and update a list of the names, nationalities and other relevant date of qualified experts provided by States Parties and communicate it to all States Parties. Any expert included on this list shall be regarded as designated for all fact-finding missions unless a State Party declares its non-acceptance in writing. In the event of non-acceptance, the expert shall not participate in fact-finding missions on the territory or any other place under the jurisdiction or control of the objecting State Party, if the non-acceptance was declared prior to the appointment of the expert to such missions.

10. Upon receiving a request from the Meeting of the States Parties or a Special Meeting of the States Parties, the Secretary-General of the United Nations shall, after consultations with the requested State Party, appoint the members of the mission, including its leader. Nationals of States Parties requesting the fact-finding mission or directly affected by it shall not be appointed to the mission. The members of the fact-finding mission shall enjoy privileges and immunities under Article VI of the Convention on the Privileges and immunities of the United Nations, adopted on 13 February 1946.

11. Upon at least 72 hours notice, the members of the fact-finding mission shall arrive in the territory of the requested State Party at the earliest opportunity. The requested State Party shall take the necessary administrative measures to receive, and shall be responsible for ensuring the security of the mission to the maximum extent possible while they are territory under its control.

12. Without prejudice to the sovereignty of the requested State Party, the fact-finding mission may bring into the territory of the requested State Party the necessary equipment which shall be used exclusively for gathering information on the alleged compliance issue. Prior to its arrival, the mission will advise the requested State Party of the equipment that it intends to utilize in the course of its fact-finding mission.

13. The requested State Party shall make all efforts to ensure that the fact-finding mission is given the opportunity to speak with all relevant persons who may be able to provide information related to the alleged compliance issue.

14. The requested State Party shall grant access for the fact-finding missions to all areas and installations under its control where facts relevant to the compliance issue could be expected to be collected. This shall be subject to any arrangements that the requested State Party considers necessary for:

    a) The protection of sensitive equipment, information and areas;

    b) The protection of any constitutional obligations the requested State Party may have with regard to proprietary rights, searches and seizures, or other constitutional rights; or

    c) The physical protection and safety of the members of the fact-finding mission.

In the event that the requested State Party makes such arrangements, it shall make every reasonable efforts to demonstrate through alternative means its compliance with this Convention.

15. The fact-finding missions may remain in the territory of the State Party concerned for no more than 14 days, and at any particular site no more than 7 days, unless otherwise agreed.

16. All information provided in confidence and not related to the subject matter of the fact-finding missions shall be treated on a confidential basis.

17. The fact-finding missions shall report, through the Secretary-General of the United Nations, to the Meeting of the Sates Parties or the Special Meeting of the States Parties the results of its findings.

18. The Meeting of the States Parties or the Special Meeting of the States Parties shall consider all relevant information, including the report submitted by the fact-finding mission, and may request the requested State Party to take measures to address the compliance issue within a specified period of time. The requested State Party shall report on all measured taken in response to this request.

19. The Meeting of the States Parties or the Special Meeting of the States Parties may suggest to the States Parties concerned ways and means to further clarify or resolve the matter under consideration, including the initiation of appropriate procedures in conformity with international law, in circumstances where the issue at hand is determined to be due to circumstances beyond the control of the requested State Party, the Meeting of the States Parties or the Special Meeting of the States Parties may recommend appropriate measures, including the use of cooperative measures referred to in Article 6.

20. The Meeting of the States Parties or the Special Meeting of the States Parties shall make every effort to reach its decisions referred to in paragraph 18 and 19 by consensus, otherwise by a two-thirds majority of Sates Parties present and voting.

Article 9: National Implantation Measures
1. The States Party shall, take all appropriate legal, administrative and other measures, including the imposition of penal sanctions, to prevent and suppress any activity prohibition to a State Party under Convention undertaken by persons or no territory under its jurisdiction or control.

Article 10: Settlement of disputes
1. The States Parties shall consult and cooperate with each other to settle any dispute that may arise with regard to the application or

the interpretation of this Convention. Each State Party may bring any such dispute before the Meeting of the States Parties.

2. The Meeting of the States Parties may contribute to the settlement of the dispute by whatever means it deems appropriate, including offering its good offices, calling upon the States Parties to a dispute to start the settlement procedure of their choice and recommending a time-limit for any agreed procedure.

3. This Article is without prejudice to the provisions of this Convention on facilitation of clarification of compliance.

Article 11: Meeting of the States Parties

1. The States Parties shall meet regularly in order to consider any matter with regard to the application or implementation of this Convention, including:

   a) The operation and status of this Convention;

   b) Matters arising from the reports submitted under the provisions of this Convention;

   c) International cooperate and assistance in accordance with Article 6;

   d) The development of technologies to clear anti-personnel mines;

   e) Submissions of States Parties under Article 8; and

   f) Decisions relating to submissions of States Parties provided for in Article 5.

2. The First Meeting of the States Parties shall be convened by the Secretary-General of the United Nations within one year after the entry into force of this Convention. The subsequent meetings shall be convened by the Secretary-General of the United Nations annually until the first Review Conference.

3. Under the conditions set out in Article 8, the Secretary-General of the United Nations shall convene a Special Meeting of the States Parties.

4. States not parties to this Convention, as well as the United Nations, other relevant international organizations, the International Committee of the Red Cross and relevant non-

governmental organizations may be invited to attend these meetings as observers in accordance with the agreed Rules of Procedure.

Article 12: Review conference

1. A Review Conference shall be convened by the Secretary-General of the United Nations five after the entry into force of this Convention. Further Review Conferences shall be convened by the Secretary-General of the United Nations if so requested by one or more States Parties, provided that the interval between Review Conference shall in no case be less than five years. All States Parties to this Convention shall be invited to each Review Conference.

2. The purpose of the Review Conference shall be:

   a) To review the operation and status of this Convention;

   b) To consider the need for and the interval between further Meetings of the States Parties referred to in paragraph 2 of Article 11;

   c) To take decisions on submissions of States Parties as provided for in Article 5; and

   d) To adopt, if necessary, in its final report conclusions related to the implementation of this Conventions.

3. States not parties to this Convention, as well as the United Nations, other relevant international organizations or institutions, regional organizations, the International Committee of the Red Cross and relevant non-governmental organizations may be invited to attend each Review Conference as observers in accordance with the agreed Rules of Procedure.

Article 13: Amendments

1. At any time after the entry into force of this Convention any State Party may propose amendments of this Convention. Any proposal for an amendment shall be communicated to the Depository, who shall circulate it to all States Parties and shall seek their views on whether an Amendments Conference should be convened to consider the proposal. If a majority of the States Parties notify the Depositary no later than 30 days after its circulate that they support further consideration of the proposal, the Depositary shall convene an Amendment Conference to

which all States Parties shall be invited.

2. States not parties to this Convention, as well as the United Nations, other relevant international organizations or institutions, regional organizations, the International Committee of the Red Cross and relevant non-governmental organizations may be invited to attend each Amendment Conference as observers in accordance with the agreed Rules or Procedure.

3. Any Amendment Conference shall be held immediately following a Meeting of the States Parties or a Review Conference unless a majority of the States Parties request that it be held earlier.

4. The Amendment to this Convention shall be adopted by a majority of two-thirds of the States Parties present and voting at the Amendment Conference. The Depositary shall communicate any amendment so adopted to the States Parties.

5. An Amendment to this Convention shall enter into force for all States Parties to this Convention which have accepted it, upon the deposit with the Depositary of instrument of acceptance by a majority of States Parties. Thereafter it shall enter into force for any remaining State Party on the date of deposit of its instrument of acceptance.

Article 14: Costs

1. The costs of the Meetings of the States Parties, the Special Meetings of the States Parties, the Review Conferences and Amendment Conferences shall be borne by the States Parties and States not parties to this Convention participating therein, in accordance with the United Nations scale of assessment adjusted appropriately.

2. The costs incurred by the Secretary-General of the United Nations under Article 7 and 8 and the costs of any fact-finding mission shall be borne by the States Parties in accordance with the United Nations scale of assessment adjusted appropriately.

Article 15: Signature

This Convention, done at Oslo, Norway, on 18 September 1997, shall be open for signature at Ottawa, Canada, by all States from 3 December 1997 until 4 December 1997, and at the United Nations Headquarters in New York from 5 December 1997 until its entry into force.

Article 16: Ratification, acceptance approval or accession
1. This Convention is subjected to ratification, acceptance or approval of the Signatories.
2. It shall be open for accession by any State which has not signed the Convention.
3. The instrument of ratification, acceptance, approval or accession shall be deposited with the Depositary

Article 17: Entry into force
1. This Convention shall enter into force on the first day of the sixth month after the month in which the 40th instrument of ratification, acceptance, approval or accession has been deposited.
2. For any State which deposits its instrument of ratification, acceptance, approval or accession after the date of the deposit of the 40th instrument of ratification, acceptance, approval or accession, this Convention shall enter into force on the first day of the sixth month after the date on which the State has deposited its instrument of ratification, acceptance, approval or accession.

Article 18: Provisional application
Any State may at time of its ratification, acceptance, approval or accession, declare that it will apply provisionally paragraph 1 of Article 1 of this Convention pending its entry into force.

Article 19: Reservations
The Articles of this Convention shall not be subjected to reservations.

Article 20: Durations and withdrawal
1. This Convention shall be of unlimited duration.
2. Each State Party shall, in exercising its national sovereignty, have the right to withdraw from this Convention. It shall give notice of such withdrawal to all other States Parties, to the Depositary and to the United Nations Security Council. Such instrument of withdrawal shall include a full explanation of the reasons motivating this withdrawal.
3. Such withdrawal shall only take effect six months after the receipt of the instrument of the withdrawal by the Depositary. If, however, on the expiry of that six-month period, the withdrawal

State Party is engaged in an armed conflict, the withdrawal shall not take effect before the end of the armed conflict.

4. The withdrawal of the Stat Party from the Convention shall not in any way affect the duty of States of continue fulfilling the obligations assumed under any relevant rules of international law.

Article 21: Depositary

The Secretary-General of the United Nations is hereby designated as the Depositary of this Convention.

Article 22: Authentic texts

The original of this Convention, of which of the Arabic, Chinese, English, French, Russian and Spanish texts are equally authentic, shall be deposited with the Secretary-General of the United Nations.

CHAPTER FOUR

AFTER THE WAR

The Nigeria/Biafra Civil War came in 1967 and ended in 1970. It rather ended with the formal proclamation of Nigeria's Head of State and Commander-In-Chief of Nigeria's Armed Forces, Gen. Yakubu Gowon of "END OF WAR" on 15TH JAN, 1970." Shortly after the pronouncement according to an Army Veteran Aniebo I.N.C., in his "FOREWORD" to Achike Udenwa's Book "THE NIGERIA/BIAFRA CIVIL WAR: MY EXPERIENCE[1], said:

"One of the most arbitrary acts of the Federal Government of Nigeria was to dismiss/discharge in 1971, all the Senior Nigerian Army Officers who had no choice but to fight on the Biafran side. Yet, the Government had declared "No Victor, No Vanquished" and had garnered a great deal of good publicity by promising a general amnesty and directing on paper that all Federal employees should be reinstated "whenever they came out of hiding." 1

The dismissal or discharge of the main actors in the losing side of the War, from the ruling Nigerian Army, debarred them from participating in the shaping of its aftermath. That was precisely what the Federal Government did when it did the following acts:

(a) Placed all the Nigerian Army Officers, who fought on the Biafran side, under a pseudo- House arrest at Owerri, with an insolent raw Nigerian subaltern in charge of their "Security",

(b) did not recognize the ranks of the officers as at the end of the War, thereby reverting them to the ranks they had at the beginning of the War.

(c) flew them surreptitiously to a nondescript Hotel in Lagos to face " a Military Tribunal" without any legal representation.

The "Tribunal" acted more like an interrogating team, the rank of officers firing prepared
questions from files.

(d) dismissed, discharged or retired all the Senior officers from captain and above (1967 ranks!), from the Army with effect from May 1967, even though the whole exercise lasted for over a year

---

[1]*Aniebo I. N. C. in his Foreword to Achike Udenwa's Book "The Nigeria/Biafra Civil War: My Experience:*

after the War ended in 1970.....".[2]

The above is the picture of what actually took place immediately after cessation of hostilities in the battle fronts. However, while the staccato of guns dimmed, the Civil War seemed to have continued in many other ways at several other fora including but not limited to contaminated areas by landmines, explosive remnants of War and other unexploded ordnance. Mines are usually unaffected by cease fire or truce.[3]

Many writers of History of the Nigerian Civil War put the dead from the unfortunate War to more than two million from both sides of the conflict. They died for the Unity of Nigeria. However, there were those who also got injured during the War in the task of keeping Nigeria one. Let us remember those Innocent Nigerians who suffered severe injuries after the War from landmines, abandoned explosive ordnance, unexploded ordnance and other explosive remnants of war left behind by the Military in their farms while tilling the ground to plant, or digging foundation of their Houses as a result of abandoned explosive remnants of War and unexploded Ordnance of War.[4]

It was a War fought without due deference to Law of War and International Humanitarian Law. Both sides to the Conflict were known to have used conventional and unconventional Landmines as they engaged each other in ground offensives and Counter-offensives in the former Eastern Region in the 30 months War. Beyond that, several millions of unexploded Ordnances (Bombs) were generously but uncontrollably deployed in various locations, Sandwiched today within 11 States out of the 36 States of the Federation.

At the cessation of hostilities in 1970, majority of these Landmines and bombs were neither removed nor destroyed, and had since then injured many people as well as claimed significant number of innocent lives. "Landmines and unexploded ordnance result in significant musculoskeletal injuries throughout the World". 4. Besides, the presence of Landmines and Bombs had since hinder and prevent access to lands which ordinarily would have been used for Agricultural, Industrial and residential purposes. Some of the lands are now thick-forests and often times tagged "Evil forests" since every effort to put to use any part or

---

[2] *Aniebo I.N.C.(ibid)*

[3] *Aniebo I.N.C. (ibid)*

[4] *Nicholas E. Walsh & Wendy S. Walsh:The Bulletin of theWorld Health Organization 2003.*

parcel of such lands result in explosion of some sort. Since 1970, Nigerian citizens in the South-East Zone who could not be killed during that War have continued to be consumed by explosive remnants of War in a rather rudderless and hapless manner until reprieve of some sort came with the introduction of the Ottawa Convention by the United Nations. [5] The Convention otherwise called Mine Ban Treaty and vice versa "prohibits the use, Stockpiling, production, development, acquisition and transfer of anti-personnel Mines"[6].

This is because in every conflict since 1938 across the globe, Anti-personnel Mines have been used extensively, often resulting in death or injury to non-combatants; and have accomplished only limited Military objectives. Other explosive remnants of war play complementary roles in decimating civilian population at cessation of armed conflicts. Explosive remnants of war are varied in forms, shape and quality. But they are largely destroyers. Explosive Remnants of War means unexploded ordnance and abandoned explosive ordnance.

Explosive Ordnance means conventional munitions containing explosives, with the exception of mines, booby traps and other devices.

Unexploded Ordnance means (uxo) explosive Ordnance that has been primed, fused, armed, or otherwise prepared for use in an armed conflict. It may have been fired, dropped, launched or projected and should have exploded but failed to do so. They are unstable explosive devices left behind during and after conflicts and pose dangers similar to landmines.

Abandoned Explosive Ordnance (axo) means explosive ordnance that has not been used during an armed conflict, that has been left behind or dumped by a party to an armed conflict, and which is no longer under control of the party that left it behind or dumped it. Abandoned explosive ordnance may or may not have been primed, fused, armed or otherwise prepared for use.

Existing Explosive Remnants of War means unexploded ordnance and abandoned explosive ordnance that existed prior to the entry into force of this Protocol for the High Contracting Party on whose territory it exists. But the one that is hardly noticeable is landmine.

---

[5] *Mine Ban Treaty*
[6] *Wikipedia, the Free Encyclopedia.*

WHAT IS A LANDMINE?

A landmine is an impediment, or a hindrance placed or buried along the axis of an advancing troop, it is meant to delay or canalize them into a predetermined line of fire of the defender. A Landmine is usually a weight-triggered or trip-wire activated explosive device which is intended to damage a target either human or inanimate, by means of a blast and/or fragment impact. It further means ammunition designed to be placed under, on or near the ground or other surface area and to be exploded by the presence, proximity or contact of a person or a vehicle.

Landmines maim and kill hundreds of people each year as well as hold entire contaminated communities hostage in the Civil War affected areas of Nigeria. They hamper and as well as hinder food and medical supplies from reaching people in need. Landmines hinder the return of internally displaced people from returning to their farms and communities. Landmines are classified into two categories: Anti-personnel and Anti-tank. An anti-tank landmine when in contact with the target aside of destroying the vehicle, it also has the capacity of incapacitating the occupants of the vehicle. The use of anti-tank mine is not banned by the Convention even though most victims end up being paralyzed in the end. Whereas the anti-personnel mine is small and it is set off either by a trip wire or a pressure switch that requires minimal pressure.

Anti-Tank Mine: - The Anti-Tank Mine is a directed mine, used against armored targets, for the protection of narrow road, especially highway and maneuvering areas. The mine can also be employed very effectively in mine field against clearance vehicle of the enemy.

The Anti-Tank Mine (ATM) is placed laterally, right angle to the driving direction of the Armored Vehicle. The target is relative to the weak armored hull (thickness of Steel max. 80mm) The Anti-Tank mine is an effective tool for quick and safe deployment during insurgency.

Description: - The body of the mine is always cylindrical, conical and made of sheet-steel spin rolled. On the front-size of the body is a special design projectile forming liner in position. The liner is embedded in high explosive 'HE' charges of approximately 9.0kg.

Its Performance: - The perforation is affected by the high Kinetic energy of the 2.8kg heavy projectile formed by detonation of high explosive (HE); at an initial velocity of approximately 2.300m/s, firing tests shows that the projectile does not disintegrate when perforating tank apron made of composite ceramic liner.

Handling of the Anti-Tank Mine: - The sighting device of the mine allows exact aiming. The mine support, consist of two fix folding legs that serve as transport for the mine. The leg supports have hinge adjustment for the vertical direction. The mine can be triggered by means of a manually operated electrical ignition device, or by means of a contact wire as well as by means of an electrical sensor.

The electrical sensor triggers the mine when a vehicle is passing the line of slight, whist wheeled vehicles do not cause a set off. The sensitivity of the electronic device can be adjusted in such a way that the mine can distinguish between light and heavy either manually or wireless or by means of a time delay switch. The safety distance behind the mine is at minimum of 30 meters, for operators in a fox hole and 100 meters for operators under cover. Anti-personnel landmines are targeted against human beings – and almost in all cases, against innocent Civilians long after cessation of hostility. They are designed to be placed under, on or near the ground, and to be exploded by the presence, proximity or contact with a person. Landmines often times, misplace their targets and expected roles during armed conflicts and against those Civilians who ignorantly attempt to pick, relocate or remove them from their erstwhile positions. The case of many "Nigerian Landmines Victims arose while they were digging the ground to lay foundations or tilling the ground for farming. "It is designed to kill or maim anything that comes in contact with it, which often includes Civilians, children and animals." They enjoy long and extended life span and can patiently lie in wait for decades. This is why 42 years after the Civil War in Nigeria they are still killing and maiming.

Anti-Personnel Landmines have their rules and regulations since their entry into War. If laid they are to be marked clearly by the Unit who laid them, and a landmine record must be kept showing date laid, where laid, size of the ground covered, quantity and density of Mines laid. Nigeria Army and indeed, parties to the conflict in the Nigerian Civil War did not keep such a record, and failure to do so has resulted in the maiming and massive killing of many innocent victims which number has swelled the number of the direct War Mine Victims and hence the need for Humanitarian Demining exercise in Nigeria.

The body of the mine is double curved and rectangular and made of plastics. In front of the body is a fragmentation face containing some steel balls embedded in a plastic matrix. The fragmentation face is formed horizontally convex and vertically concave to direct the splinters in a 60 degree, and is controlled by the vertical dispersion of the splinters. Behind the fragmentation face there is a layer of explosives, consisting of 1.3kg composition. On the back there are two protruding filing holes allowing the exact identification of the side towards friendly troops even in the darkness.

Its Uses: - The Anti-Personnel Mine (APM) is a controlled fragmentation mine that is used in a close range defense area against unprotected personnel. The Mine is also effective against thin-skinned vehicles (like jeeps, cars, truck etc). The spherical steel fragments will perforate on the body. The excellent effect of the mine is produced by the large number of steel balls in the fragmentation face. It can either be placed on the ground or fastened to a tree or another object. The standing device of the mine allows compensating irregularities of the ground, so that the mine has a solid upright position.

Handling: - the marking is relief on two protruding domes allowing the exact, identifying side towards friendly troops. The right filling hole are placed in relief "Z I" including arrows, which mark the side of the detonators.

On the other side there is a minor detonator wall which is designed to hold a detonating cord in case of an ignition in series. The mine can be set off either by means of an electrical ignition device or by means of an impact igniter.

The anti-personnel mine could be equipped with a time fuse (in range of 1 minute up to 24 hours). The standard devices of the mine consists of two pairs of legs screwed, one pair on each side of the mine. The safe distance behind the mine is 15 meters minimum in a fox, and 80 meters under cover.

How to De-arm the Mine: - The Explosive Ordnance Disposal (EOD) technician must always bear in mind the Render Safe method when dealing with mine whether planted by terrorists or by guerrilla group. That is to say, the power source if detected should be discarded from the main charge to enable the operator carry out the dismantling of the mine device.

At the commencement of the Nigeria War, the pre-civil War Nigerian Army had some large unknown quantities of anti-personnel landmines as well as anti-tank landmines in her inventory which were deployed during the War to protect, Enugu, Nsukka, and other areas after their capture from the Biafran Army. Similarly the Biafran Army also deployed Landmines at strategic areas. In the kitty of the Nigerian Army then were three types of Landmines used in the War viz. POMZ anti-personnel Landmines from the former Czechoslovakia and Russia, Ranger and Dingbat anti-personnel Landmines from Britain. There was also the introduction and use of the locally manufactured landmines which were deployed against the federal troops by the Biafran Army. As a matter of fact, the Biafran landmines otherwise called (Ogbunigwe-mass killer) in Igbo language had more devastating effects on their victims than the Conventional landmines. The Nigerian Army with all its sophistication laid Landmines within the mined areas in the territory of Biafra without records. Yet 40 years after the cessation, Nigeria waited for the United Nations, to be reminded of the need to demine the contaminated mine fields in that War. Nigeria soon forgot that an honest and sincere implementation and application of the Principle of "No Victor, No Vanquished" ought to have included the demilitarization of War affected States.

From the above, the Nigerian Army mined! Biafran Army which didn't have enough access to munitions, food and medicine relied more on the use of "Ogbunigwe" or "Ojukwu Bucket" which Radio Biafra christened "Biafran shore battery". The Biafran Army had more of Mark 4 and SMC riffles. Achike Udenwa explains the strategy of the Biafran Army in the use of Landmines; "In terms of armament, we had a couple of Landmines (Ogbunigwe) which were manned by the engineering personnel attached to us. There was a patrol team attempting to land at the Shores of Otaba. The explosion of one of the Ogbunigwe's repelled them with some casualties and we watched the survivors manage to berth in one of the creeks. This ensured they did not make any further attempt, but we kept on exchanging small arm-fire across the river"[7] It was so effective that it played very important roles throughout. As a matter of fact, the locally manufactured Biafran mines had more devastating effects on their victims than the imported ones. The "Ogbunigwe" is electronically operated and has a range of one hundred meters."[8]

It wasn't only that Nigerian Army did nothing to record mined areas in areas under its territory, it refused/ neglected to clear or remove Landmines from all the contaminated areas between 1970 and 2009, that is, 39 years before the United Nations reminded her of her obligations to her citizens. It took the intervention of the U.N. to convince Nigeria to undertake the clearance of explosive remnants of War (ERW) and unexploded ordnance when Nigeria became the 156 member of the Ottawa Convention of the 158 Members as at 2011. It is contended that the inability of Nigerian Government to embark on ridding war affected

---

[7] Achike Udenwa (ibid)

[8] Achike Udenwa *(Page 96)*

areas of ERW before now in spite of its being a State Party to the 1980 Convention on Certain Weapons (CCW) is also a total negation of the full import of Gen. Yakubu Gowon's "End of War Speech"...

One major reason Landmines, Bombs and Other Explosive remnants of War are left behind in the theatres of war is mainly owing to malfunction at the time of usage or when fired. Others are dropped, when shot or thrown at targets such as aerial bombs, mortars, grenades, cluster bombs aside of malfunctioning of primers, fuses or even as a result of abandonment. It is also thought that anywhere between 2-20 percent of munition fail to detonate on impact either because of the texture of the ground or the age of the fired munition. Also, sometimes an item of ordnance does not work as expected when it is released from the air. The Aircraft may be too low, too high or the ground conditions might not be right. In so far it has failed to detonate, it constitutes danger on the ground until someone disables or detonates it. Significant among the large quantities of mortar bombs scattered in the former Eastern Nigeria is the over-aged nature of the ammunitions with manufacture dates dating back in the early 50s.

DEMINING is defined as "the process of removing either landmines, or naval mines, from an area, while minesweeping describes the act of detecting of mines."[9] It also means the set of activities that lead to the removal of Mine and Explosive Remnants of War (ERW) hazards, including Survey, mapping clearance, marking and the handover of the cleared land.

There are two major types of Demining namely: Military Demining and Humanitarian Demining. The one is Military Demining which is the clearance of a lane or gap within a mined field to enable the continuity of military operations. It is done by the military under pressure and under the cover of darkness. It is more of a struggle to create and use the road.[10] In military demining, the Law of War applies. The other is the humanitarian demining which is the clearance of mines and explosive relics left behind by the military after cessation of conflict. It is done by civilians with military background or by personnel trained for that purpose. It is supported by bilateral convention or convention on the

---

[9] *Kenneth R. Rutherford: Peer-to-Peer Support Vital to Survivors – An article published in* <u>The Journal Of Erw And Mine Action</u>. *Issue 14.2 /Summer 2010.*
[10] *The Journal of ERW and Mine Action; Op.cit*

explosive remnants of War. [11]

The Law on military demining provides that every minefield must be clearly indicated to the enemy after cessation of Hostilities whereas the Convention on Humanitarian demining requires that when both parties cease fighting, they must come together to demine. In humanitarian demining, refusal of parties to demine could attract sanctions but in military demining, no sanction is required. Hostilities. Because of the high number of casualties caused by explosive remnants of War (ERW) that is why the United Nations insisted on a total ban on the transfer, use, manufacture and even research into mine production which is captured in the Mine Ban Treaty. Humanitarian Demining involves the carrying out of technical survey of mined areas and the deliberate marking of all mine fields found. All the Mines, once surveyed and located must be removed. In order to successfully carry out humanitarian demining, everybody in any given mined area must be enumerated before, during and after the exercise. The United States first became involved in humanitarian demining in 1988 but unfortunately it is not among the 158 High contracting state parties to the Mine Ban Treaty. However, the U.S. is an example of a country that even though refused to sign the treaty but sponsors and assists in financing and training.

Every year. Landmines kill 15,000 to 20,000 people- most of them children, women and the elderly- and severely maim countless more. Scattered in some 78 countries, they are an ongoing reminder of conflicts which have been over for years or even decades. According Nicolas E. Walsh and Wendy S. Walsh in the Bulletin of the World Health Organization 2003: "Landmines and unexploded ordnance result in significant musculoskeletal injuries throughout the world. In every conflict since 1938 antipersonnel mines have been used extensively, often resulting in death or injury to non-combatants, and have accomplished only limited military objectives." In recent years, mines have been used increasingly as weapons of terror against local civilian populations in an attempt to isolate them or force them from their communities by depriving them of access to farmlands, roads, and even necessities of life such as drinking- water and fire wood. The antipersonnel mine is small and is set off either by trip wire or a pressure switch that requires minimal pressure (typically 6 kg). It is designed to maim or kill anything that comes into contact with it. Which often includes civilians, Children and animals. Unfortunately, antipersonnel

---

[11] *1980 Convention on Certain Conventional Weapons (CCW)*

mines have a long life span: they can kill and maim indiscriminately for decades. They are not selective of their targets. Once one is in, one is in! And since the 1960 as many as 110 million mines have been spread throughout the world into an estimated 70 countries including Nigeria. Landmines are unaffected by cease-fires, truce or peace. The only way to deactivate them is by individual removal. Removal of landmines is a high risk business. Persons who engage in the business of mine removal need not be Engineers but must be skilled. They must undergo training. Even with training, mine disposal experts posit that for every 5000 mines cleared one worker will be killed and two workers will be injured by accidental explosions. Modern technology has been able to make plastic mines that are smaller and less detectable. Mines cost between US$ 3 and US$ 75 to produce but at so costs between US $300 – 1000 dollars to remove one mine. Unfortunately, their small size, design and often colour make them very attractive to children, who may pick them up thinking they are toys. Wherever and whenever it becomes expedient to demine, a lot of things are put in place such as:

Mine Risk Education (MRE): Those who live in mined areas before the mines are removed undergo mine security training aimed at reducing the risk of detonating a mine or an Unexploded Ordnance (UXO). The training is aimed at both children and grown-ups, and can substantially reduce the number of mine accidents. Drama, cartoons, posters and the likes are used in raising awareness among the population.

Information Management (IM): In order to gain an over-view of the mine problem in a given area, all available information related to the suspected and confirmed mine fields is collected, systematized and may be coupled with Geographic Information Systems. A complete survey (Non-Technical Survey and/or Technical Survey) of the mine problem in a given area, the nature of the places which have been mined, their locality and their effect, eases the prioritizing of resource use, the measurements of possible results and the devising of realistic plans for clearance.

Task Impact Assessment (TIA): TIA is a tool used actively before, during and after clearance activities, this in order to determine and measure the impact of clearance. TIA a crucial tool for NPA in determining the socio economic effect NPA's work has no people who live in, and the environment of, mine and cluster contaminated areas.

Manual Demining: This method is used worldwide. Deminers systematically search an area with metal detectors and prodders in order to locate possible mines. When a suspicious object is detected, the surrounding soil is carefully removed and the mines are defused or denoted.

Manual demining is work and time consuming, but very reliable to the defined depth, and has the advantage of not requiring large investments to get started. Manpower is recruited and trained locally, and therefore manual demining has the additional advantage of creating employment.

Explosive Ordnance Disposal (EOD) and Battle Area Clearance (BAC): EOD personnel operate as specialized separate terms or within a demining unit. Specialized EOD personnel are also used for the disposal of Custer Munitions. BAC teams are organized similarly to manual demining teams in order to undertake clearance of ERW in areas not contaminated with mines.

Mechanical Mine Clearance (MMC): Armored machines with various forms of earth removing equipment, rotating chains and

the like are driven over the minefields. The machines reveal, destroy and/or explode mine lying in the ground. Different follow-up techniques to assure that the land is safe for the end user is then applied, from visual investigation to a full demining drill depending on the situation in terms of terrain, vegetation, type of mines/ERW and the regulations in country. Mechanical mine clearance is effective in suitable areas, and has proven extremely effective mine fields, and limit the area of a search. The development of mechanical mine clearance has progressed from heavy military equipment to lighter, more flexible civilian machinery.

Mine Detection Dogs (MOD) and Explosive Detection Dogs (EDD): Dogs can be trained to detect Mines and remnant of explosives. Dogs are particularly effective in detecting mines and ERW in areas where it is difficult to determine the exact location of an ordnance and bigger areas must be verified. Also where mines have been scattered unsystematically, in difficult terrain and where mines and ERW are buried deep, dogs are an effective and sometimes the only tool that can be used. On clearance tasks, two-search procedures are readily used where initially, dogs on a search a defined area, followed by a short lash dog search, and the dog handler walks in the area cleared by the dog. So far, what has happened in the case of Nigeria is inchoat Manual humanitarian demining anchored by two companies whose Chief Executive Officers neither participated in the Civil War nor are familiar with the terrains of the South-East and South-South z ones of the former Eastern Nigeria. This is the reason any clearance effort claimed by

Nigeria is doubtful. This is apart from the fact that no organ or institution of the Nigerian Government supervised the alleged clearance exercise. How would Nigeria claim success in landmines clearance when the whole of Umuahia, Ngwaland and many other places were abandoned by the contractors on the grounds of insecurity caused by kidnapping. It is unconceivable and unimaginable what their reasons could be since kidnapping abated in the area.

CHAPTER FIVE

LANDMINES AND EXPLOSIVE REMNANTS OF WAR

During the Nigeria – Biafra conflict about 20% casualties were soldiers. But after the war approximately 80% of casualties are civilians with children more likely to die from landmine injuries than adults.....it is estimated that 50% of victims die within hours of the blast, many of them never reaching medical care that may be hours away on bad and bumpy roads. And in most cases, where there are no hospitals and even where there is, there is virtual absence of medical personnel. As for those who live depending on the country, there is a virtual lack of systems for rehabilitation professionals, financial and technical resources and a vocational rehabilitation system.

Today, some 14 UN agencies, programmes, departments and funds are active on the ground in mine-related service. They find and destroy landmines and explosive remnants of war, assist victims, teach people how to remain safe in mine-affected areas, destroy stockpiles, and encourage universal participation in the *Mine-Ban Convention*. United Nations *peacekeeping* operations often play a key role in this process. The mine-related activities of the UN system are coordinated by the UN Mine Action Service. It assess and monitors the threat posed by mines and unexploded ordinance on an ongoing basis, and develops policies and standards. The Service mobilizes resources, and advocates in support of the global ban on anti-personnel landmines. It is also responsible for providing mine-action assistance in humanitarian emergencies and for peacekeeping operations.

The UN has been actively engaged in addressing the problems posed by landmines since the 1980s. It acted decisively to address the use of weapons having indiscriminate effects when it sponsored the 1980 Inhumane Weapons Convention. In 1996, that Convention was strengthened to include the use of landmines in internal conflicts and to require that all mines be detected. Eventually, a growing public outcry, combined with the committed action of non-governmental organizations involved in the International Campaign to Ban Land Mines (ICBL), led to the adoption of a comprehensive global agreement. The landmark 1997 UN *Convention on the Prohibition of the Use. Stockpiling, production and transfer of Ant-personnel Mines and on Their Destruction (Mine-Ban Convention)* bans the production, use and export of these weapons and has nearly universal support. A United Nations

International Day for Mine Awareness and Assistance in Mine Action is observed every year on 4TH April."

One major reason landimes, bombs and other weapons are left behind is simply due to malfunctions when fired. Other remnants of Armed conflict are drooped, shot, thrown such as aerial bombs, mortars, grenades, cluster bombs aside of malfunctioning of primers, fuses or even as a result of dumping or abandonment. Howsoever, it fails to detonate it remains dangerous on ground until someone disables or detonates it.

It is worrisome to know upon proper appraisal Nigeria's attitude towards the implementation and compliance with the Ottawa Convention? The initial reaction will be to say that Nigeria Government has not uptil date domesticated the Ottawa Convention and that is the reason Nigeria is mostly unserious in the implementation of the Ottawa Convention, and the Cartegena Action Plan; and yet it has informed the world that existing laws suffice, when indeed there virtual absence of any existing law relating to landmines and other ERW's in our corpus juris.

Secondly, Nigeria has done nothing towards rehabilitation of Victims and victims' assistance. Both the Criminal Code and Penal Code operative in Nigeria do not have any provisions that can comprehensively promote the operation of the Ottawa and 1980 Conventions. It can safely be said that at best Nigeria pays lip service to the provisions of the Ottawa Convention as well as the Cartegena Action plan. The Federal Ministry of Justice has taken no steps to enable the National Assembly domesticate the Law, thus leaving the Ministry of Defence to treat the Convention with Levity and deceit. It is strongly viewed that some ministry of Defence officials who are from non-mine contaminated areas regard as a "Special favour anything done to those who caused the War"; and therefore should be allowed to die by Landmines and Bombs which they planted – the reason for the delay or reluctance in the domestication of the Law Mine Ban Treaty. Added to that, some viruses also bedevil the domestication and implementation of the Convention by Nigeria Government – they are:

- Lack of understanding
- Lack of interest and hatred
- Lack of co-ordination between the Ministry of Justice, Ministry of Foreign Affairs and the Ministry of Defence.

The Ministry of Foreign Affairs is the custodian of all Treaties and

Conventions entered into by Nigeria. It is the Ministry that is responsible for signing any convention(s) on behalf of Nigeria, and husbands these Treaties/Conventions at the same time. Nigeria has not indeed ratified the Ottawa Convention.

In May 28, 2009, Nigeria informed the Standing Committee on Mine clearance, Mine risk education, and Mine action Technologies that there were anti-personnel Mines in mined areas under Nigeria's jurisdiction or control and that Nigeria was aware of its obligation to:

"destroy or ensure the destruction of all anti-personnel mines in these mined areas as soon as possible, but not later than (10 years after entry into force" of the Convention for Nigeria). Nigeria noted that it would have a deadline of 1st March, 2012 to conclude the implementation of Article 5."

In accordance with its obligations under Article 7 of the Ottawa Convention, Nigeria reported to the United Nation among other things;

"In (a) War affected area of Eastern part of Nigeria," areas that were suspected to contain anti-personnel mines. Nigeria further reported that the types of mines would have been a "Biafran locally fabricated" explosive device (Ogbunigwe) which was used as (an) AP Landmine and that they would have been emplaced not later than January 1970."

Nigeria also reported that it had constituted an inter-ministerial committee to concern itself with mines and other explosive remnants of War to enable Nigeria meet its Convention obligations and that the Committee consisted of representatives of relevant Ministries, departments, and non-government organizations. In further response to the problems caused by explosive remnants of War including the need to fully implement Article 5 of the Convention, Nigeria set up a Mine Action Programme for South-East with the following Terms of Reference and Action plan:

(a) Mine clearance as part of a broader explosive remnants of War removal and destruction programme, including a

well-planned and implemented survey process to identify the areas of need;

(b) Mine risk education, including; (i) developing a significant programme for education of the population of South-East of Nigeria of the hazards posed by explosive remnants of War with this involving Radio and Television Campaign, poster distribution processes and training session in Villages, Markets, Churches, and

Schools throughout the affected region and

(ii) establishing a "hot-line" for populations to report explosive hazards and for taking and prioritizing on the basis of these reports.

(c) Victims assistance, particularly the enumeration of Mine victims from the Biafra / Civil War.

(d) Reporting, including by monitoring implementation and providing reports to the Ministry of Defence in part to ensure that Nigeria can comply with its Convention reporting obligation.

It is instructive to note that Nigeria is also a signatory to the 1980 CONVENTION ON CERTAIN CONVENTIONAL WEAPONS (CCW). Part of Article 2 of Protocol V on Explosive Remnants of War of the 1980 Convention thoroughly addresses Explosive Remnants of War (ERW). This convention makes it mandatory for the Federal Ministry of Defence to remove all Explosive Remnants of War (ERW) in the former War Zone.

Thus Article 3, 1, CLEARANCE, REMOVAL OR DESTRUCTION OF EXPLOSIVE REMNANTS OF WAR States that;

"Each High contracting party and party to the armed conflict shall bear the responsibilities set out in this Article with respect to all explosive remnants of War in territory under its control. In cases where a user of explosives ordnances which has become explosive remnants of War (Biafra), does not exercise control of the territory, the user i.e. (Ministry of Defence) shall, after the cessation of active hostilities, provide where feasible, inter alia technical, financial, material or human resources assistance, bilaterally or through a mutually agreed third party, including inter alia through the United Nations System or other relevant organizations, to facilitate the marking and clearance, removal or destruction of such explosive remnants of War."

Article 3(2) provides "After the cessation of active hostilities and as soon as feasible, each High Contracting Party and Party to an Armed Conflict shall mark and clear, remove or destroy explosives remnants of war in war affected territories under its control, areas affected by explosive remnants of War which are assessed pursuant to paragraph 3 of this Article as posing a serious humanitarian risk shall be accorded priority status for clearances, removal or destruction.

Article 3(3) provides, "After the cessation of active hostilities and as soon as feasible, each High Contracting party and Party to an Armed Conflict shall take the following measures in affected territories under its control, to reduce the risks posed by explosive remnants of War:

a. Survey and assess the threat posed by explosive remnants of war.
b. Assess and prioritize needs and practicability in terms of marking and clearance, removal or destruction.
c. Mark and clear, remove or destroy explosive remnants of War.
d. Take steps to mobilize resources to carry out these activities; see also sub 4 and 5 of Article 3.

Whereas Article 5 (1) provides "High Contracting Parties and Parties to an Armed Conflict shall take all feasible precaution in the territory under their control affected by explosive remnants of War to protect the Civilian population objects from the risks and effects of War. Feasible precaution are those precautions which are practicable or practicably possible taking into account all circumstances ruling at the time, including humanitarian and military considerations. These precautions may include Warnings, risk education to the Civilian population, marking, fencing and monitoring of territory affected by explosive remnants of War as set out in part 2 of the Technical annexed.

ARTICLE 8 (2) provides "Each High Contracting Party in a position to do so shall provide assistance for the care and rehabilitation and social and economic reintegration of Victims of explosive remnants of War. Such assistance may be provided inter alia through the United Nations System relevant International or regional or national organizations or institutions, the International Committee of the Red Cross, National Red cross and Red crescent Societies and their International federation non-governmental organization, or on a bilateral basis.

Article 8 (3) requires each High contracting party in a position to do so shall contribute to trust funds within the United Nations System, as well as other relevant trust funds, to facilitates the provision of assistance under this protocol.

Article 8(6) provides that "High contracting parties may submit request for assistance substantiated by relevant information to the United Nations, to the appropriate Bodies or other States. These requests may be submitted to the Secretary General of the United Nations, who shall transmit them to all High Contracting Parties and to relevant International Organizations and non-governmental organization.

Going by the Protocol 5 of the 1980 Convention, Nigeria owes her citizens the duty to clear the former Civil War affected zones of unexploded ordnances (UXO), abandoned ordnances (AXO) and Explosive Remnants of War (ERW) in the 1st three months between 1980 and 2014, Nigeria remained quite insensitive to the affected 11 States while the civilian population is gradually decimated. Article 4 of the Convention states unambiguously:

"A state party undertakes to destroy or ensure the destruction of all stockpiled anti-personnel Mines it owns or possesses, or that are under its jurisdiction or control not later than 4 years after being a signatory to the Convention."

Shortly before he left office in 2007, President Olusegun Obasanjo ordered the destruction of anti-personnel landmines in the inventory of the country's military. Chief Obasanjo did not however bother himself about dangerous unexploded devices that were buried deep down and at random in the old Eastern region which was the Theatre of War.

Nevertheless, it was late President Umaru Yar' Adua that ordered the Ministry of Defence to ensure the removal and destruction of the remaining Landmines and bombs, before the end of March 22, 2012 - United Nations deadline given Nigeria to be Ottawa Convention compliant as a signatory to the Ottawa Convention. The entire Convention requires that all signatories must within four years of joining that group, remove or destroy all stockpiles in the holding of their military. And within 19 years of that same signatory, remove all landmines buried in the ground. Nigeria is yet to take steps to exhume all weapons dropped by war planes that got stock in the ground or buried in pit latrines after the war in spite of the directive of President Goodluck Ebele Jonathan to the relevant Ministry of Defence to ensure effective and effectual demilitarization and de-contamination of Civil War affected areas of South-East and South-South till date.

However, between October 2008 and March 2009, the Ministry of Defence through its Contractors/Agent RSB Holdings Ltd., operated in 11 of Nigeria's 36 States (i.e,. 11 States contaminated by explosive remnants of War after visiting and identifying about 835 sites in about 186 Local Government Areas in Nigeria covering about 178,000 Square kilometers of Land beginning from Nassarawa State through Benue State to States of the South-East and South-South of Nigeria. About 665 locations containing landmines have been discovered and not entirely demined. Enugu had 108 Locations, Ebonyi 58, Imo 87, Cross River 67,

Abia 65, Delta 71 and Rivers 72, 3 were found in Nassarawa while 13 locations were found in Benue, among many others that are not been located because of virtual absence of equipment and appropriate technologies. But on the 2nd December 2010, at the Tenth Meeting of States Parties, Nigeria reported that four cities namely Enugu, Owerri, Port Harcourt and Markudi and their environs had been cleared resulting in the destruction of 101 POMZ type mines, 61 locally fabricated (Ogbunigwe) mines and 4,863 other explosive hazards. However, there are more Bombs in the contaminated areas than landmines – a fact which the Ministry of Defence is willing to suffocate. Mines alone do not constitute dangers to life. Information from the Ministry of Defence contractor confirms that as at May 2011, about 17519ERW and Bombs of various calibers had been removed from these contaminated areas but leaving behind more number of unexploded ordnances of War. The contractor RSB Holdings Ltd., according to its Chief Consultant – Dr. Bala Yakubu said that, "there are over 50,000 Bombs scattered all over the South-East and South-South Zones of Nigeria; notwithstanding that about 2,014 Bombs have so far been removed from Rivers State, 350 from Imo State, with Benue State recording the heaviest of the Bombs of about 250 kilograms. Quite recently, an 81mm mortal Bomb was removed from the country home of literary giant – Professor Chinua Achebe at Ogidi , Anambra State of Nigeria."[12]

It is however, obvious that the Deminers did not enter some forests which were theatres of War and yet Nigeria prides itself as having cleared the contaminations. It is imagined the type of machines and equipment they used in the process with the paltry funding by the Nigerian Government. The contractors were ill-equipped with modern machineries and earth-moving equipment as nobody saw them do this and there are no pictorials. Moreover, neither the Ministry of Defence nor Police Anti Bomb Unit supervised the alleged clearing exercise by the Deminers.

The Ministry of Defence is aware that the Ottawa Convention has more or less been honoured in breach by Nigeria; and yet about the same time in May 2011, it directed her contractor to stop the clearance of the balance explosive Remnants of War (ERW) and unexploded ordnance in the contaminated areas while at the same time, it wrote the United Nations for a refund of the sum of over N940,000.000 (Nine Hundred

---

[12] *George Opara: THE NEWS Vol. 33, Nov. 21, 30th November, 2009.*

and Forty Million Naira). All these smack of lack of understanding of the basic problems on ground. Members of the Inter-Ministerial Committee set up by the Ministry of Defence did not visit the affected States from the time the Committee inauguration and consequent commencement of work by the contractors.

A flashback to the implementation of the 1980 Convention (CCW) reveals that since after the cessation of active hostilities, Nigeria has only observed the Convention also most profoundly in breach. "Biafra" does not exercise control over the territory, Nigeria does and yet the Nigerian Government has regrettably and overtly failed to demilitarize the contaminated War areas with the result that one can safely say that the Nigerian Civil War has continued to claim lives, maim and kill the so called "Biafrans" who indeed are now alleged to have they planted the Bombs. Therefore, between 1980 when Nigeria ratified the CCW and 2001 when it equally acceded the Ottawa Convention till date not much has been done to stop the killings of innocent citizens and victims of the ERW by Nigeria Government. The actual War abated but maiming of the Civilian population and destruction of grazing animals have continued outside the main theatres of War. But if Nigeria could not and remains unwilling what has the ECOWAS done to assist Nigeria in the contaminated and War affected Areas of South-East, South-South and North-Central States. Six years before the Ottawa Convention cemented a commitment to rid the World of anti-personnel Landmines, the Organization of American States (OAS) conceived a vision to help the Governments of Central America emergence from a decade of conflict by clearing Landmines from their National territories.[13] Comparatively, since 1991, the Organization of American States (OAS) has worked to eliminate the threat of anti-personnel landmines in America. For instance, in response to a 1991 request from the newly – installed Democratic government in Nicaragua, the OAS called upon the Inter-American Defence Board – a Military adjunct of the OAS to study the Mine related problems in Central America and recommend a plan of action. Although the IADB's assessment focused primarily on Nicaragua, which was the most severely mine-affected Nation in the region, its staff also studied the landmine problem in Costa Rica, El-Salvador, Guatamala and Honduras all of which had seen the use of anti-personnel mines to some extent throughout the 1980s.[14]

---

[13] *Kenneth R. Rutherford*
[14] *Carl E. Case:A Mine Free Central Africa: How can we improve on Success: An Article.*

Sixty-four years after the Second World War, Countries like Germany, Poland and Japan are still contending with the danger of clearing Landmines, Bombs and other life-taking explosives deployed in that War. Nigeria has unfortunately been playing politics with such deadly discovery due to lack of understanding, lack of deliberate National policy to rid the War affected areas of the former Eastern Region of Nigeria of the contamination caused by both parties to the hostility. Also because of lack of interest of the Ministry of Defence representing the Federal Government in the well-being and rehabilitation of Mine Victims.

There are five pillars of Mine Action already discussed which neither Nigeria nor the regional body ECOWAS has done anything meaningful about, they are: (a) Mine Clearance (b)Victims Assistance (c) Mine Risk Education (d) Advocacy (e) Stockpile;

Of all these, Nigeria is yet to successfully comply with the standards required of her by the convention. Nigeria forgot so soon that those who survive Mine or Bomb blast typically suffer shattered limbs requiring amputation, multiple operation and prolonged physical rehabilitation. They suffer permanent disability and social, psychological and economic implication of being disabled. Being injured by a landmine is traumatic for anyone but it becomes a life-long problem when the victim is a child.

The first feeble attempt at the enumeration and rehabilitation of Mine Victims was by Ajie Ukpabi Asika – erstwhile Administrator of East Central State built a Resettlement Centre at Oji River for the resettlement of victims of the Civil War. There were about 635 of them as inmates immediately after the Civil War. As at 2009, 445 of them had died and 163 of them were alive. Of the 1163 that are alive, 277 of them were the victims of Mines. Some of them raised families while still living there and it does not bother the Government that these people ought to have been assisted, sent home and rehabilitated in line with Gen. Yakubu Gowon's "End of War Speech".

In the course of the clearing exercise by R.S.B. Holdings Ltd. Equipment remnant of War were discovered – equipment remnant of war means a machine that was used to fight the Civil War. Chief Consultant Dr. Bala Yakubu in an interface revealed that about 6 of them have so far been recovered, 4 out of which are the Biafran Red Devil while the two others are the Nigerian Army Saladin. All these are still in the locations where they have been since 1970.

The primary threat now is the result of unexploded ordnance on former battlefields about which few, if any records existed. For instance the contractors found heaps of live Bombs in the following schools:

- Aquinas Secondary School, Osu Mbano,
- St. Peter Clever Seminary, Okpuala
- Ohoba in Ohaji/Egbema Local Government Area
- St. Patrick's Secondary School, Ogbe Ahiazu Mbaise,all in Imo State, Government House

Abakaliki, Ebonyi State, Nsitubiam in Akwa Ibom State, Etche, Igwurita in Rivers State, and also in Delta State. Heaps of Bombs were also found in Ihiala in Anambra State. All these Bombs are yet to be removed!

In Abia State, the company worked in Abia North only where the team removed Bombs in Ohiafia, Bende, Uzoakoli leaving off the entire Abia South and Abia Central. And yet in paragraph 13 of a Memo titled, "Declaration of Completion of the Implementation of Article 5, Paragraph 1, of the Convention on the Use, Stockpiling, Production and Transfer of Anti-personnel Mines and on their Destruction: FEDERAL REPUBLIC OF NIGERIA, sent to the UNITED NATIONS declared as follows:

"Nigeria is now proud to declare that it has ensured the destruction of all anti-personnel mines in areas under its jurisdiction or control in which anti-personnel mines were known or suspected to be emplaced, in accordance with Article 5 of the Convention. Nigeria furthermore declares that it has completed this obligation ...."[15]

The declaration is false, totally misleading and ignisfatous. It is intended to misinform and deceive the UN. It is hardly discernible when the Ministry of Defence has not met any of its own Terms of Reference. Also there is no synergy between the Ministry of Defence, Ministry of Justice and Ministry of Foreign Affairs in almost all important Conventions and Treaties entered into by Nigeria even as it affects the 1980 Convention and the Ottawa Convention. Nigeria probably does not remember being a member or signatory to the 1980 Convention. Nigeria is unaware of the total number of Mine Victims. There is no statistics. Nigeria has not less than 178,000 Square kilometers of contaminated land Areas which have not been declared or made safe. It has not

---

[15] *The Guardian Newspaper Vol. 27, No. 11, 284 Thursday, November 19, 2009.*

rehabilitated and has no plan to rehabilitate Mine victims, 44 years since the cessation of Hostilities. Nigeria has not given any financial assistance to any victim and yet from findings, there are more than 4000 survivors and not less than 496 pre-enumerated. Meanwhile, scores of victims have died.

The pathetic story of a mother and son - Mrs. Nwogu and her only son from Etche Local Government in Rivers State, Nigeria, readily comes to mind. Both of them lost their right legs to Landmines while farming. Many of the victims who ought to have been provided for with Prosthetes, Artificial limbs or electronic equipment for movement still craw like infants. Their numerous dependants who are regarded as victims are not provided for. Another example of a victim needing help is Pa Ibiomogbo Mayor Ibiomogbo in Okaba village in Abua-Odua Local Government Area, in the same Rivers State who lost his right hand when a Landmine exploded while he was working in his farm. He has many children and dependents needing help and assistance. Mr. Cletus Akpan Ogbonna from Ukana Uwa West from Essien Udim L.G.A. of Akwa Ibom State is a mine victim who now has a partial stroke. No form of assistance has been given him. Mr. Vincent Agu – a former big time Motor Sales Businessman who went home at Ohii in Owerri-West Local Government Area, Imo State to do a House foundation had his leg shattered by Landmine. There has been no reprieve, and he spent so much taking care of himself in Europe in search of medical attention. Other known victims include: Mr Joseph Ngozi Okere, Francis Njoku, Eddie Opara, Mr Onyeanu Cyriacus Chukwuma, Miss Clementina Chinyere Chikezie, Jude Ujunwa Egbe, Mr Eze Richard, Boniface Akanwa, Miss Nkechi Osuji, Donatus Obilor, Mrs Nwogu, Mr Nwogu, Mrs Maria Okorie, Livinus Eke Nnadi, Boniface Onwuliri, Bon Okereafor, and Miss Vivian Kelechi Obasi – were all young persons when they had either their hands or legs amputated by Landmines after the end of the Civil War, to mention a few. Nze Joseph Egbujuo – Dike ukwu had his two legs chopped off by Landmines and about the same time and date and within the same environment his wife who had rushed to rescue him was also hit by a Landmine and she bled to death. What is significant here is that most of these Victims had no privilege of mine risk education and come from Ngor Okpaala Local Government Area, Imo State while the rest numbering over 496 that are still alive come from other parts of Imo, Rivers, Anambra, Enugu, Ebonyi, Delta and Bayelsa States.

It should be observed that planning process for Mine clearance so far in Nigeria is significantly flawed by lack of clarity concerning the country's

Mine situation. The ministry of defence, ministry of foreign affairs that ratified the Convention on behalf of Nigeria, and the ministry of justice have had no synergy on any action-plan at the time of ratification. All the steps taken towards implementation had no historical precedent and practically no doctrinal guidelines on how to develop mine assessment strategy. "Prior to the signatory of the Ottawa Convention and the development of international standards, there was no clear roadmap for mine Actions Programmes to follow."[16] Nigeria is worse hit!

There is virtual absence of any National Policy on the number of mines and mined or contaminated Areas on how to make such areas safe. This is probably either because those concerned are mostly Igbos or that no Igbo leader or group has cared to bring this issue to either the President or National Assembly.

There is no strategy to involve the use of mechanical and canine assets in the demining effort; and Nigeria has no equipment to assist her contractors in the Demining exercise. There is no doubt that initial planning assumption for clearance programme throughout the over 178,000 Square kilometer of the contaminated areas were affected by poorly assessed area coverage and therefore the initial funding by the ministry of defence was poor, insufficient and not based on the reality on ground. Lack of methodical survey and assessment by the ministry of defence never brought the extent of the problem to national discourse and focus so that clearance goal, targets and objective of a mine safe-Nigeria could be defined and substantially achieved. The attitude of ministry of defence officials is such that the Igbo's should be allowed to die or be killed by the Landmines and Bombs they planted! But they seem to forget that Biafran leadership in the conflict did not have enough money to procure weapons of mass destruction as the Nigerians. The ones Biafrans made were unconventional as against the conventional landmines and bombs with capacity to live longer to consume their victims. These were the ones used by Nigeria and not Biafra.

It is therefore regrettable that a former minister for defence in the Yar'Adua Administration was clearly heard expressing the opinion somewhere that the "Igbos should be allowed to be killed by the bombs they planted" without regard to the fact that bombs have no respect for tribe, creed, colour, sex and nationality.

---

[16] *The Journal of ERW and Mine Action. Op.cit*

RECOMMENDATIONS:

Nigeria should establish a Mine Action Commission or Authority and equip it with facilities to make for quick intervention now and in the future.

Nigeria should make land release, or clearance for safe land overall mine assessment and planning primary points of focus.

Develop a coherent set of National priorities and plans that can assist the deminers in their plans to reduce the dangers posed by ERW etc..[17]

Prioritizing the funding of the clearance of uxo's, axo's erw's and more particularly bombs, over 50,000 of which is said to be scattered all over the contaminated Areas of the Eastern Region. Some of these bombs sites have been identified but not isolated from sharing neighbourhood with people. Many of these bomb- sites are located in School compounds and other public places.

Nigerian government should establish reporting system and build trust and effective working relationship between communities in the affected areas.

Encourage and support the establishment of Volunteer – group that can effectively liaise with Mine – action personnel, communities and villagers.

The Mine Action and Victim Assistance Commission or Authority when established should conduct a base-line survey in the most affected and contaminated areas for physical and infrastructural rehabilitation programmes in all the affected schools and public buildings.

Develop a credible Mine / UXO risk reduction network, covering the heavily affected / contaminated villages and towns.

Get the deminers back to work with adequate funding. The Deminers need mobile equipment to run through suspected mined areas. But they should be supervised by the Mine Action Authority in liason with affected communities.

Get some of those who fought the War and who are still alive in an interface with the ministry of defence to open up on Mined Areas or

---

[17] *Cartegena Action Plan 2010 – 2014: Ending The Suffering caused by Anti-Personnel Mine.*

suspected areas.

Remove the estimated 50,000 Bombs scattered in the contaminated areas since one live Bomb can stay upto 100 years waiting patiently to consume its victims.

Honestly implement the Articles 5 and 7 of the Ottawa convention as well as the 1980 convention.

Financially assist mine victims and their dependents. To this end Nigeria needs to make yearly budgetary provisions of not less than **N1 Billion** to make these provisions to be managed by a Co-ordination Committee under the Presidency or Ministry of Defence through the Nigeria Mine Action Authority.

Build Rehabilitation and Peer-group to Peer-group Centres for the Victims in each of the war affected states in Order not to detach the victims completely from their cultural settings.

Nigeria should train up or sponsor the training of Lawyers whose work should be to follow up conventions to enable Nigerian explore some advantages. Nigeria lost the Bakassi Peninsular due mainly to the fact that the ministry of foreign affairs, ministry of justice and ministry of defence had no co-ordination on the matter. Nigeria should for the sake of unity and peace strive to avoid anything that could degenerate to civil war again as this is an ill-wind.

CHAPTER SIX

MBT AND ROAD MAP IN SELECTED COUNTRIES

The Mine Ban Treaty is the most successful disarmament legislation the world has seen. To date it covers more than 75% of the world's countries, and signed by 156 per April 2010. In December 2009 the states parties to the MBT gathered in Cartagena (Colombia) for the 2nd Review Conference to sum up the achievements so far. Landmine Monitor, the civil society driven monitoring mechanism, summed the achievements up as reported by Atle Karlsen

- *Despite the fact that 39 countries still have not acceded to the MBT, including large producers and former users like USA, Russia, China and Pakistan, the Convention has had a deep normative effect.*
- *It has not been proven that any state party has used landmines in the last years.*
- *The only countries where landmines are either used or suspected used are Myanmar, Georgia and Russia.*
- *Positive effects have also been shown on Non State Actors (NSAs) and only in seven countries had such use been proven in 2008.*
- *Of more than 50 previous producers there are just 13 countries still producing or reserving the right to produce (only India, Pakistan and Myanmar have verified the production).*
- *In relation to landmine trade the Convention has effectuated a de facto ban, also among the countries that have not acceded. Illegal trade in 2009 is minimal.*
- *In relation to destruction most countries are on their way to reach their obligations and more than 44 million landmines have been destroyed.*

ANGOLA is a country in South-Central Africa bordered by Namibia, the Democratic Republic of Congo and Zambia. Angola was plagued by civil war since independence from Portugal in 1975 until the peace accords between the government and UNITA were signed the 4th of April 2002. Mines as well as a whole other slew of traditional ammunitions and explosives were used by both sides during the conflict, making Angola one of the most mine affected countries in the world. Large portions of the country are still not accessible due to mines and ERW, and it is estimated that one fifth of the population has its day to day life affected by mines and erw. Upon request by the UN, NPA involved itself with mine clearance in Angola in 1994. Initially, the task was to map the coastal provinces and other areas pinpointed as camps for demobilized soldiers, as well as clearing the main highway between Luanda and Malanje. Due to the mine problem and the huge distances, three separate bases for clearance were established throughout the country. From 195 to 2004 these bases were located in the cities of Malanje, Lunena and Lubango. In 2003 NPA took part in the country wide survey of the problem, and became responsible for 5 provinces in the northwestern part of Angola (Malanje, Kwanza sul, Kwanza Norte, Uige, Zaire). The result of said survey created the base for strategic plans for mine clearance in Angola by national authorities (2006-2013). The strategic plan then created the basic for a large increase in funding by Angolan authorities for mine clearance. Several international donors have since chosen to pull out of Angola, but NPA has had continued support from its donors until 2010-11, albeit at a considerable reduced level compared66 to previous years.

BOSNIA HERZEGOVINA is a Country in South East Europe bordered by Serbia, Croatia, Montenegro and the Adriatic Sea. The war in Bosnia and Herzegovina has left behind a grim legacy of mines and other ERW, which can be found in almost all parts of the country. The leftover mines and ERW have a great impact on the society in Bosnia and Herzegovina and its economy. One fourth of populated places and one third of the population in Bosnia and Herzegovina is affected by mines and ERW. Most of the 11,443 mine suspected areas were identified between the former confrontation lines, stretching for more than 18,000km. The estimated size of suspected areas contaminated by mines and ERW is about 1,555 square kilometers, or 3.04% of the total land surface area. Bosnia and Herzegovina (B&H) is among the countries with the largest average number of mine and ERW casualties per million in-habitats, since 1992 until the end of 2009 there were registered 5,033 mine and ERW casualties in B&H. in the period after the war there were 1,694 casualties, of these 495 fatalities.

CAMBODIA is a Country in Southeast Asia, bordering Thailand Lao PDR, Vietnam and the Gulf of Thailand. After three decades of armed conflict, Cambodia is one of the most mine/UXO contaminated countries in the world. Cambodia experiences several hundred landmine and UXO victims per year. The Cambodia Mine Action Authorities have requested an extension on the Mine Ban Treaty Article 5, which was approved in 2009. Base Line Survey (BLS) in cooperated with all operators in order to prepare a new map defining the extent of remaining contaminated with a high degree of accuracy.

CROATIA is a Country in South Eastern Europe, bordered by Slovenia, Hungary, Serbia, Bosnia, Montenegro and the Adriatic Sea. Croatia declared its independence from the Socialist Federal Republic of Yugoslavia in 1991. The Yugoslav Army (JNA) took the side of Serb forces that fought for the construction of a break-away Serb Republic within the borders of Croatia forces continued until 1995, approximately 887.7 square kilometers of land in Croatia is still contaminated or suspected to be contaminated with mines, cluster munitions and unexploded ordnance. Almost one million people, that is, almost one quarter of the entire population lives or in some way makes use of the areas treated as mine suspected.

ETHIOPIA: Ethiopia is a landlocked country situated in the Horn of Africa, bordered by Eritrea, Sudan, Kenya, Somalia and Djibouti. Mine Action in Ethiopia is a mature activity managed by a national authority, the Ethiopian Mine Action Office (EMAO), established in 2001 and now supported by operational assets. The area identified by the Ethiopian Landmine Impact Survey (ELIS) covered 2500 square kilometers and found that more than 1.9 million people live in a total of 1,492 mine-affected communities. The threat is extensive and widespread with 10 of the 11 regions affected and ranging from pattern minefields in the north to random pattern low density suspected hazardous areas (SHA) in the Remainder of the country. Mine Explosive Remnants of War (ERW) contamination stems from a series of internal and international armed conflicts, including the Ogaden war between Ethiopia and Somalia (1977-1978), the border war with Sudan (1980), internal conflicts (1974-1991), and the Ethiopian-Eritean war (1998-2000). The ELIS also recorded 16,616 casualties, more than half of whom had been killed.

GEORGIA: Georgia is a country in the Caucasus region of Eurasia, bordered by the Black Sea, Turkey, Armenia and Azerbaijan. The war between Russian and Georgia the fall of 2008 left a large number of unexploded ordnances in Georgia. During the conflict, both sides used cluster munitions. The cluster problem was mainly limited to the conflict area, especially in the region Karteli, north of Gori.

GUINEA BISSAU: The Republic of Guinea Bissau is located in West Africa. It is bordered by the Senegal to the north and Guinea to South and East with the Atlantic Ocean to its west. According to a landmine impact survey eighty-one percent of the communities affected by ERW and landmines in Guinea Bissau are compact villages, relying on small-scale agriculture for survival. Although the overall scale of contamination and impact is somewhat limited, there is evidence from surveys that clearance will ameliorate current blocked or compromised access to agricultural and pasture land for almost half of these communities. The regions most affected are Cacheu and Oio in the north; this is mostly due to mine contamination from the Casamance Conflict. They, together with Buruntuma in Gabu region, constitute the highest priorities for clearance.

SOUTH IRAQ: The Republic of Iraq is located in the Middle East. It is bordered by Kuwait, Saudi Arabia, Jordan, Syria, Turkey and Iran. Iraq is massively affected by landmines and ERW, the result of internal conflicts, the 1980-1988 war with Iran, the 1991 Gulf war, and the conflict that has been ongoing since the 2003 invasion by the US-led Coalition. Since then, there have been almost daily attacks with car bombs and other IEDs on civilians. Iraq security forces and coalition forces indicate vast amounts of abandoned ammunitions left unsecured after the overthrow of the Saddam Hussein regime. Much of this has been plundered and is assisting ongoing insurgencies. In addition to this, ERW is currently limiting access to agricultural pasture land, and also affects other areas such as school yards and such.

JORDAN: Arab country in Southwest Asia, bordered by Syria, Iraq, the West Bank, Israel, and Saudi Arabia. The mine and unexploded ordnance (UXO) problem in Jordan derives from the 1948 partition of Palestine, the 1967-1969 Arab-Israel conflict, and the confrontation with Syria in 1970's. The minefields were limited to three major areas, the Northern Highlands, the Jordan Valley and Wadi Araba in the South. There are also UXO in a small number of areas centered in the Ajloun and Irbid governorates. According to military estimates, some 305,000 anti-personnel and anti-vehicle mines were laid on Jordanian territory. Jordan's mine action of land across 314 minefields remained contaminated with 203,094 mines. Mines in Jordan directly affect over eight percent of the population. Mine contamination blocks access to valuable agricultural land, delays irrigation and hydroelectric projects, restricts housing construction, and isolators historic and cultural heritage sites. Jordan ratified the Mine Ban Treaty in May 1999 and is committed its revised obligation to clear all landmines before May 2012.

LAO PDR: Lao PDR is a landlocked country in Southeast Asia, bordered by Myanmar, China. During the Indochina war Lao PDR experienced the heaviest aerial bombardment in history. US bombing records show an average of 176 sorties a day over nine years and more than two million tons of bombs were dropped between 1964 and 1973. A survey carried out by Handicap International in 1997 collected detailed information from 7,675 villages determining the presence of ERW, the type of land contaminated and types of UXO observed, the number of casualties caused by UXO and their impact on affected communities. Preliminary results from a recent national Victim Survey show that previous recorded accident rated have been too low, with a realistic rate of 300 new victims per year being caused by UXO in Lao PDR since 1974.

MOLDOVA: Is a country in Eastern Europe, bordered by Romania and the Ukraine. It has been recognized that 87 countries are stockpilers of Cluster Munitions. As a legacy from the former Soviet Union, Moldova had stockpiles. On the 22nd April 2010, infront of mass media and representatives from Norwegian People's Aid and OSCE the Moldovan Ministry of Defence allowed the invited guests to witness the disposal programme of its 152mm Cluster Munition Projectiles.

SUDAN: A country in North Africa, bordered by Egypt, the Red Sea, Eritrea, Ethiopia, Kenya, Uganda, the Democratic Republic of the Congo, Central African Republic, Chad and Libya. More than 21 years of civil war between the mainly Muslim north and the Animist and Christian south has created a considerable problem with landmines and UXO in central and southern Sudan. Since the civil war broke out some 4 million people have been displaced and some 1, 5 million people have been killed by manmade or natural disasters. A Comprehensive Peace Agreement (CPA) between ween the North and the South was signed in January 2005. The mine threat is found in a number of regions in Sudan. The highest contamination (excluding border areas with Egypt in the North) is found in South Sudan. The Land Impact Survey (LIS) confirms that the states of Eastern and Central Equatoria (bordering Kenya and Uganda) have been found to have the highest level of contamination, it is worth nothing that the border regions to Ethiopia have for a variety of reasons not yet been surveyed, and it is reasonable to expect that the region may be contaminated by mines and UXO threat is in fact just as significant as the mine threat. The United Nations Mine Action Program (UNMAP) report 41 casualties in 2009. The initial focus of work I Sudan was the survey and clearance of roads that had become inaccessible because of the perceived or real mine threat. The bulk of this work is now complete so the emphasis is switching towards the release of land for agriculture, return and resettlement programs, and infrastructure projects, as well as surveying and clearing un-assessed areas, and opening up secondary and tertiary routes.

SERBIA: Country located in South Eastern Europe, bordered by Bosnia-

Hercegovina, Croatia, Hungary, Romania, Bulgaria Makedonia, Kosovo and Mantenegro. Following the break-up of Yugoslavia parts of the border between Serbia and Croatia were mined. By the end of 2009 all these minefields were cleared. During the NATO bombing in 1999, NATO used cluster munitions on several targets in Serbia. Based on NPA's estimates, around 15km2 need to be cleared of unexploded cluster sub-munitions. Moreover, landmines were also used by Albanian rebel forces in southern Serbia in 2000-01. According to a hazard assessment by NPA in 2010, around 1.5 km2 are defined as suspected hazardous areas in need of further survey and mine clearance. Both unexploded cluster munitions and landmines affect agriculture, forestry, development of infrastructure and the security of the local population in affected areas. NPA cleared 1km^2 of minefields on the border between Serbia and Croatia in 2006. NPA also started a general survey project of areas affected by unexploded cluster munitions in Serbia in November 2007. NPA currently hopes to clear roughly one third of the areas affected by unexploded cluster sub-munitions in southern Serbia. The project is stipulated to last for three years, employing 35 personnel.

THAILAND: Is a country in South Asia, bordered by Lao PDR, Myanmar, Cambodia, the Gulf of Thailand, the Malaysia. Thailand has experienced intense ground warfare and deployment of a large number of landmines and littering of explosive remnants of war (ERW) in limited areas in the country. Land is still out of bounds due to landmines and ERW; the main problem being a high level of landmine contamination of the Cambodia. Thailand also receives a large number of mine and ERW victims having accidents across the border to Myanmar but the situation along this area is mainly unknown at present. According to the National; Authority the estimated area of landmine contamination is 528 square kilometers. There is also a considerable problem with explosive violence in the South of the country with a considerable number of injuries and deaths.

UGANDA: The Republic of Uganda is a landlocked country in East Africa. Bordered by Kenya, Sudan Democratic Republic of Congo, Rwanda and Tanzania. Landmines and ERW in Uganda are a result of armed conflict and civil strife over the past four decades. The main problem is in the north of the country, following many years of conflict with the non-state armed group, the LRA, and includes mines. UXO and abandoned explosive ordnances. Uganda ratified the Mine Ban Treaty on the 25th of February 1999giving it a deadline of August 1st 2009 to comply with Article 5 of the Convention. Until recently it looked as though Uganda would manage to achieve its deadline, however, with the discovery of new mined areas in the north in the border regions with South Sudan, Uganda applied for a tree year extension on the MBT deadline, until August 2012.

VIETNAM is a Country in Southeast Asia, bordered by China, Lao PDR, and Cambodia. During the last war Quang Tri and Thua Thien Hue Province provinces saw intense conflict, especially along National Route 9 from the Vietnam-Lao border towards Dong Ha Town and onto the coastal areas. During the Tet offensive in 1968 the battle for Hue city was one of the most intensive during the war and in 1972 Quang Tri province was subjected to one of the war's most extensive bombing campaigns. Almost every village in Quang Tri province was destroyed. According to statistics at that time, 328,000 tons of bombs and other weapons of explosive ordnance were used and thousands of landmines were laid. The United States combat records show that Quang Tri was the most targeted and this is where the majority of BLU-26/36 cluster bombs and M79 40mm grenades are found, according to Landmine Monitor report, 35 percent of land in central Vietnam cannot be used for cultivation or resettlement. Between 100,000 to 140,000 people became victims from unexploded munitions from 1957 and until today. Vietnam still has one of the highest civilian accident rates in the world as a result of these unexploded remnants of war. It is expected that 400 to 450 people a year will continue to become victims from the war legacy.

ZAMBIA: The Republic of Zambia is a landlocked country in the Southern Africa. Bordered by the Democratic Republic of Congo, Tanzania, Malawi, Mozambique, Zimbabwe, Botswana, Namibia and Angola. The former mine and UXO problem in Zambia stems from freedom fighters in neighboring countries having used Zambia as a safe haven. The mine problem was mainly along its borders with Angola, Congo, Zimbabwe, and Mozambique, especially in former refugee populated areas and areas previously used as guerrilla/freedom fighter camps. Landmines were used for ambush purposes, in order to deny access to areas and for protection of permanent/ semi-permanent bases within Zambia.

MOZAMBIQUE is a Country in the Southeastern Africa. Bordered by the Indian Ocean, Tanzania, Malawi and Zambia, Zimbabwe, Swaziland and South Africa. The landmine contaminated in Mozambique has its origin in three distinct phases of conflict: 1964-1975 – Minefields laid by the Portuguese as protection against incursions by the independence movement, FRELIMO. 1976-1979 - Zimbabwean independence war and the emergency of RENAMO. 1979-1992- Civil conflict between

FRELIMO and RENAMO. During all three stages, the forces loyal to the government of the day laid large numbers of mines to defend economic infrastructure and military installations, while the opposition forces often planted anti-tank mines on roads, bridges, and river crossings to inhabit government troop movement, interdict shipments, and cripple the economy. During at least the conflict between FRELIMO and RENAMO, both sides also used mines more indiscriminately, resulting in many small or low-density minefields.

WESTERN SAHARA: Western Sahara is a territory of North Africa, bordered by Morocco, Algeria, Mauritania, and the Atlantic Ocean. Western Sahara is disputed by Morocco and the Polisario Front Independence movement. According to Landmine Monitor report 2008. "Western Sahara is contaminated with antipersonnel mines, anti-vehicle mines, and explosive remnants of war (ERW), especially (cluster) sub munitions and other unexploded ordnance (UXO). According to Landmine Action, Western Sahara is one of the most heavily mined territories in the world."

KOSOVO: Is a disputed region in the Balkans Kosovo is landlocked and bordered by Serbia, Macedonia, Albania and Montenegro. From July 1999 large areas of Kosovo were contaminated with mines and unexploded ordinance (UXO) that posed an immediate threat to people's lives creating a serious obstacle to the delivery of humanitarian assistance, the reconstruction of homes, infrastructure and essential services for the rebuilding of civil society. NPA was one of first organizations to set up a demining program in Kosovo, commencing operations in July 1999. As an emergency response to the immediate mine threat posed for the remaining inhabitants and returning refugees, thirty-two experienced deminers were sent from the NPA's mine action program in Bosnia and Herzegovina. They were tasked to deal with emergency demining in the western part of Kosovo, under the direction of the United Nations. This included supervisors, deminers, medics, hose clearance personnel and dog handlers with mine detection dogs. They conducted surveys and demined in high priority task areas, such as houses, wells and schools from July to September 1999. The mine clearance program in Kosovo was always viewed as one achievable within a finite period. Despite initial projections made in 1999 that it would be a five year program, the final end date for all mine clearance operations in Kosovo was set by the United Nations Mine Action Coordination Center (UNMACC) at November 30th 2001. From that date all demining and BAC operations came under the responsibility of the Kosovo Protection Corps (KPC) and demining is still ongoing.

IRAN: Is located in the Middle East, bordered by Armenia, Azerbaijan, Turkmenistan, the Caspian Sea, Kazakhstan, Russia, Afghanistan, Pakistan, the Persian Gulf, Gulf of Omen, Turkey and Iraq. Landmines and explosive remnants of war remain in Iran from the 1980-1988 conflict with Iraq. Mines were used by both sides in large numbers. This combined with heavy shelling in many areas during the armed conflict, has caused a considerable landmine and unexploded ordnance (UXO) problem in the country. NPA worked in Western Iran along the border to Iraq in the Ihlam province in 2001-2006. This areas was an essential part of the war-theatre during the Iran-Iraq conflict. The extent of contamination is still not known with any precision.

NORTHERN IRAQ: Is a Republic in the Middle East, bordered by Saudi Arabia and Kuwait, Turkey and Syria, Jordan and Iran. The war between Iran and Iraq in the 80s, two decades with internal conflict, the gulf war, as well as the American led invasion of Iraq in 2003 has left the country with a huge problem with landmines and UXO.

SRI LANKA: Country in Southern Asia, Island in the Indian Ocean. The civil war that lasted for two decades between Singhalese government forces and Tamil rebels has left many areas heavily contaminated with Landmines and ERW. The total size of the area of contaminated in Sri Lanka is unknown. The Cease Fire Agreement that came into force in 2002 allowed for an extensive Humanitarian Mine Action Programme in the north and east. Renewed hostilities commenced in 2006, and the conflict escalated during much of 2007 and 2008. In July 2007, the army took control of the last LTTE-controlled areas on the east coast and in January 2008, the government of Sri Lanka decided to terminate the Cease Fire Agreement and a new phase of the civil war was a fact.

MALAWI: Malawi is a landlocked country in Southeast Africa, bordered by Zambia, Tanzania and Mozambique. As a result of the spill-over from the Mozambique internal conflict, there was suspicious of mines and ERW contamination at crossing points on the 1000km border between Mozambique and Malawi as well around refugee camps. There was also suspicion that 33 former Malawi Young Pioneers training bases were contaminated by Unexploded Ordinance (UXO). In addition, the Government of Malawi was concerned about the effects of flooding on the border, which could have caused migration of mines into Malawi.

RWANDA: A small landlocked country in east-central Africa, bordered by Uganda, Burundi, the Democratic Republic of Congo and Tanzania. Rwanda had a problem with landmines and explosive remnants of war

(ERW) as a result of the 1990-1994 war, from the retreat of the army and Interahamwe militias to neighbouring countries and their subsequent attacks launched from the Democratic Republic of Congo (DRC) in 1996-1998 in the northwest of the country. In a 2002-2003 assessment, four of the 12 former provinces reported a mine threat. After several years in which it's demining program had come almost to a standstill, Rwanda has, since 2006, made significant progress in reducing its mine problem. In May 2006, almost 900.000 square meters remained to be cleared of mines and unexploded ordnance (UXO) in 16 minefields in the 4 provinces. In March 2007, the total estimated area of contamination had been reduced to 885.930 square meters in 14 mined and battle areas. By late April 2007 following the completion of battle area clearance in Nyabishambi (Former Byumba province), the total suspected hazardous area (SHA) in Rwanda fell to 629.416 square meters. Due to thick bush and vegetation a machine was by far best option to release the last suspected hazardous area (SHA) within a reasonable timeframe.

GAZA STRIP: Is located in the Middle East. Explosive Remnants of War (ERW) remain in Gaza from numerous conflicts with Israel over time, the last one ended early 2009. The Gaza Strip has been surveyed and party cleared by the Palestinians, but limited support with Security assessment of collapsed buildings and some EOD operations during the reconstruction and development phase will be needed.

LEBANON: Is a Country in the Middle East bordered by the Mediterranean Sea, Syria and Israel. 15 years of civil war coupled with 22 years of Israeli occupation of Southern Lebanon has left the country with a considerable problem of mine-and UXO contamination. In 2005, 150 million square meters had been recorded as suspected hazardous areas. Approximately 33 million square meters of this has been cleared by the national army, the UN and international NGO's. A national plan is in place to clear all remaining high and medium impact communities throughout Lebanon by 2013 and remaining areas by 2015. The 2006 war with Israel in up to 500,000 new unexploded submunitions being scattered across more than 1,000 cluster strike sites. At the beginning of 2009, both the UN and NGOs reported major funding shortages to clear the remaining submunitions, which have resulted in the closing of operations and less clearance. The landmine monitor has registered a total of 709 mine/ERW casualties in Lebanon in less than 10 years (1999-2008).

TAJIKISTAN: The Republic of Tajikistan is located in Central Asia. Bordered by Kirgizstan, China, Afghanistan and Uzbekistan.

Contamination from Landmines and UXO/ERW exists within three distinct regions of Tajikistan; the Central Region a result of the civil conflict between 1992-1997; the Tajik- Afghan Border (TAB) contaminated during the 1991-1998 period; and the Tajik-Uzbek Border (TUB) contaminated with AP mines laid during 1999-2000. Most of the Tajik-Afghan and Central areas have been surveyed while the Uzbek Border is currently surveyed. According to the data gathered and information from national authorities the implications of the current landmine threat is severe. Currently, 456,790 people live in mine-affected areas, approximately 70% of which are women and children. The risk areas are usually located in hills and mountains where most villages are located. These areas negatively impact the development of the region.[18]

NIGERIA: In respect of Nigeria, the major problem stems from the fact that Gen. Yakubu Gowon's Administration was oblivious of the consequences of abandonment of the several thousands of anti-personnel landmines, UXO's, AXO's and other explosive remnants of war in the various minefields and theatres of war in the former Eastern region. A sudden realization of this following the coming into effect of the Mine Ban Treaty now led to a seemingly inchoate arrangement to tackle the problem. A proper national and/or local mechanism is required to effectively coordinate activities concerning Landmines Survivors and Victims together with other persons with disabilities. In order for this to function well and ensure service planning and implementation, an appropriate Ministry or a national commission or Authority should be established. At the time of writing, and as late as 2014, there have been many reported cases of fresh mine actions resulting to injuries to the victims particularly from the vast Ngor Okpala and Isiala Mbano Local Government Areas of Imo state; and Etche Local Government Area in Rivers state. This is in spite of bogus claims by ministry of defence of total mine clearance in the former Eastern Region of Nigeria.

---

[18] *Mine Action Port Folio 2010 - 2011*

CHAPTER SEVEN

VICTIMS' ASSISTANCE

'Victim' is defined as "the individual directly hit by a mine/erw explosion, his or her family and community" while 'landmine victims' refer more generally to those who have been injured or killed by a landmine explosion, and also their families who suffer emotional, social and financial loss and the communities that lose access to land and other resources due to the presence of landmines." This more general definition is intended to recognize that the needs of those affected by the presence of Landmines should underscore all mine action efforts. Victims assistance refers to all care and rehabilitation activities that aim to meet the immediate and long term needs of landmines survivors. "In accordance with the definition developed by the International Campaign to Ban Landmines (ICBL), the activities and concerns involved can be divided into mine categories as follows: emergency and continuing medicare, physical rehabilitation, prostheses and assistance devices, psychological and social support, employment and economic integration, capacity building and sustainability, legislation & public awareness, access and data collection" It includes, but is not limited to, casualty data collection, physical rehabilitation, psychological support and social re-integration, economic reintegration, and Laws and public policies to ensure the full and equal reintegration and participation of survivors, their families and communities in society.[19]

They have families and come from communities most of which Communities, Farms, and their Environments have been completely destroyed, degraded and rendered useless by the presence of axo's, erw's and uxo's. Laws and public policies roundly include financial compensatory damages given permanent loss of limbs and deformity occasioned by preventable injuries. Other forms of assistance include the provision and use of wheelchairs, as well as provisions for old age. This must take cognizance of African setting, customs, traditions and culture, nature and degrees of injury sustained by the victims and time-frame, and ages of Victims.

---

[19] *A framework for Mine Action programmes from a development Oriented point of view developed by the German Campaign to Ban Landmines and subsequently revised in 1997 (www. Landmine.de)*

It is submitted that Victims assistance is an obligation of State Parties to the convention on the Prohibition of the use, stockpiling, production and pransfer of anti-personnel mines and on the destruction under Article 6.
In recognition of the Central place of Victims in the fight against landmines, the United Nations policies identify victims assistance as one of the five components of mine actions. Victim assistance relies on the commitment of resources by National Governments, International organizations and private organizations. States parties to the anti-personnel mine ban convention in a position to do so are bound to provide assistance for the care and rehabilitation; and social and economic reintegration of Mine Victims. In the Nigeria context many of the victims one after the other accidentally stepped on the Landmines either while walking, or farming. Some were injured by other explosive remnants of war. Some lost one leg with a few losing both legs. Majority of them lost their hands. Those who were injured during the civil war are not counted as Victims given the definition and interpretation of who a victim is by Mine Ban Treaty.

Victim Assistance differs from person to person, age to age as well as time-frame. A newly or freshly injured victim expects to receive basic hospital treatment. An abandoned or forgotten victim whose case suddenly becomes public knowledge would require certain species of assistance such as rice, prosthetel, water bore-hole, wheelchairs, mosquito nets, seeds, toilets and other materials. Some would receive their first set of support as late as ten years after their accident due to their residency in rural locations. Many may be given support five years after the accident. These comprised of hospital treatment (this time free of charge), agricultural skills, vocational training such as sewing, motorbike repairs and hair dressing. Victim assistance should be done in a needs-based manner. Given the different conditions of victims and survivors before and after their accidents, victim's views of their future become an important point of analysis and consideration. "The overall aim of victim assistance programmes must be to fully ensure human rights for the victims of landmines and other explosive remnants of war." [20] This accords with Articles 1, 5 and 25 of the Universal Declaration of Human Rights. Section 5 specifically provides that: *"Everyone has a*

---

[20] *Mine Action and effective co-ordination: the United Nations Policy (A/56/448) Add 2 dated Sept, 1998.*

right to a standard of living adequate for the health and wellbeing of himself and his or her family."

The use of landmines, unexploded ordnance and the presence of explosive remnants of war in the fields within the territory of the former Eastern region of Nigeria despite their indiscriminate maiming and killing of the civilian population after the end of the conflict represents a serious and on-going threat to the civilian population. They will continue to cause injury and death if they remain uncleared and undestroyed; and the unfortunate victims. Having to adapt to new lifestyle from being able to write, walk, farm, cycle, and provide freely for their families has been traumatic to many of them as many have continued to show signs of depression. Some families of some of the Victims helped them with their situations by being there for them; contributing towards household finances and going as far as helping them with Housing needs and taking them to Hospitals for medical check-up, while many others have continued to suffer discrimination both by their families and communities.

They require Victims assistance not only by book such as prosthetics, wheelchairs, equipment to sustain income generating activity, but constant visits by social workers, help in setting up a small businesses, Houses, a well or borehole for drinking water as well as toilets. Money for payment of House –helps, hiring of labourers to farm for them, payment of hospital bills as some of them still have open wounds that smell as they move around. They receive negative sympathy equating to defamation and pity. As a result, some of them have developed over sensitivity to how others perceived them with their pride affected. Some members of the Public and some people see them as unclean. After their various accidents many had post-traumatic stress disorders, lingering sores and wounds that have refused to heal. Their injuries reduced them to a state of considerable helplessness as well as incapacitated them from participating in the governance of their states and the country by being unable to run around, campaign for votes, seek to be voted for and do other things to wit:

i. Many have their Arms amputated at the shoulders.
ii. Some suffered and sustained severe injuries resulting in permanent and substantial disablement.
iii. Some sustained leg injuries, total loss of two legs, and below the knee amputation of both legs.
iv. Some sustained above the knee amputation of one leg.
v. Below the knee amputation of one leg.

vi. A few sustained facial injuries and disfigurement – some male and others female.
vii. Some facial deformity of a permanent nature.
viii. A few of them still smell arising from unhealed wounds/injuries.
ix. Some of the survivors are blind while some are burnt by fire resulting from explosion.
x. The youngest Victim – a girl Nkechi Osuji who is also an orphan from Ihitte in Ngor Okpala in Imo State has one of her limbs amputated. She lives in a mud house with thatched roof. She is single with a dim prospect of marrying.

They variously come from various and varying cultures and customs where it is not possible to pull them out of their cultures, customs, communities and environments easily for purposes of putting all of them in Rehabilitation Centers or turning to learn new jobs given their various Ages and stations in life. The Nigeria State Party has not afforded any measure for the protection of victims to attain physical development in a conducive environment inclusive of taking the plight of disabled persons in so many governmental activities, buildings and road construction, social and Educational policies, inclusive of making provisions for them to get re-integrated in the society. "Victims assistance is not a stand – alone activity." It has been suggested by another writer that conscious, strategic and "active efforts should be made to integrate victim assistance activities within the framework of national and local public health, community development and violence – prevention strategies developed by national authorities." All these should form "part of broader humanitarian, reconstruction and development plans aimed to help countries recover from violent conflicts." Victims and survivors of injuries sustained through any of these means qualify to ventilate their grievance against the State or government through the enforcement of their Fundamental Human Rights through the Courts: Ecowas Court, AU Court or Nigeria Human Rights Commission and other superior courts of national governments . It is argued that if victims of landmines during any armed conflict are not entitled to compensation, I submitted that all victims and survivors of landmines explosives whether in any mined location (or nuisance locations) after the cessation of the armed conflict are entitled to enforce their Fundamental Human Rights so breached and are entitled to the award of damages by the State in control or exercising sovereignty, suzerainty or jurisdiction over the area. Payment of compensation rather than Victims assistance should be made mandatory with a baseline which can only be graduated upwards depending on the degree of injury sustained. It is suggested that the scale of damages or compensation contained under workmen compensation should be inapplicable. The Compensation should be high enough to strengthen the Mine Ban Treaty while at the same time discouraging the manufacture, production stockpile and scale of landmines.

CHAPTER EIGHT

PLEAS IN LAW

The cause of action in any Fundamental Rights matter is the infringement or likely infringement of any of the Fundamental Rights as enshrined in Section 46 of the Constitution of the Federal Republic of Nigeria 1999 (as amended) the 1999 Constitution or the African Charter on Human and Peoples' Rights (Ratification and Enforcement) Act.
Order II Rule 1 of 2009 Rules provides:

"Any person who alleges that any of the Fundamental Rights provided for in the Constitution or African Charter on Human and Peoples' Rights (Ratification and Enforcement) Act and to which he is entitled, has been, is being or is likely to be infringed, may apply to the Court in the state where the infringement occurs or is likely to occur, for redress."

There is almost a superfluity of pleas of law under which a Landmine Victim or Survivor can commence his campaign to enforce his Fundamental Human Rights or seek redress against an un-caring and negligent state party. In addition to general common Laws, the following are relevant Laws applicable in the prosecution of cases of Human rights violations arising from landmines, bombs and other explosive remnants of war injuries before the Federal High Court, ECOWAS Court and African Union Commission:
1. African Charter on Human and Peoples Rights, Articles 4,5,16,(1), (2), 18 (1) (4), 19, 22, 60 and 61 of the African Charter on Human and Peoples Rights the Honourable Court make provisions for some rights in favour of the Victims/Survivors. They also created ample duties on the Nigerian State as State party to the charter to do certain actions and perform certain duties in favour of and to the benefit of Victims/Survivors, failure of which will threaten the Fundamental Human Rights of the Victims/Survivors. 2. See also Articles 1 and 25(a) Universal Declaration of Rights 3. Mine Ban Treaty 4. Constitution of the Federal Republic of Nigeria 1999. (as amended). 5. Supplementary Protocol (A/SP.1/01/05 of the ECOWAS Court. 6. Articles 7 (a), Article II of the protocol and Rules of Procedure of the Court. 7. Article 13 (a), (6) and Articles 32 and 33 of the Rules of the Community Court of Justice, ECOWAS. 8. Evidence Act (as amended).
The African Charter on Human and Peoples Rights is not standing alone on these rights. The Constitution of the Federal Republic of Nigeria 1999 (as amended) has created similar rights in favour of the

Victims/Survivors and to approach the Courts whenever such rights are being violated or threatened. Sections 33, 34, 35 and 41 of the Constitution are relevant. These Sections lean in favour of the Victims/Survivors, as they abundantly provide the Victims with rights which the court can protect in the face of brazen disregard to the sanctity of life of the Victims, mental and physical development of the Victims in a conducive environment. The Honourable ECOWAS Court has jurisdiction to entertain cases of violations of Human Rights within member states, pursuant to the Supplementary Protocol (A/SP.I/01/05) of the ECOWAS Court. See also Articles 1, 2, 5, 6, 8, of MINE BAN TREATY. AFRICAN CHARTER ON HUMAN AND PEOPLE'S RIGHTS Article 4 clearly provides:

"Human beings are inviolable. Every human being shall be entitled to respect for his life and the integrity of his person. No one may be arbitrarily deprived of this right".

Article 5: *"Every individual shall have the right to the respect of the dignity inherent in a human being and to the recognition of his legal status. All form of exploitation and degradation of man, particularly slavery, slave trade, torture, cruelty, inhuman or degrading punishment and treatment shall be prohibited."*

Article 16(1): *"Every individual shall have the right to enjoy the best attainable state of physical and mental health."*

Article 16(3): *"State Parties to the present Charter shall take the necessary measures to protect the health of their people and to ensure that they receive medical attention when they are sick."*

Article 18(1): *"The family shall be the mutual unit and basis of society. It shall be protected by the State which shall take care of it physical health."*

Article 18(4): *"The aged and the disabled shall also have the right to special measures of protection in keeping with their physical or moral needs."*

Article 19: *"All people shall be equal; they shall enjoy the same respect and shall have the same rights. Nothing shall justify the domination of a people by another."*

Article 22(1): *"All peoples shall have the right to their economic, social and cultural development with due regard to their* *freedom and identity and in the equal enjoyment of the common heritage of mankind."*

Article 24: *"All peoples shall have the right to a general satisfactory environment favourable to their development."*

Article 60: *"The Commission shall draw inspiration from international law on human and peoples' rights, particularly from the provisions of various African instruments on Human and Peoples' Rights, the Charter of the United Nations, the Charter of the Organization of African Unity, the Universal Declaration of Human Rights, other instruments adopted by the United Nations and by African countries in the field of Human and Peoples' Rights as well as from the provisions of various instruments adopted within the Specialized Agencies of the United Nations of which the Parties to the present Charter are members."*

Article 61: *"The Commission shall also take into consideration, as subsidiary measures to determine the principles of law, other general or special international conventions, laying down rules expressly recognized by Member States of the Organization of African Unity, African practices consistent with international norms on Human and Peoples' Rights, customs generally accepted as law, genera; principles of law recognized by African States as well as legal precedents and doctrine."*

Human Rights Actions in ECOWAS Court
Competence of the Community Court of Justice (ECOWAS Court)

The Community Court of Justice, established by Article 15 of ECOWAS Treaty is the main judicial organ of the Community.

Article 15.2 of the Revised Treaty provides that the status, composition, powers, procedure and other issues concerning the Court of Justice shall be as set out in a Protocol relating thereto' The Protocol of the Court makes provisions for the jurisdiction of the Court in Articles 9 and 10.
    a. The Court is competent to deal with disputes referred to it in accordance with the provisions of Article 76 of the Treaty, by Member States or the Authority when such disputes arise between the Member States or between one or more Member States and the Institutions of the Community on the interpretation or application of the provisions of the Treaty – Article 9. 2.

b. Also, a Member State may on behalf of its nationals institute proceedings against another Member State or Institution of the Community, relating to the interpretation and application of the provisions of the Treaty – Article 9. 3.

Under Article 10 of the Protocol, the Court may at the request of the Authority, Council, one or more Member States, or the Executive Secretary and any other Institution of the Community, express, in an advisory capacity, a legal opinion on the questions of the Treaty.

The Supplementary Protocol (AP/SP.1/01/05) modifies the ECOWAS Treaty and conferred on the Court competence to determine cases of Human Rights violation that occur in any Member State of the Community. The Protocol on Democracy and Good Governance imposes on the States the obligation to apply the African Charter on Human and Peoples' Rights as well as other International Human Rights Instruments in their respective territories. The Federal Republic of Nigeria signed the ECOWAS Treaty as well as other community instruments like the Protocols on Democracy and Good Governance and on the Competence of the Community Court of Justice. Therefore, there is no doubt with respect to the Jurisdiction of the Court of Justice to adjudicate any case of alleged violation of the Human Rights that occurs in the Federal Republic of Nigeria and for which it should be held accountable as a state party.

It is certain that Article 9(4) of the Protocol relating to the Ecowas Court of Justice, as amended by Protocol A/SP.1/01/05 grants the Community Court of Justice jurisdiction to determine cases of human rights violations that occur in any Member State of the Community, without pointing out, inasmuch, the party against whom such an action may be brought.

A look at the text of the Article 9(4) may lead to the assumption that since no delimitation is done by the statute, any case of human right violation that occurs within any Ecowas member state, no matter who is the perpetrator of the alleged violation, falls under the jurisdiction of this Court. Assuming that such interpretation is correct, individuals can be sued before this Court for alleged violation of human rights. But, given that almost every dispute involving individuals can be related to human rights, the conclusion is that all those disputes, from small claims between neighbours on the fingers of their properties, through disputes between employees and employers on the amount of wages, ending in the dispute between spouses on issues like child custody and so on and so forth, would fall under the jurisdiction of the Ecowas community court of justice.

The result of such reading could not be most clear: the mere allegation of human rights violation by any individual against another individual would be enough to lead the community court of justice to replace the role of domestic courts which would become absolutely redundant. In other words, the community court of justice would metamorphose itself from an international jurisdiction into a domestic one, overwhelmed by a flood of all kinds of disputes coming from all member states. A mere moment's thought is enough to demonstrate that neither the drafters of Article 9(4) of the 2005 Supplementary Protocol on the court, nor the Ecowas Authority, the Conference of Heads of State and Government, which enacted it in a statute, would never want such a result and unrealistic task for the Community Court of Justice, a mission never conferred on any international or regional body of a similar nature. The Court may however not rely solely on the text of the statutes because sometimes it does not reveal by itself the real meaning it intends to express. In order to discover the real meaning of the text it is also necessary to take into account other elements of interpretation namely the main purpose envisaged by the statute, the social issues it intends to address, the historical context of its drafting and the role it reserves for the institutions it sets up.

However the Court being an international Court established by a Treaty and, by its own nature, it should primarily deal with disputes of international character. Therefore, it essentially applies international law where it has to find out the source of the laws and obligations which bind those who are subject to its jurisdiction. The text of Article 19(1) of the ECOWAS Protocol A/P1/7/91 is clear in this respect:

"The Court shall examine the dispute before it in accordance with the provisions of the Treaty and its Rules of Procedures. It shall also apply, as necessary, the body of laws as contained in Article 38 of the statutes of the International Court of Justice"

As an international Court with jurisdiction over human rights violation the Court cannot disregard the basic principles as well as the practice that guide the adjudication of disputes on human rights at the international level. The international regime of human rights protection before international bodies relies essentially on treaties to which States are parties as the principal subjects of international law. As a matter of fact, the international regime of human rights imposes obligations on States. All mechanisms established thereof are directed to the engagement of State responsibility for its commitment or failure toward those international instruments.

A comparative analysis of the different international system of human rights protection, be it on the universal echelon, as obtained in the case of the United Nations Committee on Human Rights (now council), or at the regional level, as in the case of the Ecowas Court or European Court of Human Rights or the inter-American Court of Human and People' Rights, confirms the said conclusion on the State responsibility.Even before the African Commission on Human Rights, the closest reference of this Court, only States parties to the African Charter on Human and Peoples' Rights are held accountable to Ecowas violation of the fundamental rights recognized in the said instrument. Up till now the responsibility of the individuals at the international level for the violation of Human Rights is limited to criminal domain, and even in such circumstances, the international courts intervene only on subsidiary grounds, that is to say, where the domestic courts cannot or fail to hold the perpetrators of such violations accountable. From what has been said, the conclusion to be drawn is that for the dispute between individuals on alleged violation of Human Rights as enshrined in the African Charter on Human and Peoples' Rights, the natural and proper venue before which the case may be pleaded is the domestic Court of the State party where the violation occurred. It is only when at the national level, there is no appropriate and effective forum for seeking redress against individuals, that the victim of such offenses may bring an action before an international Court, not against the individual, rather against the signatory State for its failure to ensure the protection and respect for the rights allegedly violated.

Within Ecowas community, apart from member states, other entities that can be brought to this Court for alleged violation of Human Rights are the institutions of the community because, since they cannot, as a rule, he sued before the domestic jurisdiction, and as such the only avenue left to the victims for seeking redress for grievance against those institutions is the community court of justice. Consequently, the Community Court of Justice does not have jurisdiction to entertain a dispute between individuals arising from alleged violation of human rights committed by one against another.

Article 4 of the Revised Treaty of the Economic Community of West African States (ECOWAS), 1993 provides for the applicability of the provisions of the African Charter on Human and Peoples; Rights to Member States of the ECOWAS.
Article 1 of the African Charter on Human and Peoples' Rights provides that:

"The Member States of the Organization of African Unity parties to the present Charter shall recognize the rights, duties and freedom enshrined in this Charter and shall undertake to adopt legislative or other means to give effect to them"

Article 2 of the Charter provides that:
"Every individual shall be entitled to the enjoyment of The rights and freedom recognized and guaranteed in the present charter without distinction of any kind such as race, ethnic group, colour, sex, language, religion, political or any other opinion, national, social origin, fortune, birth or other status".

The same African Charter on Human and Peoples' Rights, Article 22 also provides that:
"(1) All peoples shall have the right to their economic,
social and cultural development with due regard to their
freedom and identity and in the equal enjoyment of the
common heritage of mankind.
(2) States shall have the duty, individually or collectively,
to ensure the exercise of the right to development"

Article 24 provides that:
"All peoples shall have the right to a general satisfactory environment favourable to their development."

Under international Human Rights law, people whose rights are violated should have access to effective remedy. International Human Rights treaties also require the States must take steps to protect peoples' economic, social and cultural rights from actions of non-state actors that would undermine the enjoyment of those rights.

However, where the Ecowas Court, believes it lacks the requisite jurisdiction to determine any dispute resort had to Articles **88** of the Rules which provided that:
"Where it is clear that the Court has no jurisdiction to take cognizance of an action or where the action is manifestly inadmissible, the Court may by reasoned order, after hearing the parties and without taking further stepsin the proceedings, give a decision".

It is doubtful whether the same consideration could go for one of the most controversial issues in International Law which relates to the accountability of Companies, especially multinational corporations, for violation or complicity in violation of Human Rights especially in developing countries. In fact, one of the paradoxes that characterize

International Law presently is the fact that States and individuals can be held accountable internationally, while companies cannot and yet under virtually every jurisprudence corporate and companies are creations of the law which can sue or be sued.

This anomaly has been the reason for growing concern from Academia and institutions committed to the promotion and protection of Human Rights around the world. In an article entitled "Separating Myth from Reality about Corporate Responsibilities Litigation" published in the Journal of Economic law (2004) 263, 265, Harold Hongju Koh makes the following observations with respect to the issue under discussion: *"if states and individuals can be held liable under international law, then so too should be corporation for the simple reason that both states and individuals act through corporations. Given that reality, what legal sense would it make to let states and individuals immunize themselves from liability for gross violations of Human Rights through the mere artifice of corporate formation?"*

The same concern is shared by the United Nations High Commissioner for Human Rights in its Report on Corporate Responsibility and by the Committee on Legal Affairs of the European Parliamentary Assembly in its Report on Human Rights and Business presented in September of 2010.[21] The need to make corporations internationally answerable has led to some initiatives, namely the nomination of a Special Representative of the Secretary General of the United Nations whose Report titled *"Protect, Respect and Remedy: A Framework for Business and Human Rights"* (*The Ruggie Report*) is one of the greatest reference on the accountability of multinationals for Human Rights violation in the world. Despite the campaign launched by advocacy organizations towards new development, the bare truth, however, is that the process of codification of International Law has not yet arrived at a point that allows the claim against corporations to be brought before International Courts. Any attempts to do so has been dismissed on the international courts are empowered to enforce it. This understanding is widely shared among regional courts with jurisdiction over Human Rights that being the current situation at the international level, the only available alternative left to those seeking for justice against corporations has been domestic jurisdictions, as in the case of the United States where under the *Alien Tort Claims Act (1789),* it has been possible to make the American

---

[21] *Harold Hongju Koh: Journal of Economic Law (2004) 263, 265*

companies operating abroad responsible for human rights abuses in developing countries *in violation of the law of nations (international law)*.

In the context and legal framework of Ecowas, the Court stands by its current understanding that only member states and community institution can be sued before it for alleged violation of Human Rights, as laid down in **PETER DAVID V. AMBASSADOR RALPH UWECHIA** delivered on the 11th day of June, 2010. In that decision the Court held that:

"As an International Court with jurisdiction over Human Rights violation, the Court cannot disregard the basic principles and the practice that guided the adjudication of the disputes on Human Rights at the International Level. Viewed from this angle, the Court recalls that the international regime of Human Rights protection before international bodies relies essentially on treaties to which States are parties as the principal subjects of International Law. As a matter of fact, the international regime of Human Rights imposes obligation on States. All mechanisms established therefore are directed to the engagement of State Responsibility for its commitment or failure toward those international instrument. From what has been said, the conclusion to be drawn is that for the dispute between individuals on alleged violation of Human Rights as enshrined in the African Charter on Human and Peoples' Rights, the natural and proper venue before which the case may be pleaded is the domestic court of the State party where the violation occurred. It is only when at the national level, there is no appropriate and effective forum seeking redress against individuals, that the victim of such offenses may bring an action before an International Court, not against the individuals, rather against the signatory State for failure to ensure the protection and respect for the Human Rights alleged violated. Within ECOWAS Community, apart from Member States, other entities that can be brought to this Court for alleged violation of Human Rights are the institutions of the Community because, since they cannot, as a rule, be sued before domestic jurisdiction, the only avenue left to the victims for seeking redress for grievance against those institutions is the Community Court of Justice".

CHAPTER NINE

RESPONSES TO MINE BAN TREATY

NIGERIA'S RESPONSE I:
"The Convention on the Prohibition of the Use, Stockpiling, Production and Transfer of Anti – Personnel Mines and their Destruction commonly referred to as the Mine Ban Treaty (MBT) or Ottawa Convention entered in force in 1999. The ultimate goal of the convention was to "put an end to the suffering and casualties caused by anti – personnel mines that kill or maim hundreds daily". The Treaty stipulates that all ratified State Parties (157 and counting) are obliged to (among others) destroy and prohibit the use of anti – personnel mines in mined areas and stockpile, seek international co-operation and provide assistance to victims, ensure transparency measures. Article 6 of the Treaty encompasses the duty of each State Party to provide needed assistance to victims of landmines. It states, "Each State Party in a position to do so shall provide assistance for the care and rehabilitation, and social and economic reintegration, of mine victims and for mine awareness programmes." The Mine Ban Treaty also presents Victim Assistance to be reached with support from various organizations; bilateral and multilateral organizations.

However, some concerns were raised over the years on the limited space victim assistance covered in the Treaty. Consequently, in 2004 and 2009, two conferences were held to review the progress made so far and to address concerns over some of the Articles. For instance in 2004, in the Nairobi Action Plan (NAP), the State Parties adopted a five year plan 2005 – 2009 wherein victims assistance amongst other items, was given a comprehensive outlook. Action IV of the plan covered a total of 11 articles, which encompassed obligations on assistance to be provided within the framework of victim's needs and rights. In addition to this, the Nairobi Action Plan established a guide to State Parties to comply with the stronger obligation of Victim Assistance in the Mine Ban Treaty. The article further highlighted the need to capture victim assistance within the broader disability, human rights and development structures. Nigeria ratified the Ottawa Convention on 23 July, 2001 while the Convention entered into force on 1st March, 2002. Initially, in accordance with its obligations under Article 7 of the Convention, Nigeria reported no areas known or suspected to contain mines. However, in 2009, news reports surfaced suggesting that anti – personnel mines formed part of a residual threat posed by explosives remnants of war (ERW). This residual threat was from the 1967 to 1970 conflict between Nigeria and the self-declared Republic of Biafra. This conflict involved a series of ground offensives and counter – offensives, resulting in significant amounts of Explosive Remnants of War (ERW) left after the conflict. This included landmines laid by parties to the conflict. Few, if any, records were kept of laid minefields; and majority were both 'nuisance' mines as well as "classical" minefields. That is to say, both conventional and unconventional landmines were used by parties to the conflict in the War that cost Nigeria not less than one million dollars per day to prosecute the War which lasted for 30 months. Some of these landmines as stated before there were nuisance landmines scattered indiscriminately. Nigeria laid mines in the War Affected areas without records as required by both International Humanitarian Law, the Conventions and Law of Armed Conflict.

In the same month but on 28 May, 2009 precisely, Nigeria informed the Standing Committee on Mine Clearance, Mine Risk Education and Mine Action Technologies that it was uncertain if references made to anti – personnel mines in press reports were accurate. Nigeria further informed the Standing Committee that, with these news reports having surfaced, it knew that it must "make every effort to identify all areas under its jurisdiction or control in which anti – personnel mines are known or suspected to be emplaced" in accordance with Article 5, paragraph 2, of the Convention. All the areas where the Nigerian Civil war was fought have since 1970 when the War ended fallen due and under the jurisdiction and control of the Federal Republic of Nigeria. Following this development, Nigeria informed the Standing Committee that it had contacted the Implementation Support Unit of European Union to acquire the necessary Technical assistance to investigate the situation and that a visit, on the basis of funding having been made available through the European Union's "Joint Action" in support of the Convention, would proceed in July, 2009.

It was not too long, Nigeria informed the United Nations that should the results of a technical investigation findings in a determination that there are anti – personnel mines in mined areas under Nigeria's jurisdiction or control, Nigeria was aware of its obligation to "destroy or ensure the destruction of all anti – personnel mines in these mined areas as soon as possible, but not later than ten years after entry into force" of the convention for Nigeria. Nigeria noted that it would have a deadline of 1 March 2012 to conclude implementation of Article 5 of the Mine Ban Treaty. In the information Nigeria submitted in 2009 in accordance with its obligations under Article 7 of the Convention in which it reported of the presence of ERW's, "in war affected areas of Eastern Part of

Nigeria", that is, areas that were suspected to contain anti – personnel mines. Nigeria further reported that the type of mines would have been a "Biafran locally fabricated" explosive device (Ogbunigwe) which was used as (an) Anti – Personnel (AP) landmine and that they would have been emplaced "not later than January 1970". Indeed, the two types of Landmines on ground were the conventional type Mines imported by Nigeria mainly and Biafran type "Ogbunigwe".

Nigeria also reported that it had constituted an Inter – ministerial committee to concern itself with mines and other explosive remnants of war to enable Nigeria meet its convention obligations and that the committee consisted of 15 representatives of relevant ministries, departments and non-governmental organizations. The Inter – ministerial committee set up by the Hon. Minister did not meet for once and neither visited the War Affected Parts of Nigeria nor were members sincerely concerned with the clearance and removal exercise. The committee did not assess the extent of environmental degradation and did not assess the continued decapitation and destruction of lives, of human beings as well as of animals and/or the consequences on families and their communities. The mission hastily concluded that a fully viable and functional structure has been put in place to address the problems caused by explosive remnants of war in Southeast Nigeria, where the contamination has been causing casualties for the past 40 years. In response to that observation, Nigeria entered into a contract with a commercial Company **RSB Holdings Nig. Ltd.** to set up a mine action programme in the Southeast Nigeria. The terms of contract required the company to undertake inter alia the following actions:

a. *Mine clearance as part of a broader explosive remnant of war removal and destruction programme, includinga well-planned and implemented survey process toidentify the areas of need.*

b. *Mine risk education, including (i) developing a significant programme for education of the population of Southeast Nigeria of the hazards posed by explosive remnants of war with this involving radio and television campaign, poster distribution process and training sessions in villages, markets, churches and schools throughout the affected region and (ii) establishing a "hot – line" for populations to report explosive hazards and for tasking and prioritizing on the basis of these reports.*

c. *Victim assistance, particularly the enumeration of mine victims from the Biafran/Civil War.*

d. *Reporting, including by monitoring implementation and providing reports to the Ministry of Defence in part to ensure that Nigeria can comply with its Convention reporting obligations.*

The contractors were also required to develop two databases: one for recording the mine and uxo victims in Nigeria and the second for recording the basic details of mines and uxo found and dealt with during operations. Subsequently, The Company operated in 11 of Nigeria's 36 States (i.e., the 11 States contaminated by explosive remnants of war). Between October and December 2008 it surveyed all potentially affected States in Southeast Nigeria with 186 Local Governments visited to gather data. Between January and March, 2009, a confirmatory survey was undertaken with 835 locations visited. In the process of executing the Contract some areas of Nasarawa, Benue, Enugu, Ebonyi, Imo, Rivers, Bayelsa, Anambra, parts of Abia were visited with many more areas left untouched in Abia Central – Isiala Ngwa, Azumiri, Obioma Ngwa, Okpuala Ngwa and parts of Bayelsa.

In December, 2010, at the 10th Meeting of State Parties, Nigeria reported that four cities namely Enugu, Owerri, Port Harcourt and Makurdi had completely been cleared of erw's. No mention was made of other states of Southeast and South - South with existing Mine fields. This information arose from imagination than from reality as the Inter-ministerial committee did not supervise the clearing. The Nigeria police anti-Bomb Unit was not also involved. That story is also debunk as nobody issued Land Clearance Certificate as required by the convention and none has been issued till date. Consequently, Nigeria declared that it has ensured the destruction of all anti – personnel mines in areas under its jurisdiction or control in which ant – personnel mines were known or suspected to be emplaced, in accordance with Article 5 of the convention. Nigeria furthermore declared that it completed this obligation but that in the event that previously unknown mined areas are discovered after this date, Nigeria will:

a. Report such mined areas in accordance with its obligations under Article 7 and share such information through any other information means such as the Intercessional Work Programme, including the Standing Committee meetings.
b. Ensure the effective exclusion of civilians in accordance with Article 5; and,
c. Destroy or ensure the destruction of all anti – personnel mines in these mined areas as a matter of urgent priority, making its needs for assistance known to other States Parties, as appropriate.

Nigeria's claim is bogus and the truth about the exercise shrouded in uncertainty occasioned by failure of the Supervisory Ministry because areas such as Isiala Ngwa, Ohanku in Aba, Azumiri, Akwete, Methodist Boys Uzuakoli, Umuahia South, Umunwanwa, Udo are yet to be demined. There are more than 50,000 Live Bombs yet to be removed which are scattered in many parts of South - east and South – south Zones of Nigeria. For instance three bombs, were removed from the Government House Owerri, Imo State, Nigeria in 2011. Three other bombs were exhumed by an Earth-moving machine while clearing a building project site within the same government house premises.

In addition marked Bomb Dumps and Bomb Danger Sites indicated and mapped out at the compounds of the following Public Schools in Imo State where children are schooling are yet to be removed by the Nigeria government 44 years after the Civil War. They are: *Aquinas Secondary School, Osu Mbano, Peter Clever Seminary, Ngor Okpala, St. Patrick's Secondary School , Ogbe Ahiara, Mbaise, Ahiara Technical School, Nnarambia, Central School Ngugo Ikeduru, Magistrate Court Hall Umuagwo, Ohaji, Umuokanne – Ohoba Road, Ohaji, Alaka – Ohoba in Ohaji, Central School Eziama Oparanadim in Ahiazu Mbaise, Obitti-Awara in Ohaji, Akpuru Nnorie in Ngor Okpala, Umuopara Isiala Oparanadim Biafran Refinery dump, St. Ephraim's Imerienwe, Orduga in Umuokanne Bomb-dump Site, Paternoster Secondary School in Mpam Ekwerazu, all in Imo State; L.A. School Etche in Rivers state; Methodist Boys School Uzuakoli in Abia state; Bomb Dumps Locations at Ihiala in Anambra State and Nsit – Ubim in Akwa-Ibom State* where the Company RSB Nigeria Limited group lost three of her Staff when they inhaled gases emitting from a Bomb Location while trying to exhume the Bombs from an Air Force Plane crash site during the Civil War. The Aeroplane had some Bombs in it at the time of crash. The Contractor ran away with his team leaving the environment more dangerously contaminated. This is precisely at the site of Nigeria Air Force plane crash at Akwa-Ibom. Gas emission from the site indicate the use of chemical weapons by parties to the conflict. Besides, the Biafran side had a chemical Bombs site at Akwa Ibom State which was abandoned and has remained un-attended to by the Nigeria Government till today. Maiming, killing and injuring of Civilian Population by Landmines, Explosive Remnants of War and other UXO's and Bombs in their various communities are still continuing and threatening. Farmlands have been abandoned and people have not been going to their farms since their accidents because of fear that the mines and bombs are still littered all over the place.

The degree of Contamination by erw in the Eastern Nigeria varies between 40 80%, so also the Victims. In the course of the exercise by

RSB Nig Ltd, Rivers and Imo States turned out over 7,149 and 6,730 Explosive Remnants of War respectively, followed by Abia, Anambra, Akwa Ibom, Ebonyi, Enugu and Cross Rivers. Others are Benue, Nasarawa and Delta States. There are still many Abandoned Unexploded Ordnance (AXO), Unexploded Ordnance (UXO) and Explosive Remnants of War (ERW). The cause of more deaths after the cessation of Hostilities in 1970 has been mostly due to Explosive Remnants of War left by the Nigeria Army. In all, the Ministry of Defence through her contractors claimed to have cleared and destroyed more than 17,519 ERW while 45% of the land in the East remains uncleared of ERW as at 8th September, 2014 and yet on the same day, the Hon Minister for Defence declared at the same occasion of Stakeholders Meeting on "The Role of International Donors in Assisting Mine Victims in Nigeria" hosted by the same Hon Minister, that Nigeria had complied with Articles 5, 6, 7 of the Ottawa Convention by clearing and removal of erw in the war contaminated areas - a position that is false. Both Landmines and Explosive Remnants of War pose a serious, ongoing and continuing threats to members of the Civilian population in the various contaminated communities and environments. These weapons can still be found on roads, footpaths, farm lands, forests in and around surrounding houses, schools, government house in the South-east and South-south zones.

The continuing threats and infractions deny the people access to some basic needs and freedom of movement, as well as limit their abilities to attain adequate, effective and effectual physical and mental Health and development as they are almost perpetually traumatized. The presence of these weapons or the thought of the possibility of these weapons being around has constituted psychological Health Hazards, hypertension and stress to some of them particularly those of them above the age of 40. All these constitute veritable threats to the communities, families of their inalienable rights contained in S. 46 of the Constitution of Nigeria and African Charter as well as in Other Human Rights instruments.

==========================

NIGERIA'S RESPONSE II:
(NIGERIA FOREIGN MINISTRY ADDRESS TO
UNITED NATIONS)

Mr. President,

"Nigeria would like to report on her efforts in recent times in the implementation of the Ottawa Convention. It was recently discovered that some mines and UXOs existed in certain states of the South Eastern region of the country where a civil war fought over 40 years ago, precisely between 1967 and 1970. In, actual fact, at the end of the war, the Nigerian Government had used the Armed Forces and Police deminers to clear the war arena of mines and UXOs, including locally fabricated mines called OGBUNIGWE. Some must have been inadvertently left behind. Therefore in 2008, the Nigerian Government carried out humanitarian demining to free all lands in that part of the country from danger and accident caused by unexploded Remnants of relevant provision of the Ottawa Convention, in particular Article 5. The demining was carried out by private demining contracting/consulting company called RSB Holding Limited.

The Government further constituted an inter-Ministerial Committee to monitor the activities of the Contractor. Specifically, four (4) cities and their environs namely: Enugu, Owerri, Port-Harcourt and Makurdi were cleared in the exercise. A total of 4863 ERWs were destroyed. The destroyed ERWs consisted of 101POM2 types, 61 Locally Fabricated Mines called OGBUNIGWE. We can report to this August Assembly that there are no more Landmines contaminated areas in Nigeria after the extensive exercise. Nevertheless, to take care of any reports that may come up of EWR, the consultant is kept on site to carry out any required action, Nigeria is therefore confident that by the March 2012 deadline for demining, there should be no more ERWs in the civil war affected areas and all lands will be free for normal use. Indeed, the lands have already been released to the inhabitants. And I seize this opportunity to acknowledge request of the Implementation Support Unit (ISU) to visit Nigeria in order to confirm that Nigeria is mine-free. That request currently undergoing administrative processing and ISU will hear from us soon, so that they can assist in the drafting of our Declaration of Completion, to be formally tendered thereafter. I also need to mention that prior to the commencement of mine clearance in Nigeria, there was an extensive sensitization exercise as well as advocacy on mine risk education in order to prevent accidents among the people of the area. That in part contributed to the successful conduct of the humanitarian demining exercise because, inhabitants of the areas were able to lead deminers to some contaminated areas. I recall that at the June meeting, we had reported elaborately on activities in the area of the mine risk education as well as in the area of victim assistance. Since then, there has been no new report of ERWs explosion, accident or injury.

I wish to give a brief update of Nigerian's action in response to the Cartagena Action Plan. In connection with Victim Assistance, as it was reported in June by the Nigerian delegation, total number of landmine victims in Nigeria stands at 367, out of which 64 are physically incapacitated. The Government has collated an extensive data base on the victims. This includes the nature of their injuries. A need assessment programme is already in place, aimed at identifying the specific areas of needed assistance of each victims. This is part of the comprehensive master plan of the Government which has already made provision for these victims of mines, UXOs and ERW in the current budget of the Defence Mistry. This provision is expected to take care of their medical care, rehabilitation, social re-integration, skill development, self-help, vocational training, income generation, basic education as well as assistance to their families. This means that in the meantime, victim assistance will be a part of the Defence ministry's annual budget and in the nearest future, ERW victims and other disabled persons will be brought together under a common platform. Nigeria also recently ratified the Conventional on the Rights of persons with Disabilities.

Having said this, I would like to assure that Nigeria is fully committed to the letter and spirit of the Ottawa Convention, as we are up to date in rendering our annual transparency report. Furthermore, I wish to confirm that administrative and legislative procedures for the domestication of the OTTAWA convention are in progress. The Government recently constituted an inter-ministerial Committee under the Federal Ministry of Justice to review the status of all treaties or instruments in the International Humanitarian Laws with a view to advice on their implementation at the national level. Indeed, the intention of Government is to stigmatize and criminalize nationwide the use, Local Production, stockpiling and transfer of those inhumane items such as mines in Nigeria.

I will conclude by assuring that Nigerians remains an advocate of the full implementation of the Ottawa Convention and a conscientious believer in the attainment of a mine free world. Thank you for your attention."

Address delivered by Amb. Maria O. Laose, Director, International Organization Department Ministry of Foreign Affairs, Abuja – Nigeria Being Nigeria Statement at the 10th Meeting of States Parties to the Ottawa Convention Geneva, Switzerland 29 Nov. – 3 Dec. 2010

===========================

NIGERIA'S RESPONSE III:

As part of Nigeria's response, an Inter-ministerial Committee was set up. The Committee was made up of 25 members. They were:

MEMBERS OF THE INTER – MINISTERIAL COMMITTEE ON HUMANITARIAN DE-MINING

1. Ministry of Defence Mr. H. Ogundiya — Chairman
2. Ministry of Foreign Affairs   Mrs. V.N. Okeke -Member
3. Ministry of Environment Mr. Kasimu Bayero -Member
4. Defence Headquarters Gp Capt EM Eno -Member
5. Army Headquarters   Lt. Col. GA Ngugban - Member
6. Naval Headquarters Cdre MB Ajibade -Member
7. HQ NAF Air Cdre Agbeche -Member
8. Nigerian Police Force HQ ACP Uzowuru Godson -Member
9. Nigeria Security & Civil Defence Dr. EA Adeoye -Member
10. SA II/HMOD Alh. Jaafar Iman -Member
11. SA/HMSD   Barr. Ayodeji Akande -Member
12. Living Earth Nig   Mr. Arikpo Arikpo -Member
13. PSO-HMOD Gp Capt VI Aikhomu -Member
14. Asst. Director (Press) MOD Barr Bukhari Bello - Member
15. Director Procurement (MOD) Mr. St Echono - Member
16. Director Legal (MOD) Barr. Bukhari Bello - Member
17 HMOD Nominee Prince Lawson I. Aroh - Member
18 DJSD (MOD) BM Gamawa -Member
19. Iansa Women Network Ms Mimido Achakpa - Member
20. Ministry of Defence   -   Mr. Sam Eno
21 Ministry of Defence   -   Mr. Ikpeme Esuabana
22 Ministry of Defence   -   Mr. AF Famakin
23 Ministry of Defence   -   Mrs. RCJ Ahuchaogu
24. Ministry of Defence   -   Mrs. JO Okunorobo
25 Ministry of Defence   -   Ms Joyce Akponor

Unfortunately, this Committee never sat for once. Members did not also undertake any visit to the Civil War contaminated areas. This Committee also did not supervise the activities and claims of the contractors hired by the Ministry of Defence.

==========================

NIGERIA'S ATTITUDE IV:
Brief On The Effort At The Removal, Clearance And Destruction Of Explosive Remnants Of War (Erw) Recovered From The Former Civil War Zone Of Eastern Nigeria
1. "Nigeria formally accented to the Ottawa Convention on the 27th of September 2001, because of the presence of landmines in Nigeria, while the Convention became mandatory on Nigeria on

1st March 2002 as a result of the entry into force of the Convention. By this act, Nigeria signed the Ottawa Convention alongside 156 nations of the world making Nigeria along with some forty eight other African countries member of the State Party to ban the use of landmines in wars by her Armed Forces and also compelled to clear all APM buried in the ground.

2. The Ottawa Convention, otherwise known as the Mine Ban Treaty (MBT) "Prohibit the use, stockpiling, production and transfer of Anti-Personnel mines and their destruction". On this Convention, we have led the Ministry by our profession service, which was verified and commended by the UN to enable Nigeria fulfil her obligations fully two years ahead of time and is awaiting the United Nations APM Clearance Certificate. This can be confirmed by the Ministry's team that went to Geneva where they received a standing ovation on our excellent works.

3. Similarly, Nigeria is also a signatory to the 1980 Convention on Certain Conventional Weapons (CCW). BELOW IS AN EXTRACT OF Article 2 of Protocol V on Explosive Remnant of War of the 1980 Convention on Certain Conventional Weapons, which addressed Explosive Remnants of War. This Convention makes it mandatory for the Federal Ministry of Defence to remove all ERW in the former war zone. The Constitution says that; "Existing Explosive Remnants of War means, unexploded ordnance and abandoned explosive ordnance that existed prior to the entry into force of this Protocol for the High Contracting Party on whose territory it exist". ThusArticle 3, 1; Clearance, Removal or destruction of Explosive Remnants of War States that;

*"Each High Contracting Party and party to an armed conflict shall bear the responsibilities set out in this Article with respect to all explosive remnants of war in territory under its protocol. In cases where a user of explosive ordnance which has become explosive remnants of war (Biafra), does not exercise control of the territory, the user {i.e Ministry of Defence} shall, after the cessation of active hostilities, provide where feasible, inter **alia technical, financial, material or human resources assistance**, bilaterally or thorough a mutually agreed third party, including inter alia through the united Nations system or other relevant organizations, to facilitate the making and clearance, removal or destruction of such explosive remnants of war".*

4. In compliance with the provision of this Article in our zeal to

save the lives of our fellow Nigerians located in these contaminated area, we sourced funds to remove over 17,519 ERW as at May 2011 this year when the Ministry asked us to stop the clearance of ERW. The calls for the removal and discovery of ERW is unending, from the time the Ministry asked us to stop to date, we have received over so many SOS calls from communities threatened by ERW. The completion of this project left to the discretion of the Ministry of Defence. The UN does not accept partial clearance of ERW just like the case of the removal of Landmines." - *Dr. Bala Yakubu Chief Consultant to Ministry of Defence on Humanitarian Demining and CEO Deminers Concept Nig. Ltd*

============================

NIGERIA'S RESPONSE V:
AGENDA
1. Opening Prayer
2. Chairman's Opening Remark
3. Adoption Of Minute Of Meeting Dated 13th March, 2013.
4. Matters Arising
   (a) Payment of Contractor   (b) Victim Assistance Plan
5. Any Other Business
6. Closing Prayer

Insensitively of Nigeria State Party to the Ottawa Convention towards the welfare as well as well-being of Mine Action Victims led the Victims/Survivors to file a suit at the Sub-regional ECOWAS Court of Justice Abuja – Nigeria in *Suit No. ECW/CCJ/APP/06/12."* This became an historical mile-stone in the History of landmines where Mine Action Victims took a State Party to Court. This is the first of its kind in all the countries with landmine problems. While the matter is still pending, the Nigerian Government, through the Chief Law Officer and Attorney-General of the Federation acting on the instruction of the President of Nigeria - Dr. Goodluck Ebele Jonathan opted for out of Court settlement through a letter from the Attorney-General of the Federation dated 11th March, 2013 and Reference MJ/CIV/ABJ/190/12. Consequently, two meetings were held in the office of the Solicitor-General of the Federation. Below is the proceeding of 1st meeting. The proceeding of the second meeting was not allowed to see the light of the day by officials of the Federal Ministry of Justice who were overwhelmed by the startling revelations and quantum of evidence against the attitude of the Federal Government towards Nigeria Civil

War contaminated areas and Victims/Survivors.

1.0 **COMMENCEMENT**:
1.1 The meeting commenced at 12.30pm with an opening prayer by Dr. Emeka Uhegbu.

2.0 **OPENING REMARK:**
2.1 "The Solicitor-General of the Federation and Permanent Secretary (SGF/PS) welcomed everyone present to the meeting, noting that all parties to the meeting were duly represented. He then requested for self-brief introduction by those present and it was promptly done.

   2.2 SGS/PS in his remark informed the meeting that it was unfortunate that the meeting was sitting over the subject matter of Landmines and Bombs at a time like this. He explained that the meeting was just a preliminary one and its essence was to enable parties look into the matter and proffer suggestions on ways that will foster an amiable out of Court settlement of the matter which was already before the ECOWAS Community Court of Justice. He hoped and prayed that the meeting would proffer a lasting solution to the issue so as to enable us advice our political heads and ensure the settlement became a reality.

2.3 The SGF/PS informed the meeting that it was preferable to listen to the Applicant's Counsel followed by the Contractors and staff of the Federal Ministry of the Federal Ministry of Defence, respectively before deliberations commenced. This was noted as appropriate."

3.0 **HIGHLIGHT OF THE MEETING**
3.1 The director Civil (DCL) at the instance of the SGF/PS gave the highlight of the meeting to include, the case before the ECOWAS Community Court; the reliefs sought by the Applicants and the need for settlement of the matter as directed by Mr. President. She noted, without prejudice, that the essence of the meeting was to see the possibilities of amicably resolving the matter out of Court and urged parties to leave out technicalities, deal strictly the facts on ground of the case and see how Justice can be armed at.

4.0 **VICTIMS APPLICANTS' COUNSEL'S ADDRESS**
The Victims were represented by a team of Lawyers: Chief Uzoma Onyeike, Chief Ike C. Ibe, Chief Noel Agwuocha Chukwukadibia who indeed anchored the pleadings, and Barr.

Alex Williams.

4.1 With the permission of the SDS/PS, one of the Victims/Applicant's counsel Chief Noel Agwuocha Chukwukadibia, addressed the meeting on the subject matter of the case and the victims position on the issue. He thanked the meeting and thereafter gave a brief address on the subject matter which he said affected 11 (eleven) States of the Federation of Nigeria. He narrated the alleged ordeal and plight of the victims, especially their health conditions. He lamented the unbearable condition in which the residents of the war affected states are subjected which made them live by with unexposed ordnance and explosive remnants of the Nigerian Civil War over 42 years now.

4.2 According to him, "stockpiles of live bombs, remnants of war explosive and other war relics used, some of which were buried in the ground in the identified locations such as school compounds, farm lands, and homes as well as other public places still littered the eleven (11) States,

4.3 He said that no record was kept by the Nigerian Army of these case. These weapons left in the identified places has led to huge migration of the indigenes from their communities to other parts of Nigeria,

4.4 He added that the presence of massive bombs in the identified communities has deprived the indigenes of access to their communities, farm, lands, schools and other public places and hampered development of the communities. He mentioned that those weapons have the capacity to last up to 300 years. He said that those who did not partake in the Civil War are being subjected to danger everyday by the continuous existence of the explosive in the communities,

4.5 He lamented that their people were maimed and killed in hundreds and the survivors could not cultivate their farms rather they depended on other people for food. He emphasized more on the dangerous nature of the explosive which when denoted could contaminate the whole environment making them unsafe. This scenario he said had claimed two lives recently,

4.6 He stated further it was part of the social responsibility of the Federal Government to clear the explosive remnant which he acknowledged Government had commenced action on but later stopped work in April 2011. As a result they wrote to different people even to the President asking why work was discontinued when about 50,000 bombs which covered up to 178,000 square kilometer area still remained uncleared. These facts emanated in the Court Action,

4.7 In conclusion, he noted that the most affected victims were women and children some of which were not born during the war and that they want adequate provisions to be made for the victims as they were not prepared to gloss over the issue. He however urged the Ministry of Justice and the Ministry of Defence to undertake a visit to the affected areas and establish the facts alleged,

4.8 Finally he was asked what he wanted Government to do for his clients Chief Chukwukadibia who is one of the counsel for the victims said that he was adopting the writ/ claims which he pleaded in court pending before the ECOWAS Community court of Justice but added that first and foremost the Contractor RSB Holding/Demminers Concept Nig. Ltd must go back to work immediately and continue the clearing and destruction of the dangerous explosives still littered all over the war affected States in Nigeria namely; South East, South South and parts of North Central Zones of Nigeria. He requested the Ministry of Defence to compel their contractor to destroy the over 6,000 bombs stockpiled at the largely populated residential area in Owerri Imo State capital. He also pleaded with Government to assist the unfortunate victims of these explosives nothing that the assistance must consider each victims peculiar circumstance and nature of injuries. He said he disagreed with the conventional way of quarantine of victims for rehabilitation nothing that our culture rejects that method of assistance."

CONTRACTOR'S RESPONSE:

4.9 Dr. Bala Yakubu on behalf of the CONTRACTOR sued as 4th and 5th Defendants also addressed the meeting at the instance of the SGF/PS using point demonstration to derive down his point. "In his response, he said that he was engaged by the Federal Government through the Ministry of Defence sometime in January 2009 to clear all the Landmines/explosive deposit form the Civil War in the whole 11 States in the South East and South South regions of the Country. He further stated that his scope of duties including providing technical survey of every battlefield in the affected States and part of North Central in Nigeria as well as to enumerate Landmines victims.

4.10   In the course of diligently executing the contract of clearing landmines the contractor found numerous and more dangerous bombs, unexploded ordnance and explosive remnants of war. These he reported to his principal the Federal Ministry of Defence which directed that the contractor cleared both ordnances at the same time while the contractual agreement would be redrafted and re-executed by both parties.

4.11   It was the due process required to effect this Agreement and the release of the funds that took time until the contractor was no longer able to continue his work without funds. Dr. Yakubu said he was asked at a stage to stop further clearing of the explosives remnants of war by the then Minster of Defence Chief Adetokunbo Kayode SAN when Dr. Yakubu insisted on being paid to enable him continue the clearance. He said that despite the stop work order by the Hon. Minster he found it difficult to pull out his men from the field because of the danger they were living with through the Mine Risk Education and Mine Awareness Campaign which he conducted. Dr. Yakubu said he left a skeletal staff at the Nigerian Mine Action Center Owerri to react while requesting for payment which payment remained unpaid despite repeated demands.

4.12   Dr. Yakubu further stated that the suit pending before the ECOWAS Court would have been unnecessary if the Ministry of Defence had listened to him and had taken charge of the issue because Federal Government (FG) has done a lot to ensure that the issue is resolved but that the Ministry of Defence was frustrating the effort of Federal Government.

4.13   He confirmed that all the landmines have been cleared leaving the explosive remnants and that he would require 3(three) years to clear up the remaining explosive remnants from the affected areas.

4.14   He however expressed appreciation to the Defence Ministry for engaging them in the first place to do the work and said that in the process of their work, they had enumaread mine victims, types of injuries sustained and the nature of the assistance required. All these were presented to the Defence Ministry. He further stated that they had files and their forms filled. He also suggested that if Government agreed, he would issue ID card to them, to enable the FG take care of them.

4.15 He emphasized that Demminers cleared up to 226 Local Government area of the 11 affected States of which 7 of the States were visited by the United Nations (UN) to see what the FG had done so far over the Landmines. Regrettably no Minister was there, however Nigeria was rated 70% contaminated. Mr. Yakubu said that the UN representatives praised Nigeria for a job well done which qualified Nigeria to be appointed repertoire on stockpile destruction with Belguim and German as co-chairs. He regretted that Nigeria was not living up to that position neither did the government appreciate the company that worked hard for such accolade.

4.16 The contractor further drew the attention of the members on the UN's convention which stipulated that in the event of war between two opposing parties, the victor will clean up the environment hence in this circumstance it behoved the FG to do so accordingly.

4.17 He also informed the meeting that after one year of clearing the contaminated areas his company would issue the clearance certificate if there no incidence of explosion in the area. He said that the UN would refund all the money spent to the country in appreciation of her compliance to the obligations of the convention if the programme was followed through.

4.18 He further explained that they were asked to stop work 2010 by the then Minster of Defence without payment for the work done so far despite their latters, numbering up to 200 up-dating Defence ion the dangers ahead but no serious attention was given to them.

4.19 He remained the meeting that the 4th April of every year was Landmine victims' day and it was on that date last year that he wrote to the President concerning this issue and the danger the unexploded ordnances continued to pose for the citizens in the war affected places. The President approved the immediate payment of the sum of ₦649million in November, 2012 and directed that the money should be released to the contractor immediately o enable then go back it work. The President also directed that efforts be made to settle the matter out of Court. Dr. Yakubu said that up till date no effort was made to pay him to enable him go back to work. He said that he was still recovering bombs and that he is ready to go back to work if the meeting was released to him.

4.20   In his own contribution the field Administration and Director of media RSB Holding/Deminers Concept Nig. Ltd Dr. Emeka Uhegbu said that he is surprised that the exercise was not captured in the 2013 Budget despite repeated pleas by his company to the Ministry of Defence for payment of the outstanding bill since 2010. He wondered whether the fund for the clearing of the remaining unexploded ordnances would ever be budgeted for if the fund for the job already was not in 2013 budget.

4.21   In his own remark the counsel represented the 4th and 5th respondents in the case filed at ECOWAS Court of Justice Chief Charles H. T. Uhegbu said that he was sure that someone influential in the Ministry of Defence was working very hard to ensure that these dangerous ordnances were not cleared from the South East and South South geopolitical zones of Nigeria. Barr. Uhegbu said that he wondered why the President of Nigeria would approve the payment of the money owed a contractor in writing since November 2012 and went further to direct the immediate payment of the money due to the sensitive nature of the job; and yet up till date 5 months later the Ministry of Defence and that of Finance were displaying serious acts of insubordination to the President of this country. It was amazing he said. The President called for a meeting in which he approved money for us to continue our work and settle the matter out of Court but nothing has been done to pay us till now.

4.22   In his conclusion, he said that he was prepared to go back to work if he was paid his money and that he would require a longer period to complete the work because he has to put the necessary machinery in place."

4.23   The SGF/PS inquired from the contractor the nature of the assistance he talked about, he said paying them for work done, providing the victims with prosthesis which would be maintained regularly, providing the victims with financial assistance as was suggested by one of the Defence Minister to the tune of ₦250, 000.00 per victim. He added that the victim assistance was at the discretion of the government but UN had made the military ordnance a base line. Counsel for the alleged victims disagreed with the government accepting the contractor baseline as the yardstick victims assistance.

4.24   On that note the DCL opined that there was no need to join issues on at the moment on whether or not we are bound to follow the convention. This may be resolved at a later date when the meeting got to this position. The essence of this meeting was to chart a course that would allow palliative measure by government.

4.25 The Applicants' Counsel interjected and commented on the issue of the amount so far suggested by the Minister for the victims saying that it was unreasonable, that they were not consulted before reaching the agreement but the SGF/PS intervened and assured them that everything would be taken care of amicably.

MINISTRY OF DEFENCE (MOD) ADDRESS:

4.26 At the instance of the SGF/PS, Director of Legal Services Ministry of Defence introduced the Deputy Director of Joint Services Department in the person of Mr. Sam Eno to give the response on behalf of MOD nothing that he was versed with the issue particularly with respect to payment and management of the contract relating to the subject matter.

4.27 While thanking the SGF/PS for the opportunity provided by the meeting, Mr. Eno informed the meeting that he started the Victims Assistance Programme and that he was aware of the issues that led to the suit now pending in Court. His address covered 4(Four) points which includes Contract, Victim Assistance Master Plan, Contamination Cartagenal Action Plan and Stockpiles.

4.28 On the issue of the Contract, Mr. Eno said Federal Ministry of Defence engaged the contractors sued as 4th and 5th Defendants in the suit pending at the ECOWAS Court to enumerate landmines victims arising from the Biafra/Nigeria CIVIL War, remove landmines, as well as stockpiling and destruction of mines with the agreed contracts sum to be fully paid upon completion of the contract obligation of phase 1.

4.29 He stated further that the contractor thereafter demanded payment for work done in phase 11 without approval of MOD and outside the scope of the contract terms. Upon verification and evaluation of the work done and the need to ensure the safety of indigenes in the affected states, the work done was approved, renegotiated and a fresh fee was approved for payment, the contractor was then asked to return to work.

4.30 He said that while the issue of non-payment was still going on, the contractor abandoned the work emphasizing that he would only continue upon payment of the outstanding sum. MOD on the other hand did everything possible to ensure that the contractor was paid and returned to site but the paucity of funds remained an impediment. He noted that the MOD has approved that work should continue and the modalities for payment of the contractor's fees was on-going. He also acknowledged that the said approval sum in question was not captured in the 2013 budget.

4.31 On the issue of the Master Plan for victims, he said that Mr. President approved a 5 (five) years rolling plan for victim assistance and that the sum of ₦128million Naira for 514 victims was proposed to Mr. President as initial compensation to the Landmine Victims. On the issue of contamination of land and environment, he stated that it was beyond the MOD and suggested that Applicants approach the Honourable Minster of Environment for necessary action. Dr. Eno conclusion that Mr. President does not want the issue to get to Court.

HOPE ALIVE ORGANISATION'S ADDRESS:

4.32 At the instance of the SGF/PS the representatives of a nongovernmental organization the **Hope Alive organization** also made their presentation noting that they came into the issue sometimes in 2010 and expressed their concern and sympathy for the landmine victims. He added that they have continued to assist the victims with the view of ensuring that their hopes were kept alive and urged the Ministry of Justice to foster the resolution of the matter and ensure that the victim hope and future was kept alive.

5.0 **RESOLUTIONS:**

5.1 After the above deliberation on the issue, it was unanimously resolved as follows:

a) There was a contract between Federal Government and RSB Limited now known as Deminers Concept Nig. Ltd.

b) The continuation of the contract was important to clear the explosive remnant in the affected areas in the country and the presidential approved has been obtained in that regard.

c) The Attorney General of the Federation and the Minister of Defence shall liaise with the Minister of Finance, Director General of Budget and other necessary persons to facilitate the release of the money to the contractor

d) Compensation to victims would be worked out in a manner that will be acceptable by all parties. To this end, a report about the continuation of the contract and the issue as to figures to be presented to Mr. President shall be discussed.

6.0 **CLOSING REMARK:**
6.1 There being no other matter to be discussed, was adjourned to the 4th of April 2013. SGF/PS noted that the Applicants are free to come with their expert.
6.2 Mr. Chabki said the closing prayer and the meeting accordingly closed at 3.00pm.

C. I. NEBO (Mrs.)   **R.M.S SHITTU (Mrs.)**
Secretary   *Secretary*

========================

NIGERIA'S RESPONSE VI
FINDINGS OF FACTS IN THE FIRST MEETING

"It was found that there was a contract between the Federal Government and the 4th and 5th Defendants - RSB Holdings Ltd (Demminers Concept) Nig Ltd.

It was found out that in removing of Landmines, the contractor discovered more bombs, UXO's, AXOS and ERWs and with the consent of the 2nd and 3rd Defendants, the contractors commenced removal of all these explosive remnants of war.

Midway into the clearing/removal exercise, the 2nd defendant, Hon. Minister for Defence ordered the contractors to stop the task of removing the UXO's, AXOs, E.R.Ws.

It was found out that the contamination of the victims/Plaintiffs still subsist and is on-going in the war affected areas.

It was found out that there is stockpile of bombs at Mine Action Center, Owerri.

It was found out that between 178,000 and 212,00sq. kilometers of land are affected.

It was found out that market, public buildings, residential homes, farmlands and trees are contaminated and affected as disclosed by the film/slide.

It was found out that the massive presence of these contaminants in the Plaintiffs/Victims environments have indeed impede and still impede access to farm and cultivable lands.

It was found out that at the end of hostilities receding soldiers abandoned most of these contaminants and government did nothing to embark on Mine Risk Education/Mine Risk Reduction Education which resulted in the injuries suffered by surviving victims and that many had died.

It was found out that if clearance/removed work is completed a certificate of clearance declaring land safe will be issued for now there is none.

It was found out that any money spent by Government on clearing/removal will be refunded by the United Nation as stated by the consultants.

It was found out that people in the war affected/contaminated areas are still being maimed and injured on daily basis and such victim are abandoned to their own devices and fate by the government.

The need for the proper establishment of a Mine Authority or the elevation of the present Mine Action Center, at Owerri was underscored to continue monitoring given the longevity of Mine, Bombs, UXOs, AXOs and ERWs.

RESOLUTIONS:
It was resolved that everything be done to pay the contractors and compelled to go back to work before the next adjourned meeting. That every other discussion on the writ should be left till the next meeting.

On the 4th of April, 2013, till date all the representatives of the parties again met at the same venue and discussion were held and findings made in furtherance of peaceful settlement of the Suit. With the above findings made and agreed upon, the Nigerian Government became afraid and between 4th April, 2013, there has been no other meeting. The government side has done all within its power to scuttle any further meeting. The moment a new Director of Civil Litigation Mr. Taiwo Abidogun came in, the process of settlement out of ECOWAS Court was stalled.

Following an earlier Order made by the Hon. ECOWAS Court, the new Director of Civil Litigation Mr. Taiwo Abidogun led a Federal Government delegation to visit the Stockpile of Bombs by the Federal Government of Nigeria as well as Bomb-sites at various places in Imo State. The delegation comprises:

1. Mr. Taiwo Abidogun – Dir, Civil Litigation, Ministry of Justice
2. C.I. Nebo (Mrs.) – Ministry of Justice
3. R.M.S. Shittu (Mrs.) – Ministry of Justice

4. Barr. Benny Chabki – Ministry of Defense

The delegation was received at Owerri Capital – Imo State of Nigeria by Dr. Bala Yakubu – Chief Consultant to the Ministry of Defense on Humanitarian Demining exercise, Dr. Emeka Uhegbu – Field Administrator and Director of Mediaand Barr. Charles Uhegbu – Attorney and Legal Adviser to the Deminers.

On the side of the Victims were Barr. Noel Agwuocha Chukwukadibia, Barr. Uzoma Onyeike, Barr. Ike C. Ibe, Barr. Alex N.N. Williams and members of Hope Alive World Outreach – an N.G.O., Amb. Moses Emeanuru, Pauline Ijeoma Ufom (Mrs.) Etuk John Essien and Prince Charles Ozuzu. The delegation was also received by about 43 Mine Action Victims who indeed filed the Suit against the Federal Government of Nigeria at the ECOWAS Court, Abuja including a good number of residents and stakeholders of the New Owerri residential neighbourhood. Officials of National Television Authority (NTA) and Development of State Security Service also attended.

At the end of the visit which was at the instance of ECOWAS Court, the delegation confirmed the presence of stockpile of Bombs and other explosive remnants of war as well as various Bomb-dump sites. However, rather than continue the process of settlement out of Court, the Ministry of Justice went behind and retained the service of external solicitor Femi Falana & Co. to fight the Victims in Court. In order words, to continue the Suit in Court even while negotiation and peaceful settlement have not broken down. That is Nigeria's attitude towards the implementation of Mine Ban Treaty and the Cartagena Action Plan.

CHAPTER TEN
ACCESS TO ECOWAS COURT

INTRODUCTION:
The Community Court of Justice, (ECOWAS Court) was established pursuant to the provisions of Articles 6 and 15 of the Revised Treaty of ECOWAS. Protocol **A/P1/7/91** relating to the Community Court of Justice clearly states that the Court is the principal legal organ of Ecowas with the main function of resolving disputes relating to the interpretation and application of the provisions of the Revised Treaty, Protocols and Conventions. The primary objective of the administration of justice is to render justice according to law. The Court is enjoined in Article 9.1.of its Protocol to ensure the observance of law and of the principles of equity in the interpretation and application of the provisions of the Treaty. The Protocol further enjoins the Court to establish its own Rules of Procedure. For any Court of record, Rules of Procedure are important, because they regulate the proceedings of the Court. The Rules of Procedure of the Community Court of Justice have been formulated to regulate the proceedings of the Court. It is expected that lawyers wishing to appear before the Court should be very familiar with the provisions of the said Rules.

COURT PROCEDURE
As stated in the aforementioned paragraph, Article 32 of the Protocol of the Community Court of Justice empowers the Court to establish its own Rules of Procedure to be approved by Council. Pursuant to this provision, the Court formulated its Rules of Procedure, which was approved by Council vide Regulation **C/REG/04/8/02** of 28th August 2002. The approved Rules of Procedure of the Community Court of Justice of the Economic Community of West African States has been published in volume 41, August 2002, of the Official Journal of ECOWAS.

The procedure of the Community Court of Justice is governed by the Protocol and the Rules of Procedure of the Court. Proceedings before the Court shall consist of two parts: written and oral. Written proceedings shall consist of the application entered in the Court, notification of the application, the defense, the reply or counter-statement, the rejoinder and any other briefs or documents in support. See Article 13 (1) - (3) of the Protocol and Articles 32-51 of the Rules of Procedure. The Oral Proceedings shall consist of the hearing of parties, agents, witnesses, experts, advocates or counsel. See Article 13 of the Protocol and Articles

52 -58 of the Rules of Procedure.

THE APPLICATION

Cases may be brought before the Court by an application addressed to the Court Registry. See Article 11 of the Protocol. By virtue of the provisions of Article 33 of the Rules of Procedure, every application shall state;

i. the name and address of the Applicant
ii. the designation of the party against whom the application is made
iii. the subject matter of the proceedings and a summary of the pleas in law on which the application is based
iv. the form of order sought by the applicant
v. where appropriate, the nature of any evidence offered in support
vi. an address for service in the place where the Court has its seat and the name of the person who is authorized and has expressed willingness to accept service.
vii. in addition or instead of specifying an address for service, the application may state that the lawyer or agent agrees that service is to be effected on him by telefax or other technical means of communication.

THE DEFENSE

Article 35 of the Rules of Procedure provides that within one month after service on him of the application, the Defendant shall lodge a defense stating:

a. the name and address of the defendant
b. the arguments of fact and law relied on
c. the form of order sought by the Defendant
d. the nature of any evidence offered by him

REPLY AND REJOINDER

The application initiating the proceedings and the defense may be supplemented by a Reply to be filed within one month from the date of receipt of the defense and by a Rejoinder by the Defendant within one month from the date of that receipt of the Reply by the Applicant. See Article 36 of the Rules.

NOTICE OF REGISTRATION

It is also a requirement under the Rules of the Court that Notice of the Registration of an Application initiating proceedings be given in the Official Journal of the Community. The Notice shall state;

a. the date of registration of the Application
b. the names and addresses of the parties
c. the subject matter of the proceedings

d. the form of order sought by the applicant
   e. A summary of the pleas in law and of the main supporting arguments. See Article 13 (6) of the Rules.

It should be noted that the Notice of registration is significant because it serves the purpose of putting members of the public on Notice, so that interested persons who may wish to intervene in the proceedings, can do so. See also Article 21 of the Protocol which empowers any interested Member State to intervene in a dispute before the Court. By virtue of Article 89 of the Rules of Procedure of the Court, an application to intervene must be made within six weeks of the publication of the Notice of registration. See also Article 59 (4) The application for intervention shall contain:
   a. The description of the case
   b. The description of the parties
   c. The name and address of the intervener;
   d. The intervener's address for service at the place where the Court has its seat
   e. The form of order sought, by one or more of the parties, in support of which the intervener is applying for leave to intervene
   f. A statement of the circumstances establishing the right to intervene, where the application is submitted pursuant to Article 21 of the Protocol.

REPRESENTATION BEFORE THE COURT: AGENTS, ADVISERS AND LAWYERS

Article 12 of the Protocol of the Court provides that each party to a dispute shall be represented before the Court by one or more agents nominated by the party concerned, and the agents may request the assistance of one or more Advocates or Counsel who are qualified to appear in Court in their area of jurisdiction. A lawyer acting for a party is required to lodge at the registry of the Court, a certificate showing that he is authorized to practice before a Court of a Member State or of another State which is a party to the Treaty. See Article 28(3) of the Rules. Provisions have also been made in the Rules for Agents, Advisers and Lawyers appearing before the Court to enjoy immunity in respect of words spoken or written by them concerning the case or the parties. See Articles 28, 29 and 30 of the Rules. The Court may however exclude from the proceedings any Adviser or Lawyer whose conduct towards the Court or a Judge is incompatible with the dignity of the Court. See Article 31 of the Rules.

JUDGE – RAPPORTEUR
In the trial of cases before the Court the Judge – Rapporteur plays an important role. The main task of the Judge – Rapporteur is to make a preliminary report to the Court in respect of an Application. The preliminary report shall contain recommendations as to whether a preparatory inquiry or any other preparatory step should be undertaken. The measures of inquiry that the Court has ordered shall also be conducted by the Judge – Rapporteur. Where the Court commissions an expert's report, the expert works under the supervision of the Judge - Rapporteur. See Articles 39, 41 and 45 of the Rules.

PREPARATORY INQUIRY
After the conclusion of the written proceedings, the President of the Court fixes the date on which the Judge – Rapporteur is to present his preliminary report to the Court. Upon his recommendation, the Court shall decide what action to take. The following measures of inquiry may be adopted:
    a. The personal appearance of the parties
    b. A request for information and production of documents
    c. Oral testimony
    d. The commissioning of an expert's report
    e. An inspection of the place or thing in question. See Articles 39 and 41 of the Rules and Article 16 of the Protocol

ORAL PROCEDURE
After the completion of the preparatory inquiry, the President fixes the date for the opening of the oral procedure. The proceedings shall be opened and directed by the President who shall be responsible for the proper conduct of the hearing. The Court may summon a witness of its own motion or on application by a party. After the conclusion by the parties, the President shall declare oral procedure closed. See Articles 50 - 57.

QUORUM
Pursuant to the provisions of Article 14 (2) of the Protocol, the Quorum of the Court consists of the President and at least two other Judges. The sitting of the Court shall comprise of an uneven number of its members i.e. 3, 5 or 7. The dates and times of the sessions of the Court shall be fixed by the President. The Court may however choose to hold one or more sessions outside its seat of Court. Where the Court has been convened and it is found that there is no quorum, the President shall adjourn the sitting until there is a quorum. The sitting of the Court shall be public, but the Court may sit in camera at the request of one of the

parties or for reasons, which only the Court may determine. See Articles 21 and 22 of the Rules and Articles 26 (1) and 27 of the Protocol. It is submitted that it is necessary to amend the provisions of Article 14 (2) of the Protocol in order to ensure that two panels of the Court can seat at the same time or seat without the President.

LANGUAGES
Article 87 of the Revised Treaty makes provisions for the official and working languages of the Community. The Rules of Procedure of the Court provide that the official languages of the Court shall be English, French and Portuguese. The language of a case shall be chosen by the Applicant, except that where the Defendant is a Member State, the language of the case shall be the official language of that State. The language of a case shall be used in the written and oral pleadings of the parties, the supporting documents, and in the minutes and decisions of the Court. See Article 25 of the Rules.

THE JUDGMENT OF THE COURT
The Court's deliberations upon what its judgment shall be takes place in a closed session, and only those Judges who were present at the oral proceedings are entitled to take part in the deliberations. Every Judge taking part in the deliberations shall state his opinion and the reasons for it. The conclusions reached by the majority of the Judges after final discussion shall determine the decision of the Court. The Judgment of the Court shall be read in open Court and shall state the reasons on which it is based. See Articles 23, 60, 61, and 62 of the Rules and Article 19 of the Protocol.

EXECUTION OF JUDGMENTS
Article 62 of the Rules provides that the Judgment shall be binding from the date of its delivery. Article 22 (3) of the Protocol enjoins all Member States and Institutions of the Community to immediately take all necessary measures to ensure the execution of the decisions of the Court. Finally Article 15 (4) of the Revised Treaty provides that 'Judgments of the Court of Justice shall be binding on the Member States, the Institutions of the Community and on individuals and corporate bodies''
It has been observed that the above provisions are not adequate for the enforcement of the decisions of the Court. More elaborate provisions have been made in the proposed draft supplementary Protocol of the Court. The proposed new Article 24 reads as follows:
1. Judgments of the Court that have financial implications for nationals of Member States or Member States are binding.
2. Execution of any Judgment of the Court shall be in the form of a

writ of execution, which shall be submitted by the Registrar of the Court to the relevant Member State for execution according to the rules of civil procedure of that Member State.
3. Upon the verification by the appointed authority of recipient Member State that the writ is from the Court, the writ shall be enforced.
4. All Member States shall determine the competent national authority for the purpose of receipt and processing of execution and notify the Court accordingly.
5. The writ of execution issued by the Community Court may be suspended only on the authority of a decision of the Community Court of Justice.

INTERPRETATION AND APPLICATION OF ECOWAS PROTOCOLS

Without being repetitive the Community Court of Justice was established as the principal legal organ of ECOWAS. The main function of the Court is the interpretation and application of the provisions of the Revised Treaty, Protocols and Conventions. The Treaty defines "Protocol" as an instrument of implementation of the Treaty and having the same legal force as the Treaty. In discharging this responsibility, the Court is enjoined to ensure the observance of law and of the principles of equity. As aptly stated in the preamble of the Protocol of the Court (**Protocol A/P.I./7/91**) "the essential role of the Community Court of Justice is to ensure the observance of law and justice in the interpretation and application of the Treaty and the Protocols and conventions annexed thereto" The Protocol defines Treaty to mean "The Treaty of the Economic Community of West African States and includes Protocols and conventions annexed thereto"

PRINCIPLES OF INTERPRETATION OF TREATIES

In international law, there are three basic principles that International Tribunals use in resolving the problems of interpretation of Treaties. The first relates to the actual text of the Treaty and the analysis of the words used. The second approach looks at the intention of the parties adopting the Treaty while the third deals with the object and purpose of the Treaty. However, any true interpretation of a Treaty in international law will have to take into account all aspects of the Treaty, from the words employed to the intention of the parties and the aims of the Treaty.

Article 31 (1) of the Vienna Convention declares that a Treaty shall be interpreted in good faith in accordance with the ordinary meaning to be given to the terms of the Treaty in their context and in the light of its object and purpose. It has often been emphasized that the interpretation of a Treaty must be based above all upon the text of the treaty especially where the words are clear and unambiguous. In such a situation, the natural and ordinary meaning of the terms of the Treaty must be applied. The Community Court of Justice applied this principle in the case of OLAJIDE AFOLABI V FEDERAL REPUBLIC OF NIGERIA where it held that the text of Article 9 (3) of the Protocol is clear and unambiguous and applied the provision by holding that only Member States can institute proceedings before it on behalf of their nationals. The point has therefore been made, that in discharging the responsibility of interpretation and application of the Treaty, Protocols and Conventions of ECOWAS, all the Court has to do where the texts are clear and unambiguous, is to simply apply the text.

ECOWAS PROTOCOLS
Since the primary responsibility of the Community Court of Justice, is the interpretation and application of the Revised Treaty and the annexed Protocols and Conventions, it is necessary to give a brief status Report of these legal instruments. In a Report titled "Status of Ratification of the ECOWAS Revised Treaty, Protocols and conventions as at 30th June, 2004" presented to the 52nd Session of the Council of Ministers, the Executive Secretary of ECOWAS gave the following details:
1) That between 1978 and 31st January 2004, 45 Protocols and Conventions were signed.
2) Those as at 30th June, 2004, 36 Protocols and Conventions have entered into force. They include:
3) Protocol **A/P1/7/91** on the Community Court of Justice
4) Protocol **A/P2/8/94** relating to the Community Parliament
5) Protocol **A/P1/12/99** relating to the Mechanism for Conflict Prevention Management Resolution Peacekeeping and Security
6) Protocol **A/PI/01/03** relating to the Definition of the concept of Product originating from Member States of the Economic Community of West African States (ECOWAS)
7) Protocol **A/P2/01/03** relating to the application of Compensation Procedures for loss of revenue incurred by ECOWAS Member States as a result of the Trade
Liberalization Scheme.
8) Protocol **A/P1/5/79** relating to free movement of persons, residence and establishment
9) Protocol **A/SP3/5/81** relating to Mutual Assistance on Defense
10) Protocol **A/P3/5/82** relating to the definition of Community Citizen
11) Supplementary Protocol **A/SP2/7/85** on the code of conduct for the implementation of the Protocol on free movement of persons, the

right of residence and establishment.
12) Supplementary Protocol **A/SP1/7/86** on the second phase (right of residence) of the Protocol on free movement of persons the right of residence and establishment
13) Supplementary Protocol **A/SP2/5/90** on the implementation of the Third Phase (Right of Establishment) of the Protocol on Free Movement of Persons, Right of Residence and Establishment.

CHAPTER ELEVEN

VICTIMS AND HUMAN RIGHTS

An essential element to the advancement of Fundamental rights is the inclusion of Landmine survivors and Victims into the broader sector of disability and the linkage of both sectors to international human rights sectors. Non-governmental organizations and Mine Action Centre where such is established can instill requisite knowledge of relevant, national legislation, and national and international guidelines to promote and protect the rights of Landmine Survivors, Victims and persons with disabilities.

Chapter IV of the Constitution of the Constitution of the Federal Republic of Nigeria (as amended). S. 46(1) provides:
"Any person who alleges that any of the provisions of thischapter has been, is been or likely to be contravened in any state in relation to him may apply to a High Court in that State for redress."

S.46(2)
"Subject to the provisions of this Constitution, a High Court shall have original jurisdiction to hear and determine any application made to it in pursuance of the provisions of this section and may make such order, issue such writs and give such directions as it may consider appropriate for the purpose of enforcing or securing the enforcement within that State of any right to which the person who makes the application may be entitled under this Chapter."

Assuming, without conceding that any claim has a Common law origin, it is important to state here that having been guaranteed by chapter IV of the 1999 Constitution, African Charter on Human and Peoples Rights, the Universal Declaration of Human Rights, the Mine Ban Treaty and the Cartagena Action Plan, they have now been elevated above ordinary Common Law by the Laws codifying them and making them enforceable – by this Honourable Court.

Generally, negligence remains part of the Law of Tort. But any aspect of negligence which is isolated and elevated into a code creating duties, rights as well as the enforceability of the duties and rights is no longer ordinary Common Law. See Article 61 of the African Charter on Human and Peoples Rights. (Supra). See the case of **Mrs. Yetunde Zainab Tolani Vs. Kwara State JSC & Ors.** (2009) LPELR-CA/IL/2/2008, the Court of Appeal of Nigeria held thus:
"Consequently, the Court guar d these Fundamental Human Rights very

jealously. Therefore Law or Act is perpetrated against the provisions of the Fundament Rights of any individual which is against the spirit of the Constitution would not be allowed to stand. The spirit of the Constitution must stand firm at all times and to ensure that this is done, the superior Court have constantly held in a plethora of cases that the human right of the individual should no account be subsumed or swept under the carpet in favour of other laws no matter how well pivoted that law may be."

See also ***NASIRU BELLO & ORS VS A.G. OYO STATE (1986) 5 NWLR (PT. 45) 828. ATTORNEY GENERAL OF CROSSS RIVER STATE & 2 ORS VS CHIEF OKON (2007) ALL FEDERATION WEEKLY LAW REPORT (PT. 395) 370; TIMOTHY VS OFOKA (2008) 9 NWLR PART 1091 PAGE 204; W.A.E.C. VS AKINKUNMI (2008) 9 NWLR PART 1091 PAGE 151; NAFIU RABIU VS STATE (1981) 2 NCLR 293; MOHAMMED VS OLAWUNMI (1990) NWLR (PT 133) 458."***

There is nowhere in the body of Ecowas Court Rules where it is prescribed that an aggrieved party must come under Writ of Summons. Instead, the Fundamental Rights Enforcement Procedure Rules 2009, made pursuant to Chapter IV of the Nigeria Constitution recommends commencing Fundamental Rights Enforcement claim or complaint through any process known to law. However specifically, the Rules of Ecowas Court of Justice have prescribed the means by which an aggrieved party may approach this Court for redress and that is what is envisaged by Order II Rule 2 of the said Fundamental Rights Enforcement Procedure Rules 2009. See also, Articles 32(1) (3) (4) (5), 33(1) (2) of the Rules of the Community Court of Justice.

The Rules of Ecowas Court of Justice enjoins parties coming before the Honourable Court to seek justice to come via an "APPLICATION" made pursuant to Written Procedure and Articles 32 (1), (2), (4), (5), 33 (1), 34, 36 (1) (2), 39 and addressed to the "Chief Registrar" of the Ecowas Court of Justice. See Article 11(1) (2) of Protocol A/P.1/7/91 on the Community of Justice. The Procedure stipulates the type and mode of Application required by the Ecowas Court Rules.

The Rules of Ecowas Court contemplate both Written and Oral evidence unlike the FREP Rules made pursuant to S. 46(1) of the 1999 Constitution which permits of only the use of Affidavit evidence. See also Article 13 of Protocol A/P.1/7/91.

The Ecowas Court Rules is of its own nature permitting the "Judge – Rappoteur" to look at the suit and processes filed to determine and present his preliminary report to the Court after or where all or any of the things contained in the subsections of Article 39 would have taken place. It is only after that would have happened that the Honourable Court shall decide what action to take upon the Recommendations of the "Judge – Rappoteur".

Actions or Suits affecting issues on Human Rights violations may be conveniently anchored and copious founded on the guaranteed rights of a citizen (Nigerian, Ecowas, African) as enshrined in Chapter IV of the 1999 Constitution, African charter on Human and Peoples rights, the charter on universal Declaration of Human rights, Mine Band Treaty and other international Human Rights instruments as well as general principles of Law as prescribed by Articles 60 and 61 of the African Charter.

When the principal complaint of an Applicant is on Human Rights issues and the continuous violations and infraction of Applicants Fundamental Human Rights guaranteed by Chapter IV of the Constitution of the Federal Republic of Nigeria 1999 (as amended) particularly S. 33(1), 34, 35, 41 and 46(1) (2) thereof, the Forum of the Ecowas Court is convenient. It is submitted that by virtue of Articles 60 and 61 of the African Charter on Human and Peoples Rights, all manner of persons who have cause to approach this Court, shall have their cases entertained.

Article 60 provides:
"The Commission shall draw inspiration from international law on human and peoples' rights, particularly from the provisions of various African instruments on Human and Peoples' Rights, the Charter of the United Nations, the Charter of the Organization of African Unity, the Universal Declaration of Human Rights, other instruments adopted by the United Nations and by African countries in the field of Human and Peoples' Rights as well as from the provisions of various instruments adopted within the Specialized Agencies of the United Nations of which the Parties to the present Charter are members.

Article 61 provides:
"The Commission shall also take into consideration, as subsidiary measures to determine the principles of law, other general or special international conventions, laying down rules expressly recognized by Member States of the Organization of African Unity, African practices consistent with international norms on Human and Peoples' Rights, customs generally accepted as law, general principles of law recognized by African States as well as legal precedents and doctrine.

The African Charter permits and allows recourse to common Law principles of Law recognized by African states as well as legal precedents and Doctrines.

Under the African Charter on Human and Peoples Rights – Chapter IV – "APPLICABLE PRINCIPLES" the Commission, or indeed, the Court before whom an application such is presented can draw inspiration from International Law on Human and Peoples Right – see Article 60. Article 61 allows the Commission (or indeed the Court) to have recourse to general principles of Law such as the Tort of Negligence as well as legal. The Court to take into consideration subsidiary measures to determine the principle of Law applicable in any case brought before this Honourable Court.

It is submitted that Environmental Law encompasses the Law of Tort, nuisance, strict liability offence, trespass, negligence, damages for environmental wrong, property law, land law, riparian rights and other related Areas. See Article 24 of African Charter. See also THEODORE OKORONKWO: THE LAW ON ENVIRONMENTAL LIABILITY: Cap 2; Pg. 18.

Article 19 of the Protocol of Ecowas Court provides that:
"The Court shall examine the dispute before it in accordance with the provisions of the Treaty and its Rules of Procedure. It shall also apply, as necessary, the body of laws as contained in Article 38 of the Statues of the International Court of Justice."

Article 38 of the Statute of International Court of Justice (ICJ) provides:
"The Court whose function is to decide in accordance with International Law such disputes as are submitted to it, shall apply:
(a) International Conventions, whether general or particular, establishing rules expressly recognized by the contesting States.
(b) International customs, as evidence of a General practice accepted as Law.
(c) The general principles of law recognized by Civilized Nations.
(d) Subject to the provisions of Article 59, Judicial decisions and teachings of most highly qualified publicists of the various nations, as subsidiary means for the determination of Rules of Law."

The Hon. Ecowas Court can apply the general Principles of Law recognized by civilized Nations. In the case of Aegean Sea Continental Shelf (GREECE Vs. TURKEY) ICJ Report 1976 at 15 – 16, the Court applied the provision of Article 38(1) (c) of the statute of the International Court of Justice to protect rights of an individual in the interim where the rights are infringed upon in accordance with the principles of Law recognized in municipal systems and jurisprudence of the Court.

It is my opinion that the Law of Tort of Negligence is applicable in aid of Cap IV of the 1999 Constitution of the Federal Republic of Nigeria and all the relevant Fundamental Human Rights provisions guaranteed as well as relevant Articles of African Charter aimed at preserving, and protecting Fundamental Human Rights of Citizens.

CHAPTER TWELVE

LOCUS STANDI OF LANDMINES VICTIMS TO SUE STATE PARTIES TO MINE BAN TREATY (MBT)

One bizarre impression often bandied about by Lawyers and academics about the Nigerian/Biafra Civil War is that there can be no Legal inquisition on the events that took place then within the Biafran enclave which has since 1970 fallen due and under the control of the Federal Republic of Nigeria. While the situation has remained that way since the cessation of hostilities, it is apparent that no Law (Decree) limited or abrogated the justiceability of actions, inactions or omission arising from the events of that war happening after January 15, 1970. It was neither contemplated nor reasoned by the Nigeria Authorities that the huge chunk of arms and ammunitions released to the fighting Nigeria Soldiers to crush Biafra before the cease-fire did not return to the armoury but were largely abandoned at the various theatres of war. Those that could work unsupervised continued to ravage the civilian population after the war. This included majority of people who were born after 1970 or whose mothers had not been born by 1970. If the alleged participis criminis in the Nigeria – Biafran War are not allowed to seek redress or damages arising from injuries sustained during the Civil War, the same argument cannot go with those who did not participate in the war as well of those injured Victims who were born between January 16, 1970 and any time after till date.

"Article 10: Access to the Court
Access to the Court is open to the following
a) Member States, and unless otherwise provided in a Protocol, the Executive Secretary, where action is brought for failure by the Member State to fulfil an obligation;
b) Member States, the Council of Ministers and the Executive Secretary in proceeding for the determination of the legality of an action in relation to any Community text;
c) Individuals and corporate bodies in proceedings for the determination of an act or inaction of a Community official which violates the rights of the individuals or corporate bodies;
d) Individuals on application for relief for violation of their human rights; the submission of application for which shall:
   i) Not be anonymous; nor
   ii) Be made whilst the same matter has been instituted before another International Court for adjudication;

e) Staff of any Community institution, after the Staff Member has exhausted all appeal process available to the officer under the ECOWAS Staff Rules and Regulations;

f) Where in any action before a court of a member State, an issue arises as to the interpretation of a provision of the Treaty, or the other Protocols or Regulations, the national court may on its own or at the request of any of the parties to the action refer the issue to the Court for interpretation."

Therefore, anybody born at any date between January 16, 1970 till date who happens to be injured by any of those abandoned weapon within the area now under the control or supervision of the Federal Government, in so far as it falls within the former Eastern region must necessarily have the locus to sue or seek redress in court.

b) On *locus standi*

The Hon. Ecowas Court considered the issue of Locus standi in the case of The Registered Trustees of the Socio-Economic Rights & Accountability **Project (SERAC) VS The President, Fed. Rep. of Nig & 7 Ors. Suit No: ECW/CCJ/APP/08/09 and Ruling No: ECW/CCJ/RLL/07/10 (2010) CCJELR, Pg 231, 248**.

With respect to the alleged lack of locus standi by the Plaintiff, the analysis of the Court firstly relies on the nature of the dispute brought before it for adjudication. In fact, the claim presented in the application is related to the alleged violation of the Human Rights of the people who inhabit the Region of Niger Delta. The framework presented in the initiating application is not only of violation of an individual's rights, but of rights of entire communities as well as environmental devastation without sufficient and protective intervention from public authorities.

There is a large consensus in international law that when the issue at stake is the violation of rights of the entire communities, as in the case of the damage to the environment, the access to Justice should be facilitated.

Article 2 (5) of Convention on

"Access to information, Public Participation in Decision – Making and Access to Justice in Environmental Matter" defines the *"public concerned"* with environment protection as *"Public affected or likely to be affected by, or having an interest in the environment decision-making. For the purposes of this definition nongovernmental organization promoting environment and meeting requirements under national law shall be deemed to have an interest".*

Article 9 of the same instrument confirms the access to justice to the public concerned as defined in Article 2 (5).

Although the Convention is not a binding instrument on African States, its importance, as a persuasive evidence of an international communist opinion Juris in allowing NGOs to access the Courts for protection of Human Rights related to the environment, cannot be ignored or underestimated by this Court. The capacity of NGOs to lodge complaints related to Human Rights is also recognized by the American Convention of Human Rights which provides in its Article 44 "that any person or group of persons, or any non-governmental entity legally recognized in one or more member states of the organization, may lodge petitions with the Commission containing denunciations or complaints of violation of the Convention by a state party". This more liberal locus standi has been welcomed and recommended for the African Continent (Magnus Killander, The African Regional Human Rights System and other Regional Systems: A Comparative Analysis, in Judiciary Watch Report, Publication from The Kenyan Section of the International Commission of Juris, page. 182)

It is my strong believe that both the High Court of a State and the Federal High Court of Nigeria are adequately empowered by the Constitution of the Federal Republic of Nigeria 1999 to handle issue affecting the Fundamental Human Right of Citizens. But with respect to the Federal High Court particularly, it can assume jurisdiction to try only when such issues derive from Section 251 of the Constitution. Section 251(j) makes provision for Munition and Explosives, thus, bringing the triable issues of Bombs and other Explosive Remnants of War within the jurisdictional ambience of the Federal High Court.

In case of the jurisdiction of the Hon. ECOWAS Court to assume jurisdiction over Human Rights issues, the Treaty and the Protocols abundantly clothe the ECOWAS Court with the powers to handle Fundamental Human Rights infractions of individuals and corporate bodies within ECOWAs member states.

Locus Standi and Actions in Representative Capacity

Just as a litigant may question the 'locus standi' of any party especially that of its plaintiff in any case, it is legitimate to question the 'Locus Standi' of applicant in matter of enforcement of Fundamental Human Rights. This was the position under the 1979 Rules. The same applies to actions and applications brought or defended in a representative capacity. The other party is at liberty to raise objection to that effect. The big question left for Applicants coming in a representative capacity is: how can all the people supposedly represented have the same cause of action? Quite a lot of legal authorities were cited to illustrate the position of the law. The general position of the law then is that it is completely inappropriate to commence representative actions in human rights proceedings. However, with the commencement of the Fundamental Human Rights (Enforcement Procedure) Rules 2009, it does appear that actions in representative capacity or in public interest have become acceptable in Fundamental Rights Litigation. This position is well founded in view of the clear provisions contained in the preamble to the new Rules. This is provided in preamble 3 which sets out the overriding objectives of the new Rules. One of such objectives is set out in paragraph e (i to v) which provides as follows:

e) "The court shall encourage and welcome public interest litigations in the human rights fields and no human rights case may be dismissed or struck out for want of locus standi." In particular, human rights activists, advocates, or group as well as any non-governmental organizations, may institute human rights applications on behalf of any potential applicant. In human rights litigation, the applicant may include any of the following:
i) Anyone acting in his own interest
ii) Anyone acting on behalf of another person
iii) Anyone acting as a member of or in the interest of a group or class of persons
iv) Anyone acting in the public interest and
v) Association acting in the interest of its members or other individuals or groups

The above provision puts paid to the twin issues of 'locus standi' and representative actions with regard to applications for enforcement of fundamental human rights. The provision is very clear and unambiguous. No human rights case may be dismissed or struck out for want of 'locus standi'. The class of applicants bring an application to enforce the fundamental rights of members of the public or an individual. Any member of a group or a class may commence an application not just for himself and in his name but also in the mane of members of the group or class. Anyone could represent anyone and the application would be valid. This is operational under the chapter IV of this Constitution Order 3(a) and particularly 3 (b) provide in part that for purposes of advancing Applicants rights and freedom, the Court shall respect Municipal, Regional and International Bills of rights cited to it or brought to its attention or of which the Court is aware, whether these Bills constitute instruments in themselves or form parts of larger documents like Constitutions, Such Bills as mentioned earlier include:
i. The African Charter on Human and Peoples Rights and other

instruments (including protocols) in the African Regional Human Rights System.
ii. The Universal Declaration of Human Rights and other instruments (including protocols) in the United Nations Human Rights System.
iii. Statute of International Court of Justice.
iv. Constitution of European Union.
v. African Union Commission.
vi. European Union Constitution

The African Charter is unique. The Court is referred to **OSHEVIRE Vs. BRITSH CALEDONIAN AIRWAYS LTD (1990) 7 NWLR (PT. 163) – 489 -507 R.2.** It is strongly contended that the African Charter is concerned with the protection and preservation of both Fundamental Human Rights as well as peoples Right

It is submitted that the 1999 Constitution and the Fundamental Rights (Enforcement Procedure) Rules 2009 made pursuant thereto allow for the expansion and purposeful interpretation and application of the provisions of the African Charter with a view to advancing the protections intended by them. See S. 3(b) of the Rules: "The overriding objectives of these Rules are:
(a) ……………………………………..
(b) "For the purpose of advancing but never for the purpose of restricting the <u>Applicants</u> rights and freedoms, the Court shall request municipal, regional bills of rights cited to it or brought to its attention or of which the Court is aware, whether these bills constitute instruments in themselves or form parts of larger documents like Constitutions."

See Abo S. 46(1) of the 1999 Constitution is a constitutional provision which does not limit the time within which a citizen or anybody whose rights are violated or about being breached or likely to be infringed, can bring an action for the enforcement or securing the enforcement of his Fundamental Human Rights.

In the case of **C.A. Savage & 2 Ors Vs. M.O. Uwaechue (1972) 3 SC. 214** THE Supreme Court per Fatayi Williams (J.S.C) as he then was in defining the term "Cause of Action" said:
"A Cause of Action is defined in Shroud's Judicial Dictionary, as the entire set of circumstance giving rise to an enforceable claim. To our mind, it is, in effect the fact or combination of facts which give rise to a right to sue and it consists of two elements – the wrongful act of the Defendants which gives the Plaintiff his cause of complaint and the consequent damage. As Lord Esher said in ***COOK Vs. GILL (1973) L.R.***

*8 C.P. 107 and later in **READ Vs. BROWN (1888) 22. Q.B.D 128 (CA)**, it is every fact that it would be necessary for the Plaintiff to prove, if traversed, in order to support his right to the judgement of the court, (See also **KUSADA Vs. SOKOTO NATIVE AUTHORITY DC** 131/68 delivered on 13th December, 1968, where the definition in READ Vs. BROWN (Supra) was referred to with approval)."*

A Cause of Action arises when an injury is caused to a person or property by any harmful waste or substance which has been disposed or dumped on any land or territorial waters or Contiguous Zone or Exclusive Economic Zone of Nigeria or its inland waterways. See S.12 (1) Harmful Waste (Special Criminal Provisions etc) Act. Cap F10 LFN, 2004. "Injury" or "Damage" includes death of, or injury to any persons (including diseases or any impairment or physical or mental conditions) S 12(2). See **IBRAHIM VS OSIM (1987) 4 NWLR (PT.67) AT 365:**
"In law, a Cause of Action is the entire set of facts or circumstances giving rise to an enforceable claim which is depicted by the statement of Claim." **IBRAHIM VS OSIM** (Supra).

"It also includes all those things necessary to give a right of action and every fact which is material to be proved to entitle the Plaintiff to succeed." See also **PATKUM INDUSTRIES LIMITED VS NIGER SHOE LIMITED (1985) 5 NWLR (PT 93) at 134.**

It is trite that the cause of action is found either in the Writ of Summons or in the Statement of Claim embodying the pleadings.

It is further submitted that a cause of action means the fact or facts, which establish or give rise to a right of action and it is the factual situation which gives a person the right to judicial relief. It is the entire set of circumstances giving rise to an enforceable claim. "It includes every fact which the defendants will have the right to traverse. See **RINCO CONSTRUCTION CO VS. VEEPEE IND. LTD (2008) 9 NWLR (PT. 929) 85 PP. 96 – 97 Para E – A.**

When Victims get more traumatized, their environments getting more degraded as to prevent them getting back to their farms for Agricultural to produce food for themselves/family, they should not stand-by and wait until they die.

It is therefore erroneous and inconceivable to contend that a Human right infraction is Statute barred when the wrong or violation are still subsisting.

It is contended that the continuous violation, breach and threat to the Victims or Survivors Fundamental Human Rights leading to the need to enforce or secure the enforcement of their Fundamental Human Rights will at all times ground actions for the enforcement of the Fundamental Human Rights of anybody or individuals who fall into this group.

Making land safe and free from continued contamination to enable the Applicants/Respondents (Victims) get back to farming and Agriculture in their various Communities and Environments where they come from are Human Rights Issues which cannot be flattered by any limitation statute. See Definition of Victims in Landmine Monitor 2008.

See JALLCO LTD Vs. OWONI BOYS TECH. SERVICES LTD (1995) 4 NWLR (PT. 391) 534; Para E-G, where the Supreme Court of Nigeria has this to say per Mohammed JSC.

"Time begins to run for the purpose of Limitation Law when there is in existence a person who can sue and another who can be sued and when all facts have happened which are material to be proved to entitle the Plaintiff to succeed."

Where in challenging the infringement of Fundamental Rights, where such infringement is continuous, time bar will not catch up with it.

In Uzoukwu & Ors Vs. Ezeonu II & Ors (1991) 6 NWLR (PT.200) 708 at 759 – 760 the Court of Appeal (Per Nasir P.C.A) held;

"The only complaint was in respect of a condition precedent to the exercise of jurisdiction. Learned Counsel submitted that the action was statute barred as it was not brought within twelve months. I have already stated above that this was a very narrow interpretation of the evidence. I am satisfied that the learned trial judge could exercise his jurisdiction as the various elements of complaint were not only within 12 months but were also alleged to be continuous. The respondents have not proffered any evidence to the contrary."

A group of individuals/victims who have suffered the same fate and who have been injured by Landmines or other explosive remnants of war can bring action by and for themselves as a collectivity. This will include their families and communities in view of the definition of who a victim is by MBT and pursuant to Article 10(d) of the Protocol.

In PAULINUS NWAEZE Vs. ENUGU STATE COMMISIONER OF POLICE & ORS (2001) CHR 445, one of the grounds of the Preliminary Objections raised by the Respondents was that the action was incompetent as it was filled after 12 months. In rejecting the Objection AHANAONU J. held:

"Coming to the second term of the Objection based on limitation of time prescribed by ORDER 1 RULE 3(1) of the said Rules, I have no hesitation in agreeing with the counsel for the Applicant that the act

complained of has continued. The act has in the detention of the Applicants motorcar. Although the detention of the said car began in May, 1997, it has continued till date. Order 1 Rule 3(1) does not therefore apply to this case. I therefore, overrule the second Objection also."

It is my view that when reliefs claimed by an Applicant fall within same specific rights enumerated in chapter IV of 1999 Constitution of Nigerian 1999 as amended and African charter on Human and Peoples Rights (Ratification and Enforcement Acts), cause of action shall guarantee unfettered access to court.

There is nothing in plea of limitation of time to defeat the long and lingering violations, breach and infringement of any Applicants Fundamental Human Rights once such act of continued violations and infringement is unabated and subsisting.

Identifying, mapping out as well as making Bomb Dumps and Locations with Danger signals at various locations in the various Communities where Victims or Survivors come from without removing them for destruction creates a situation of continuous violation of the Fundamental Human Rights of the victims or survivors. The mere knowledge of the location of some of Landmines - these Bombs in so far as they affect the psyche, affect the physical and mental Health of the Victims or Survivors amount to infractions and threat to the Fundamental Human Rights. Once the contaminations and degradation of Victims environment and Communities is a Human Rights Issue and this ought not to be affected by statute of limitation.

In so far the Victims and/or survivors cannot move about freely and their Rights are circumscribed by the limitations and injuries imposed as well as inflicted on them, it will be unsafe to conclude that their Environment provided them with one as contemplated by African Charter. The conclusion that has been thrown up is that the plea of limitation of time or statute of limitation is a defence not available in Human Rights cases except where statute makes specific provision that should exist for the formation or operation of that defence. See **Adepoju Vs. Oke (1999) 3 NWLR (PT. 594) 154 at 169; Taiwo Vs. Taiwo (1958) 3 FSC 80 at 182; Moss Vs. Kenrow (Nig) Ltd (1992) 9 NWLR (PT. 264) 207 at 224.**

Besides, Order III of the Fundamental Rights (Enforcement Procedure Rules, 2009) provides:
"An Application for the enforcement of Fundamental Rights shall not be affected by any limitation statute whatsoever."

The wordings of this order is very clear and unambiguous. Time would never be a barrier in bringing an application for enforcement of Fundamental Human Rights so long as this Rule remains in force. There is no doubt that this Rule would override the Limitation Act so long as the subject matter deals with enforcement of Fundamental Human Rights.

The ECOWAS Court is enjoined to have recourse to National, Municipal and International Laws while determining any matter brought before it.
Stockpile of Bombs is at best a hazardous waste. "Hazardous waste" means any waste or a combination of wastes that exhibits ignitable, corrosive, reactive or toxic characterization and poses a substantial danger, now or in the future, to human, or animal, life and which therefore cannot be handled or dispose of without special precautions.
S. 33(1) of the 1999 Constitution states that "every person has right to life and no one shall be deprived intentionally of his life". The stockpile of Bombs within the residential neighbourhood inhibits as well as limits the full enjoyment of life of affected residents. In the interpretation of matters concerning the Fundamental Rights of the Citizens of this country as guaranteed by the Nigerian Constitution, the courts should adopt a liberal attitude unless of course, in those cases where a narrower interpretation will best carry out the spirit, objective and intention of the Constitution: **OSAWE VS REGISTRAR OF TRADE UNIONS (1983) 4 N.C.L.R. 556**, HC Bendel State.

Considerable care and originality must be employed whenever the courts are called upon to interpret its provisions and in the discharge of the duty the courts ought always to bear in mind the circumstances of our people: **DR. BASIL UKAEGBU V ATTORNEY GENERAL OF IMO STATE (1985) 1 S.C.N.L.R 212**.

In the exercise of the right to life along with S.20 of the Constitution and S.24 of African Charter confirms a right to a healthy environment which right enures to Applicants. See **EZEUGO V. STATE** (2013) LPELR-19984(CA) (Page 116, paragraphs D-F) Per SAULAWA, J.C.A. Under the 1999 Constitution (supra),
"Every person has a right to life; a right to dignity; a right to personal liberty; a right to fair hearing; a right to private and family life; a right to freedom of thought, conscience and religion, et al. See Sections 33-43 of the 1999 Constitution as amended (supra). These are the everlasting fundamental inalienable rights to which every citizen of this country is entitled." See **EZEADUKWA V. MADUKA & ANOR (1997) LPELR-8062(CA)** page 45-46, paragraphs F-A) Per TOBI J.C.A (As he

then was)

"Right to dignity of the person entails that no person shall be subjected to torture or to inhuman or degrading treatment." Torture in this regard is mental torture to which Applicants are subjected to which is capable of snuffing life out of the person should the stockpile of Bombs remain there as vulnerable as they are. This right seems to protect the right of citizens against environment degradation.

Torture in the regard is mental torture as a Survivor goes to bed every day and wake up with the thought of possible Bomb explosions whether activated by natural persons, hoodlums or by an act of god. See **ABACHA & ORS. V. FAWEHINMI** (2000) LPELR-14(SC) (Pp. 31-32, Paragraphs F-G) per OGUNDARE, J.S.C.

"By Cap. 10 the African Charter is now part of the laws of Nigeria and like all other laws the courts must uphold it. The Charter gives to citizens of member states of the Organization of African Unity rights and obligations which rights and obligations are to be enforced by our courts, if they must have any meaning. It is interesting to note that the rights and obligations contained in the Charter are not new to Nigeria as most of these rights and obligations are already enshrined in our Constitution. See Chapter IV of the 1979 and 1999 Constitutions." Both the African Charter and the Constitution abundantly provide for the protection and preservation of peoples Fundamental Human Rights. It is contended that the right of Freedom of movement, particularly not to be allowed to leave their homes, organize ceremonies within the environment as at when and how they want it, will be empty without a concomitant right not to be deprived of the opportunity of moving about in their environment.

The High Court, Lagos State has held that Freedom under the Constitution should not be restricted to physical freedom, that is ability to move about freely, but also extends to mental freedom so as not to hinder the ability to move about freely, if the concept of freedom under the Constitution is to be meaningful. See **AKOKHIA VS C.O.P. (1984) 5 NCLR 836, Bode J**, H.C. Lagos. The African Charter, Article 24 proclaims that the right to a satisfactory environment for development is a Human Right. This development includes Human development and welfare. **In Gani Fawehimini Vs Abacha (1996) 9 NWLR, Part 475, P. 710.** The Court held that Article 24 of the African Charter can be relied upon by a Nigerian to enforce his environmental right instead of relying on S.20 of the Constitution which is not however, justiceable. This right is sine-qua-non to Victims/Survivors enjoyment of life and any limitation to the exercise of such right tantamount to the breach of Applicants Fundamental Human Rights guaranteed.

The presence of these Bombs and other Explosive Remnants of War constitute and amount to threats and infractions of the Applicants Fundaments Human Rights guaranteed by the 1999 Constitution and the African Charter. Wherever Bombs are stockpiled where they ought not to be stockpiled is capable of killing or causing sicknesses and disease when stockpile where people live. Similarly, wherever Bombs or other explosive remnants of war are abandoned, this constitutes on-going threat to life. This is capable of constituting some danger to people's health and where this occurs, it amounts to infraction of Fundamental Human Rights.

The elements of our own Environment include the following: (i) Hydrosphere - (water), (ii) Lithosphere - (land), (iii) Biosphere – (plants, organisms and animals), (iv) Atmosphere - (energy, light and gases)
According to Chambers English Dictionary, Pollution means: *"to befoul physically, to contaminate, make (any feature of the environment) offensive or harmful to human, animal or plant life to make unclean morally, to defile ceremonially, profane."*
While S. 37 of the NESREA ACT define "pollution" to mean, "Man-made or man-aided alteration of chemical, physical or biological quality of the environment beyond acceptable limits and "pollutant" shall be construed accordingly.

From, the foregoing definitions, that pollution means any human activity or activities such as those of the Respondents that impede the ecosystem adversely to the advantage of man and thereby impairing the natural environment and Environmental rights places duties on the state to prevent Pollution and ensure the conservation of water resources.
Live Bombs of assorted types, hand grenades and other instruments and weapons of mass destruction when stockpiled in such a place where weapons of such nature with capacity to wipe out humanity at any mistake or explosion are not ordinarily dumped or stocked or stockpiled in any form including earthen man-holes artificially made or dumped ignorantly.
Stockpile in places where they ought not to be constitute a violation of affected persons Fundamental Human Rights to life, liberty, right to a healthy physical and mental health of Citizens who live within the neighbourhood. It is unarguable that the mere presence of the Bombs in any environment constitutes mental torture and a veritable threat and thus

violates Applicant's Fundamental Human Right to S.34(1)a of the Constitution as well as Articles 5, 6 of African Charter on Human & Peoples Right.

The conclusion to be drawn where such exists in that people's right to freedom of movement is hampered, restricted and this time not by a lawful order but by the presence of these stockpile of Bombs which is a breach of their right to freedom of movement guaranteed by S. 41(1) of the Constitution of the Federal Republic of Nigeria 1999 as amended and Article 24 of African Charter. The more Bombs stay in contaminated environments the more deadly they become. Bombs are high risk objects and are vulnerable. Stockpile of Bombs in places where they ought not to be can lead to sicknesses and deaths. The recovering of Bombs from various destinations and stockpiling them, dumping them in earthen hole, exposing them and other UXO's and AXO's to visibility and to the knowledge of the Victims/Survivors can diminish life and life expectancies; and indeed when it comes with such fears and stress, they can kill. Also such actions and activities constitute enormous threat to life of the Victims/Survivors which life can be cut short either physically or psychologically.

After the cessation of hostilities in 1970, many returnee refugees and fugitives found abandoned Bombs at their Homes and Villages which they collected and dumped into pit Latrines without considering future development projects. All those are bombs waiting to consume Nigerian citizens who may be involved or engaged activities requiring excavation or exploration. By burying or dumping the Bombs in earthen holes and man-made holes, without covering those holes, rain water that enter such holes are not baled out but disappear or seep into the surrounding soil to pollute and contaminate underground water aquifer. See the case of **Ballard V Gomlinson (1885) 29 Ch.D 115.** In this case, neighbouring properties each had wells sunk into a chalk aquifer. The claimant used water from his well for the purpose of brewing. The defendant allowed sewage and refuse to enter his well and these found their way into the common source of underground water with the consequences that the water became unusable for the claimants brewing purposes. It was held that the claimant was entitled to extract water percolating beneath his land and the defendant had no right to contaminate this. Accordingly, the claimant was awarded an injunction and damages. The enjoyment of life and preservation/protection of same can only be done by one whose duty it is to do so, does that only in safe, secure and uncontaminated Environment.

The stockpile or dumping of these dangerous and hazardous bombs have colossal consequences on the environment where the victims/survivors live which continues to threaten and violate the Victims/Survivors Fundamental Human Rights to life, liberty, security and movement within the environs. These bombs enchased with metals suffer gradual Applicants Environment. Stockpile of Bombs causes a lot of damage, injury to health leading to deaths in most cases.

The Right to life and clean environment is profoundly recognized in **GBEMERE VS. SHELL PET. DEV. COMPANY NIGERIA & ORS IN SUIT NO. FHC/CS/13/153/2005** (Unreported Decision) of Benin Fed High Court, decision of 14th Nov, 2008, accorded this recognition. Also **in OKPARA VS SHELL PET DEV COMPANY NIG LTD Suit No. FHC/PH/CS/518**, unreported decision of Fed High Court, Port Harcourt division, decision of 29 Sept, 2006. The above two cases represent a compelling and positive jurisprudential basis by court to interpret the right to life to accommodate environmental right to clean and healthy environment. The facts of the above two cases are akin and relate to Gas flaring.

The Nigerian Constitution S.33 (1) has created a duty on the State Party and strengthened by Articles 4, 5, 16(1) (2), 18(1) (4), and 24 of the African Charter on Human and Peoples Rights, to ensure the preservation of life by dutifully removing, clearing, and destroying Bombs and other Explosive Remnants of War from the contaminated neighbourhood. It is therefore safe to further argue that S.35 (1) of the 1999 Constitution having guaranteed the right to life and having created a duty on another not to cause loss of that life (or destruction) to that life, the only way to enjoy right to life as guaranteed by S.33 (1) of the Constitution and the African Charter is to ensure that anyone who has a duty to preserve it, does not take it unconstitutionally. Not to do that or refusing to do so, amounts to infractions of any affected persons guaranteed Fundamental Human Rights.

Environment can be defined as the "surrounding external conditions within which man or any organism for that matter lives. Man depends on the resources in the environment for shelter, for his sustenance and meeting basic needs such as air, food, water and clothing." Black's Law Dictionary (Fifth Edition) 1979 Page 479 defines "Environment" in the following terms: "The totality of physical, economic, cultural, aesthetic and social circumstances and factors which surround and affect the desirability and value of property and which also affect the quality of

Peoples' lives, the condition, instances or forces which influence or modify elsewhere." "Environment" has also been defined to include, "water, air, land and other livings animals."

"An Environmental right has been defined as "the right of individuals and peoples to an ecologically sound environment and sustainable management of natural resources conducive to sustainable development." See Theodore Okonkwo: THE LAW ENFORCEMENTAL LIABILITY. 2ND ED. page 709

The Court also recognized that Environmental degradation can give rise to a violation of Human Right. See **Kokoro – Owo Vs. Lagos State Government** (1995) 6 NWLR 760 at 765.

It is therefore my believe that the violation of Human Rights are directly linked to environmental harm which threaten and is capable of shortening the lives of people who need not wait to be killed by explosion or contaminations.

The right to a healthy environment is related to the right to an adequate standard of living. It means that all people have the right to live in an environment that is safe and adequate for their health and well – being. Without a healthy environment, people cannot attain an adequate standard of living and are exposed to potentially harmful surroundings.

Source: Page 4 of Newsprint Newspaper Vol. 8 No. 71 June 4 – 5, 2012 titled "EXPLOSIVE STOCKPILE OWERRI RESIDENTS IN DANGER." The concept of this right is relatively new. It has however developed due to the increasing recognition that many human activities can have a degrading impact on the environment which in turn has a negative impact on people's health.

The right includes the right of all people to participate in decisions that relate to the environment and to have access to courts or other bodies where appropriate. For example, the public should be consulted in relation to development applications, particularly where the development plans to destroy or modify part of the natural environment. Government are required to be accountable and transparent in relation to their decisions that impact on the environment and they should be responsive to the questions and concerns of the public. In addition to the right to a healthy environment, all people have a duty to protect the environment in every way they can. This can take forms and includes, for example, recycling, riding a bike instead of taking and car as well as installing solar water heaters.

The constitution of a country guarantees basic human rights and provides guiding principles for society. The rights and the obligations that are expressed in the Constitution belong to each person and community in Nigeria. In Nigeria we are fortunate to have a Constitution that recognizes a healthy environment as a basic human right. This is not the case in all countries. (Okonkwo Theodore, Ph.D.: ENVIRONMENTAL LAW Multi- Disciplinary Approach - Page 640.

CHAPTER THIRTEEN

BOMBS

"A Bomb is defined as a hollow metal shell, fitted either with explosives for causing destruction on bursting or with smokes gas, or incendiary material." "An explosive is a chemical compound which were properly initiated, suddenly generates much heat and gas highly in excess of the original volume of the chemical compound thereby exerting in its summon dings sudden and intense presence this resulting in a heavy bang." These could be military or homemade bombs which remain in whatever state they are found pretending to be friendly unless tampered with or triggered off. The life span of a bomb could be very long. Some world war 11 bombs were very recently sighted at Rhine River in 2012.

TERRORISM
Terrorism is a systematic intimidation or a method of governing or securing political, social, religious, economic or other freedom by violence.
U.S. Laws (18 U.S.C. 3077 defines, "Terrorism as an act of criminal violence that intends:
(a) intimidate or coerce a civilian population
(b) influence the policy of the government by intimidation or coercions
(c) to affect the Conduct of a government by assassination or kidnapping.
Terrorism also means "the use of threats, by a cohesive group of persons to cause violence and achieve its aims". Baljit singh describes terrorism as a threat or use of symbolic violent acts aimed at influencing political behaviour" According to Dappa Sogbere terrorism also means "the use of threats, by a cohesive group of persons to cause violence and achieve its aims". "It is also a violence directed at wider audience and targets, involving a deliberate violation of societal norms, to create impact and fear."

Peter Chalk has opinionated that terrorism's aim is to destroy societal status quo by gradually removing the structure which ultimately gives society its strength". On his own, Cindy Combs describes terrorism as a "synthesis of war and theater, a dramatization of the most proscribed kind of violence perpetrated on innocent victims, thereby creating a mood of fear."

Baljit Singh sums up terrorism as, "a threat or use of symbolic violent acts aimed at influencing political behavior." All these suggest that terrorist acts are for ulterior motives, usually perpetrated against innocent victims in order to weaken the bonds between the legitimate government and the society.

Terrorists are mobile and move from one target to another. Strategically, terrorists will likely shift from more protected targets to less protected ones. In Nigeria, terrorist activities take place on both protected and unprotected areas. We have seen it take place in United Nations building in the Federal Capital Territory, Abuja, more in churches than in mosques, in parks and market places. This is the key to defensive measures. Terrorists are often times, non-state armed groups.

Section 1 (2) of Terrorism (Prevention) Act 2011 defines **"act of terrorism"** to mean an act which is deliberately done with malice; aforethought and which:

a) may seriously harm or damage a country or an international organization;
b) is intended or can reasonably be regarded as having been intended to-
i) unduly compel a government or international organization to perform or obtain from performing any act;
ii) seriously intimidate a population;
iii) seriously destabilize or destroy the fundamental political, constitutional, economic or social structures of a country or an international organization; or
iv) otherwise influence such government or international organization by intimidation or coercion; and
c) involves causes, as the case may be-
i) an attack upon a person's life which may cause serious bodily harm or death;
ii) kidnapping of a person;
iii) destruction to a Government or public facility, a transport system, an infrastructure facility, including an information system, a fixed platform located on the continental shelf, a public place or private property, likely to endanger human life or result in major economic loss;
iv) the seizure of an aircraft, ship or other means of public or goods transport and diversion or the use of such means of transportation for any of the purposes in paragraph (b) (iv) of this subsection;
v) the manufacture, possession, acquisition, transport, supply or use of weapons, explosives or of nuclear, biological or chemical weapons, as well as research into, and development of biological and chemical weapons without lawful authority;

vi) the release of dangerous substance or causing of fire, explosives or floods, the effect of which is to endanger human life;
vii) interference with or disruption of the supply of water, power or any other fundamental natural resource, the effect of which is to endanger human life;
d. an act or omission in or outside Nigeria which constitutes an offense within the scope of a counter terrorism protocol and conventions duly ratified by Nigeria.
e) an act which disrupts a service but is committed in pursuance of a protest. However, demonstration or stoppage work is not a terrorist act within the meaning of this definition provided that the act is not intended to result in any harm referred to in subsection (2) (b) (i), (ii) or (iv) of this section.

Non-state armed groups include organizations carrying out armed rebellion or insurrection as well as a broader range of non-state entities, such as criminal gangs and state-supported proxy.

Methods of Preventing or limiting the activities of Terrorists:
To prevent or limit the activities of terrorists the following actions must be taken:
i. Ensure that everybody abandons his/her luggage for whatever reasons and walk freely.
ii. Treat all abandoned luggages and briefcases with suspicion.
iii. Sensitive places should be installed with detectors and trained Explosive Ordnance Disposal (EOD) men detailed to handle the equipment.
iv. Ensure effective security coverage of sensitive areas at all times.
v. Report any suspected movement
vi. Report any strange person or visitor or guest
vii. Dial the Department of State Security (DSS) or Police
viii. Install CCTV cameras in major streets and public places.

Bomb Detection:
Bomb detection is the duty of the EOD search team. In other words, police men at check points, security officers in other government departments, firms and corporations e.g. the Nigeria Customs Officers, as well as officers in the Postal Telecommunications and Courier Companies also detect bombs during their routine checks. In carrying out these checks, some security equipment are employed. The explosive detectors are employed in the search of personnel, cars, parcels, fabricated leather, boxes, offices and shops, and other suspected places.

The metal detector is also used in searching persons, parcels and places not expected to have heavy metal alloys content. This is so commonly used at public places where a lot of people are expected to enter the door way. A detector could be of immense help in the stadia, churches and mosque. An explosive detector could be fooled and deceived by certain types of perfumes. A physical search must therefore be carried out to ascertain the availability or presence of a bomb. In cases of letters and parcels, an X-ray machine may be employed for confirmation. In advanced countries the services of sniff dogs in searching for explosives is usually used. This is one of the best methods of bomb detection as the sniff dogs' accuracy in explosive detection has been 95% correct.

Bomb Scare: - This is a Device that shares some characteristics with improvised explosives device with notable absence of actual explosives component. These characteristics include identifiable power source, circuit board with exposed wiring and electrical tape.

Bomb warning: - A stunning piece of news of an explosives warning sign that a bomb is about to explode.

False Alarm: - A false alarm is also called a nuisance alarm, a phony report of an emergency, causing unnecessary panic, and or bringing resources (such as emergency services to places where they are not needed per time.

Hoax: - A hoax is deliberate attempt to deceive or trick people into believing or accepting something which the hoaxer knows to be false.

Bomb Threat Awareness And Counter Terrorism:

Bomb threat should not be taken for granted. Persons receiving threats by telephone should endeavor to remain calm and dial Police of DSS numbers. No arrest shall be effected on the person passing the information even if it turns out to be false.

Home Made Bombs (HMB)

Due to the restrictions placed on the sale of commercial explosives, terrorist find it difficult to acquire explosives. Terrorists are therefore forced to produce their own explosives by manufacturing Home-Made-Bombs.

The materials used are: Sugar, Soap, Petrol, Fuel Oil (Paraffin/Kerosene), Aluminum Powder, Fertilizer or Ammonium Nitrate (AN), Weed Killer 'Ammonium Chlorate' (AC)

Improvised Explosive Devices (IED): - These are those devices placed or fabricated in an improvised manner incorporating destructive, lethal, noxious, pyrotechnics or incendiary chemicals designed to destroy, kill, disfigure, distract or harass. They may incorporate military stores, but are normally device from non-military components.

These may be described as booby traps, or devices placed or fabricated in an improvised manner, incorporating destructive, lethal, obnoxious pyrotechnics or incendiary chemicals designed to lath, maim, destroy disfigure or distract. Examples of an Improvised Explosive Device (IED) is the Biafran – type "Ogbunigwe". It is potent enough and extremely dangerous to de-arm manually. Terrorist and suicide Bombers oftentimes rely on the use of IED. That terrorist acts are for uterine motives, usually perpetrated against innocent victims in order to weaken the bombs between the legitimate government and the society". Reter Chalk agrees with him and says that terrorist accord to destroy societal status quo by gradually removing the structures which ultimately given society its strength." While Cindy comb could not agree more when he described terrorism as a synthesis of war and the theater, a dramatization of the most proscribed kind of violence. Perpetrated on innocent victims, thereby creating a mood of fear. Terrorism is hardly targeted at more protected targets than less protected targets. It is akin to a poor man venting his annoyance on an equally poverty stricken person for his being poor. Terrorists will in most cases shift from areas that the camera might catch them in areas inhabited or occupied by the less prolonged. This is the reason Terrorist are often go slot-times.

TYPES OF EXPLOSIVES
(1) Low Explosives
(2) High Explosives
(3) Velocity of Detonation
(4) Commercial Explosives
(5) Types of Nitroglycerine
(6) Dynamite
(7) Blasting Gelatin
(8) Gelignite
(9) Nitroglycen and Ammonium Nitrate
(10) Ammonium Nitrate
(11) Retaining cord.

Low Explosives (LE): - These are substances which explode rather than denote. This takes place on the surface of a substance and burns layer by layer. The rate of burning of explosives greatly increases when confined and is proportional to the degree of confinement.

Use of Low Explosives: -
As propellant or disruptive agent in pyrotechnics; and in demolition

stores – safety fuse

High Explosive (HE):- These are substances which denotes. A demotion takes place when a shock-wave travels through a substance breaking up the molecular structure of the substance. The explosive is manufactured in such a way that its molecular arrangement is in detestable state and the slightest agitation by heat, shock or impact cause the molecules to break up and recombine in more stable forms. In the process of braking-up, the molecules release heat and gas, building up pressure that break up the container into small fragments. The stable molecule normally formed after denotations are CO_2, H_2O and N_2.

Velocity of Detonation: Speed
This is the velocity with which the detonating wave travels through the substance. It is measured in meters/second.
The denoting wave loses energy in bringing air gaps; and it is not affected by the degree of confinement or ambient temperature. The power of an explosive depends on the volume of gases produced.

Commercial Explosives: -
This can be divided into two groups namely:
High Explosives; and Demolition Accessories

DEMOLITION AND DETONATION
Bombs are classified into two main categories, namely the terrorist's bombs and the military bombs. Unlike the terrorist bombs, military bombs undergo well refined and standardized factory processes in the course of manufacture. While the terrorist bombs are unstable and not specific in shape, the military bombs are shapely structured and stable. They therefore require different treatment in handling and demolition. The method employed in the detonation of terrorist bomb is known as "operator disarm" the Bomb. While that of the military bomb is called "Demolition".

The following situations may affect the physical structures (both internal and external) of military bombs with adverse diminishing values, thereby requiring demolition: expiration; poor storage conditions; unprofessional handling; uncontained exposure to adverse weather condition. The inherent danger posed by bombs that are subjected to or suffer the above conditions demand that such bombs be disposed off in a safe and efficient manner.

The following guidelines are preferred in conducting demolition exercise: -

Demolition will not take place unless under direct supervision for a qualified demolition officer.

The demolition ground be well specified and must be located far from residential areas.[22]

At least 24 hours prior to the time of demolition, a public announcement should be made of the intended demolition exercise. Public address system or the media could be utilized for this purpose. The police and the Hospital Authority within the area should be alerted.

Demolition should be carried out during the hours of the day only. Demolition exercise is prohibited, if it is raining, the cloud base is exceptional low or there is thunder storm and when the visibility is less than the safety distance i.e. firing point, due to fog or mist.

Written instructions must be served on all personnel engaged in the demolition exercise which shall define specific duties assigned to each person and the method to be adopted. A comprehensive list of item taken to the demolition ground should be documented. Items consumed should be noted and physically checked. Spectators are prohibited in the demolition zone.

All entrances to and exit from the demolition ground should be properly manned by sentry post which should be equipped with red flags mounted in pole of about 8 feet high. If practicable, the services of ambulance and first aid team should be secured.

Bombs no matter the size should be diffused in pits which should be created in relation to the sizes of bombs to be demolished. Effective communication arrangement should be worked out between the demolition officer, the guards and other men deployed for the exercise during demolition.

Records of Bombs, demolished and the materials expended should be kept at the end of each exercise. Records of injuries must be kept and in the event of serious injuries, demolition operations must be stopped pending detailed investigation. No unauthorized access should permitted during this period.

---

[22] Dappa Sogbere Ph.D: A Hand Book of imstructions on Explosive Ordnance Disposal (EOD) In The Nigerian Police Published 2012 by Keny & Brothers Enterprises, Asata Enugu, Nigeria

Naked light is not permitted during demolition unless for the purpose of initiating the charges by safety fuse. No smoking is allowed, a fire extinguisher is acquired.

Where necessary firing bunkers should be constructed, sand bags or natural features used as shields. The demolition ground will remain closed until "all clear signal" has been given.

Handling, Transportation and Storage of Explosives

The handling, transportation and storage of explosives as prescribed in the Explosives Act and Regulations of 1997 requires trained and experienced persons or EOD Officer to tamper or deal with explosives.

Those who handle explosives, stay or work where explosives are stored must take precautions to prevent accident, fire or explosion, and unauthorized persons from having access to the explosives. Responsible persons should be made to take charge of explosives and a written authority issued to such persons by the owners of the explosives.

There should be no smoking in the vicinity of the explosives. No naked light or any instrument likely to cause fire or explosion should be brought or kept near the explosives.

All thefts of explosive should be reported immediately.

Outside the regulations, it is essential to note the underlined precautions: -

There should be no eating while handling explosives.

Avoid scratching, touching or cleaning the face or other parts of the body while handling explosives. After handling explosives, ensure the hands are thoroughly washed using soap and a good quantity of water.

Ensure that the explosives are not spilled on the clothes. Should this occur soak the clothes in clean water, then was with soap and sufficient water before use.

Explosives splashed on the floor should be removed with the aid of saw dust, a base and water.

Transportation by Road: -

The Explosives must be securely loaded. No other goods of a dangerous or inflammable nature should be loaded in the same vehicle. In the same vein, no passenger for hire or reward should be carried in any conveyance carrying explosives.

Detonators should not also be conveyed in the same means of transportation with other explosives. It is very dangerous to permit or allow unauthorized and untrained persons to have access to the explosives or conveyance.

Any explosive that escapes from its container should be collected and disposed off and all traces removed from the conveyance. It is important to stress that explosives must be protected from fire and any form of accident. What this means is that care and caution must be employed while Explosives are in transitu.

It should be covered with tarpaulin or other spark resisting material except when it is conveyed in a covered container.

The person in charge of conveyance of explosives by road should ensure the following: -

No stopping within 100 meters of a village or town.

No keeping of explosives within 100 meters of a road or railways at night time.

No vehicle carrying explosives should be loaded above 75% of its authorized load.

Persons carrying explosives should not proceed within 100 meters of a railway except when crossing same by a recognized path for the purpose or railway use.

At resting place, explosives should be guarded.

Transportation by Rail & Air: -
Persons in charge of the conveyance of explosives by Rail and Air should observe the same regulations as in road conveyance and any other regulations that the appropriate Airport authority might take.

Transportation by Sea
The Ship Master or the shipping agents should notify the port's officer at least 24 hours before the expected arrival of the ship conveying the explosives. Under International Law, Ships carrying explosives should fly flag B of the International Code of Signal, and by the night show a red light at the foremost head, visible for at least $2^{1/2}$ kilometers.

The Ship Master should detail an officer to supervise the loading and off-loading of the explosives.

The importer should send a fit and responsible person to supervise the loading, unloading and transportation of the explosives to the firm's magazine. The police particularly the Explosive Ordnance Disposal (EOD) Command should be notified of the arrival of the Ship and should send representatives and where necessary provide an escort to ensure that the regulations on handling, transportation, and storage of explosives are not violated.

Importation: - the permit to import explosives is issued with form 7 first schedule, by the Inspector-General of Police or in case of Explosives for mining purposes, issued by the Chief Inspector of mines. In most cases, approval of the supervising Minister is sought and obtained.

Storage: - Explosives should be stored in licensed storage boxes, stores houses and magazines. The Minitry of Solid Mineral Resources is in charge of issuing these licenses in Nigeria.

Approved Storage Limits:
Storage limit   **Cap. 64 Section 42**
Detonators   -   100 pieces and below
Explosives   -   45.36kg (100 Lbs) and below

Explosives Storage
Detonators   -   Over 1000 but not more than 10,000 pieces.

Magazine:
Detonators   -   Over 10,000 pieces
Trade Powder   -   Over 902.20kg (2,000 Lbs)
Other Explosives   -   Over 113.40kg (250 Lbs)

Types of Magazines
There are three types of magazines for the storage of explosives. These are:- Surface Magazine, Floating Magazine, and Underground Magazine.

Ammonium/Explosives Grouping
4. -   PE 4 Gelatin
5. -   GP
6. -   Small Arms Ammo
8. -   Cordtex, Grenades, Mortar and Rocket
9. -   Pyrotechnics
10. -   Detonator
12. -   SMK WP Ammo e.g. Grenades
13. -   Chemical Ammo e.g. Chemical agent 43 CS Irritant/pellet irritant
15. -   Ammonium with inflammable liquids or gel[23]

Explosives that could be Isolated and Stored Together
Below are the permissible group that may be stored together in a building and those that could be stored separately. 9, 10, 12, 13 are to be stored separately 5, 6, 8, 10 with container transverse 15, 6 could be stored together. 4, 6, could also be stored together. Every place where

---

[23] *Dappa Sogbere*

explosives are stored must be indicated by means of the word "**Danger**" underneath it, "**Explosive**" or "**Detonators**" as the case may be and below these, the registered number of the storage boxes, store house or magazine written. When a store is not in use the doors, should be locked and the key kept with the person is charge of the explosives. Theft or loss of explosives should be reported immediately to the police or the nearest Inspector of Mines.

Precautionary Measures
Minimum number of persons should be employed.
No instrument of iron or steel should be used for tampering if preferable with minimum force applied.

Detonators must not be left unattended to and must be the last to be connected to the charges. Persons deployed should quickly move away from the demolition ground as soon as detonators are connected to the charges.

When the charge is ready all, persons other than the officer detailed to fire the charge will withdraw to the natural shields or firing bunkers as the case may be. In a situation where several charges are to be fired separately by safety fuse, the fuse must be arranged to fire at intervals of not less than ten seconds.

The officer detailed to fire a charge electrically must retain in his possession, the key to the exploder or in case of batteries should be in his proper control and will be the last to leave the demolition ground before firing. Under no circumstances should firing cables be connected to the leads of the exploder or batteries at this stage.

Before Firing
- The officer must satisfy that the sentries are at alert.
- Inform all groups employed that firing is about to begin.
- Obtain acknowledgement from the sentries before firing order is given.

After Firing
No person should be allowed to enter the danger zone or move from the place of safety until "All Clear" signal has been given by the officer in charge. When several charges are being detonated simultaneously by means of safety fuse or electrically, the officer in charge must allow the following time to lapse before inspection. This is called a soak-time

period, the essence is to allow the pollutants or flakes that may have adverse effect on human to dissipate.

If initiated by safety fuse - 30 minutes
If initiated electrically - 10 minutes

Misfire
This is a situation whereby a charge fails to explode after initiation. These could cause as a result of:
Broken Cable
Faulty Power Source
Defective detonator
Earthed cable
Faulty or expired detonation cord
Faulty connection
The following precautions should be observed in the event of misfire: -
No one will be permitted to approach the charge until ten minutes have elapsed from the time of firing, if initiating electrically, or by safety fuse thirty minutes is required. The misfire will then be dealt with by as few people as possible. The charge will not be touched or removed unless, it is absolutely necessary. If accessible, the charge which has misfired should be rendered harmless by detonating a fresh charge.

Demolition Accessories – Detonators: - these are similar to military detonators. Electric and non-electric types which are divided into three groups namely: -
Standard
Delay
Seismic.

Dappa Sogbere took time to enumerate them as follows:
BASIC EOD EQUIPMENT
Jamming System,
Wheel Barrow,
Electric Detonator,
Detonating Cord,
Safety Fuse,
Mail Scan,

EOD Protective Clothing 'EOD SUIT',
Short Gun,
CCTV Camera,
CCTV,
Jungle Tape,

Electronic Stethoscope,
EOD/IED Electrical Disruptors,
EOD Search kit,
Hook and Line,
EOD Tool Kit,
Mine Detector,
Bomb Detector,
Bomb Blanket,
Letter Bomb Detector,
Hand Held Metal/Weapon Detector,
Letter Bomb Visualizers,
Bomb Disposal Trailer,
Walk-Through Explosives; and
Detector (Sniffing Door Way)

Jamming System Dictation Equipment: - The HP Jammer system is a full modular, designed with basic subunits and all channels pre-adjusted and assembled, to complete system. It is very easy and fast to change any subunit in case of damage. No special tools or measurements are required. It is only a normal screw driver is needed.

The Wheel Barrow or EOD Robot: - this machinery is very important to the EOD Operative. It is used as remote delivery system. It was originally produced as a remote grapnel for removing suspected vehicles from places which are of public interest that could be damaged as a result of any explosion. The wheel barrow currently used by the Nigeria Police Anti-Bomb 'EOD' Command is the MK 7 type or version, though with modern technological break through, it has undergone series of improvement.[24]

The prime mover is racked, giving the machine a stair climbing ability and a fine driving control with the use of ramps, it is capable and able to lead and unload itself from a Land Rover or any vehicle. The basic vehicle or machinery weights 185kg, and the complete system has a total weight of about 370kg, the MK 7 system is powered by two (2) 12 volts lead/Acid batteries which provide power for approximately 2 hours of continuous usage depending on the task and the skill of the operative. It is fitted with a close circuit television (CCTV). This machine is capable

---

[24] *Dappa Sogbere:*

of carrying out various remote assignments. The basic tasks of the machine are as follows: - To break the window of a suspected vehicle and deposit explosive or incendiary charge for a controlled explosion.

A tow rope i.e. Hook and line, used to tow a suspected vehicle with a bomb, away from the main target.
To carry and deposit explosives or place the explosives or incendiary charge in a suspected vehicle for controlled explosion.
Deliver and deposit projectile or remove mats or carpets suspected of booby trap.
Delivers aimed through CCTV and can fire a shot gun for a disruptive attack.
The wheel barrow is a robot machine which can withstand relatively large explosion without any person sustaining serious damage. Invariably the basic chassis remains unchanged.

Electric Detonators: They are similar to military detonators. Their color and leads varies with companies as well as countries of manufacture. They are normally wrapped in paper packets holding 10, 50 or 100

Safety Fuse: It is a slow burning gunpowder filled cord, which

burns at the rate of 30 seconds per foot. They are covered with, blue fabric or white cotton spiral yarn.

Mail Scan- x ray System: This equipment enables the EOD operative to take an X-ray of an object and examine the contents therefore to ensure a bomb free environment. The three levels of x-ray power help out the operator to see into the contents of any package or brief case however density packed.

EOD Protective Clothing ('EOD Suit'): The EOD Suit is a unique combination of fragments of resistant materials. The suit has 6 separate parts; ballistic helmet, torso protector, including protection for arms, front and back, collar, leg chaps with foot protector, groin protector, and molded face/chest shield. The face/chest shield is a molded glass reinforced plastic and polycarbonate which offers excellent resistance to high velocity fragments and maximum acoustical and visual clarity. The 5 body protectors are light weight Kevlar, cover with heavy duty, flame retardant nomex fabric, with Velcro closures for "quick release" removal system. The sizes are in medium-large (5" 11" and taller)

Shot Gun: This is a 12 bore shotgun mounted to the wheel barrow with 5 shot recoil loaded automatic gun mounted for attacking the bomb and extension tubes with firing solenoid and connecting cable to the wheel barrow or EOD robot.

CCTV: As the name implies – it is a close circuit television mounted to the robot for easy operational method involve in the handling of the EOD robot or wheel barrow, with the aid of the camera mounted on the machine, one is able to watch and operate the vehicle from the CCTV to its desired target.

CCTV Camera: It is a video camera attached to the machine which evolves the recording of scene during the EOD operation.

Jungle Tape: It is a back insulating tape commonly used by EOD operatives in binding open electrical wires or cables.

Electronic EOD Stethoscope: This electronic stethoscope was developed and designed for EOD improvised explosive device applications. The principle involved is the application of sound waves emanating from clock work type fuse or other similar mechanism in parcels, luggage, brief cases or other container. These sound waves are picked up by sensor, amplified and relayed to the operator's headset via a cable. The stethoscope carrying case complete with all the components that makes up the unit. An advantage of this stethoscope s that it can be deployed either by an operator or by remotely controlled robot vehicle.

Improvised Explosive Device Electrical Disrupters: The disrupter is the safest tool for dealing with Home Made Bombs IEDs. It will disarm the Bomb without damage to property or injury to people. the disrupter is essentially water cannon which projects a slug of water into the package containing the I.E.D. The water travels through the air, bits and penetrate, even plywood, box or thin metals, as if it were solid projectile. As it decelerates by collision, its properties revert to normal and it splashes in all directions inside the package, but still with sufficient energy to disrupt everything in its contents, breaking electrical circuits and separating detonator from main charge. All this happens so rapidly, the process is complete well within few milliseconds. Depending on the size, construction and design of the Bomb and the skills of the user, the success rate is accurate more than manual de-arming and no one needs to be hurt since the disrupter must be placed close to the package. The short effective range is consistent and rapid.

EOD Search Kit: This is a specially selected kit for explosive ordnance recognizance allowing the technician full flexibility in assessing the threat and deciding how to deal with a potentially explosive device.

Hook and Line: Although a relatively small piece of equipment, the hook and line is of great importance to the EOD operator, it is used to: - shake or tumble a suspected IED, so as to eliminate some anti-handling devices.
It is designed to move a suspected I.E.D from its intended target or area. It is also used to remove the contents of an I.E.D after it has been opened.

EOD Tool Kit: This is a well proven and modified EOD tool. The kit comes, complete in a red steel portable tool box, with 2 self-locking drawers and lid, with all the required tools for an EOD operator or technician.

Mine Detector: This is high sensitivity metal detector, designed to detect buried mines and concealed weapons. It uses the latest pulse induction electronic circuit with increased sensitivity and stability. This technique is considerably advance on the more conventional types of mine detectors which rely on tuned oscillators in their detection circuit, this can discriminate against small objects and will work effectively in adverse conditions such as damp soil, undergrowth and underwater. The controls are mounted on a small lightweight belt mount pack which contains the electronics and incorporates the battery pack. The electronics are in solid state and consist of six plugs in modules mounted on one circuit board to facilitate servicing. The detector can be used with earphones or special loudspeaker unit connected to the control. It is supplied with either a rechargeable sealed lead acid battery or a dry cell carrier. It is used in accessible places.

Bomb Disposal Blanket: It is made of specially designed ballistic nylon with fiber resistant coating. The bomb blanket will contained explosion from a large variety of Bombs, sixteen square feet of coverage providing substantial protection, yet the bomb blanket is light enough (25 lbs) to be carried by one man. In high magnitude explosions the blanket rises to a parachute configuration while the sides drop to contain the blast.

Hand Held Metal/Weapon Detector: Portable metal/weapon detector is a compact lightweight, durable, easy to operate. Fully adjustable, one knob turning permits use in virtually any situation. So sensitive that it will detect a paper clip at a distance of two inches, and will only sound the alert when larger objects are present. The unique faraday shield type coil delivers pinpoint accuracy ferrous and non-ferrous is instantaneous, audibly through its $2^{1/4}$ speaker and visually with a light emitting diode LED.

EOD Trailer: It is used for transportation of suspected bombs, volatile substances and dangerous chemicals; it is designed to meet the need of Anti-Bomb Technician and industrial safety organizations with maximum efficiency. It carries the dangerous item gently and safety in its net suspension system. If an explosion should occur the blast is vented upward from the towing vehicle. Easily maneuverable, it can be brought or materials, since the bomb trailer has its own remote loading system.

The EOD Safety Light Probe: A hand held battery operated light source with a 6" (152mm) long and 1/8" (3mm) fiber optic light probe. The lamp is totally contained in the handle and the light "piped by the fiber optic probe is therefore cold (and safe) so that the probe can be inserted into a suspected parcel.

Walk- through Explosive/Weapon Detector (Sniffing Doorway)
Buildings and staff are often at risk of bombing by terrorist groups. The problem is eliminated by screening of people entering the building. False alarms can be rapidly dismissed and real bombs (and the planter) can be caught at the entrance. The security procedures can be manual but this is costly and can become ineffective. An entirely automatic system like the entry scan, gives a consistent level of security. It brings explosives sniffing the same convenience that metal detecting arch ways brings to arm detection. In order to avoid a higher false alarm rate, sensitivity has been improved by a great factor. Red and green control lights are attached to the entry scan and each person has to wait in the archway until his test is completed. If he moves before time an audible "illegal exist" alarm is given which is distinguishable from the true explosives alarm. This could be achieved by fast mode operation, for highest sensitivity. The instantaneous signals are the integrated over a full ten seconds to give a sensitivity equal to that of the very best portable explosives detectors, much faster than a head-to toe search. The operation is compatible with metal detectors. It has inbuilt metal detecting arch that serves dual purposes.

Protection Level: Since Home Made Bombs vary greatly as to blast and fragmentation characteristics, it is difficult to specify protection level and impossible to guarantee that such threat will be defeated. However, a large number of tests have clearly demonstrated that the bomb blanket provides protection which is equal to or greater than any similar device now on the market. The bomb blanket will suppress at least 90% of the fragments generated from essentially all expedient Bombs. In the event of an explosion, the bomb blanket will "fail safe" i.e. will not cause additional hazard.

Letter Bomb Detector: This is a precision electronics instrument that provides reliable security against letter bombs. It is fast, easy to use and is designed for continuous operation. The detector can examine hundreds of letters in just minutes. An audio signal will sound when electrically conductive materials (all known letter bombs contain metal used either in electrical circuits or as a means of mechanical detonation) is detected and remains until instrument is reset. A calibrated control permits simple adjustment to different level of sensitivity to avoid alarms for harmless objects such as paper clips and staples. Advanced solid state circuitry provides excellent long term stability.

Letter Bomb Visualizer: This is a valuable investigative aid as well as a tool to prevent undue embarrassment. The unique chemical solution creates a "window" in envelopes permitting the investigator to actually see what the contents are. Spraying letter bomb visualize on an envelope makes opaque paper temporary transparent, thus eliminating the need to open the parcel.

How the Letter Bomb Visualizer Works: Visualizer is a special chemical compound which "wet" paper in such a way as not to destroy the fibers or cause most inks to run. It is similar to an x-ray or fluoroscope. It works in a way that the investigator is permitted to see the content of an envelope for a brief period of time. By simply spraying the solution and examine the contents. The solution evaporates in 60 seconds or less returning the paper to normal. Visualizer and eliminates harmless nail while dramatically discovering explosive triggering devices.

Rear Hand Generators: This is designed to meet the requirement of a small lightweight electrical energy supply, to be used as a means of initiating an electric detonator.

Strike Exploders: This is more portable and handy exploders; it is small and lightweight and can produce enough power to overcome total series lead of 400 ohms and it uses a 6 volts battery and produce 80,000 candle power. It produces a parallel intense beam and could trigger off a light sensitive device or change at a distance of 50 meters.

EOD Technics

EOD Procedure: This refers to the training and modes of action for access to, recovery, rendering safe, and disposal of explosive ordnance or any material associated with an EOD incident.

Access Procedure: This is the action taken to locate exactly or gain access to unexploded object (UXO) or improvised explosive devices (IED).

Rendering Safe Procedure: It is the application of special explosive ordnance disposal (EOD) methods and tools to provide for the interruption of function or separation of essential components to prevent an unacceptable detonation.

Render Safe: An improvised explosive device (IED) is rendered safe when the essential components of the IED have been separated, and are not joined in any way, example, main charge, detonator, power source and switching mechanism separately from each other.

Neutralized: This is when the functions of improvised explosive devices have been disrupted.

Controlled Explosion: This is an occasion when EOD Technician or operator neutralizes an IED during rendering safe procedure; the explosion may cover the use of a standard item of disruptive equipment, or the use of a demolition charge to destroy the device.

Safe Waiting Period or Soak Time: This is the length of time applied by an EOD technician or operator during which he will not make a personal approach to an IED, and during which IED if timed, would normally by expected to function or explode, it may be adjusted periodically to counter changes in terrorist.

Final Disposal Procedure: The final disposal procedure of explosive ordnance may include demolition of burning in place, removal to disposal areas, dumping at Sea or any other appropriate means.[25]

In those days of Boko Haram insurgency in Nigeria, the EOD Command of Nigeria Police Force has suddenly come to public glare as the Ministry of Defence has fallen to public scrutiny with the military complaining about lack of Arms and modern Ammunition. It has therefore become necessary for the military and the Nigerian public to know what happened to huge Ministry of Defence votes in the past 35

---

[25] *Dappa Sogbere:*

years if Nigerian Soldiers are again fighting Boko Haram insurgents with similar military equipment they used to fight Biafra 44 years ago.

All these have been by various write rs to aid national security but not so much is on ground as a visit to many EOD Commands in the country revealed how ill-equipped these departments are. What most Nigeria Police State Command have in their kitty are mostly vehicles with bold inscription - ANTI-BOMB UNIT. They lack basic equipment to confront challenges. In 2011, two 81mm bombs were exhumed by earth-moving machine directly in front of and within the premises of Nigeria Police Anti-bomb Unit, behind Government House, Owerrri, Imo State. The Police had to invite officials of Deminers Concept Nig. Ltd to assist it remove the Bombs. The media also covered the news.

APPENDIX I

GLOSSARY:

Mine and Landmine:
Further Means ammunition designed to be placed under, on or near the ground or other surface area and to be exploded by the presence, proximity or contact of a person or a vehicle.

Demining: Means the set of activities that lead to the removal of Mine and Explosive remnants of War (ERW) hazards, including Survey, mapping clearance, marketing and the handover of the cleared land.

Anti-personnel Landmines: According to the Mine Ban Treaty, an antipersonnel mine "means a mine designed to be exploded by the presence, proximity or contact of a person and that will incapacitate, injure or kill more persons.

Anti-vehicle Landmines: According to the Mine Ban Treaty, an anti-vehicle mine is a mine designed "to be detonated by the presence, proximity or contact of a vehicle as opposed to a person."

Cluster Munition: According to the Convention on Cluster Munitions, a cluster munition is "A conventional munition that is designed to disperse or release explosive sub munitions each weighing less than 20 kilograms, and includes those sub munitions." Cluster munitions consist of containers open and sub munitions. Launched from the ground or air, the containers open and disperse sub munitions (bomblets) over a wide area. Bomblets are typically designed to pierce armor, kill personnel, or both.

People with Disabilities: The Convention of Rights of Persons with Disabilities defines people with disabilities as "those who have term physical, mental, intellectual or sensory impairments which, in interaction with various barriers, may hinder their full and effective participation in society on an equal basis with others."

Disability: Disability is an evolving concept that interacts with various factors and hence is seen as a social model adapting to different contexts. It encompasses concepts of people with disabilities, impairments and so on.

Explosive Remnants of War: (ERW) (Under Protocol V to the Convention on Conventional Weapons). Means the unexploded ordnance and abandoned explosive ordnance that excludes mines, booby-traps or other devices.

Mined Area: According to the Mine Ban Treaty, mined areas are areas, which are dangerous due to the presence or suspected presence of mines.

Survivors: Survivors are persons injured as a direct consequence of landmines and ERW.

Victims: According to the Mine Ban Treaty and Convention on Cluster Munition, victims are "all persons who have been killed or suffered physical or psychological injury, economic loss, social marginalization or substantial impairment of the realization of their rights" caused by the use of weapons of war. In this light, there are two types of victims:

(i) Direct victims are persons injured or killed as a direct consequence of landmines and ERW;

(ii) Indirect victims include families and communities that suffer economically or otherwise due to the presence of contamination.

Victims Assistance: According to the Mine Ban Treaty Convention on Cluster Munition, victim assistance includes (not limited to) "casualty data collection, emergency and continued medical care, physical rehabilitation, psychological support and social integration, economic integration and laws and public polices to ensure the full and equal integration and participation of survivors, their families and communities in society."

Victim Compensation: Includes money payable to Mine Action Victims who did not participate in the battle/hostilities and all those who were born after the war and became injured by landmines. It includes their families and communities.

Landmine Survivor: Refers to any individual who has been directly injured by a landmine explosion and has survived the accident.

Landmine Victims: Refer more generally to those who have been injured or killed by a landmine explosive and also their families who suffer emotional, social and financial loss and the communities that lose access to land and other resources due to the presence of landmines.

Mine Action Centre: Refers to those organizations given the authority to plan and coordinate Mine Action activities in country.

Explosive Remnants of War (ERW) also refers to ordnance left behind after conflict. Explosive weapon that for some reasons fail to detonate as intended.

Unexploded Ordnance (UXO) These unstable explosive devices are left behind during and after conflicts and pose dangers similar to landmines.

Abandoned Explosive Ordnance (AXO) is explosive ordinance that has not been used during armed conflict but has been left behind or dumped by a party to an Armed Conflict, and which is no longer under the control of the Party that left it behind or dumped it. Abandoned Explosive Ordnance may or may not have been primed, fused, armed or otherwise prepared for use. The term refers to munitions that were designed to explode but for some reason failed to denotate: Unexploded sub-munitions are known as "duds".

"Contaminant" means any solid, liquid or gaseous matter, any odour, or any form of energy whatever source.

"Environment" includes water, air, land and all plants and men or other animals living therein; and the inter-relationships which exist among these.

"Pollution" ordinarily means the man-made or man-induced alteration of the chemical, physical or biological quality or the environment and "pollutant" shall be construed accordingly.

"Water" means all accumulations of water, surface and underground, natural and artificial, public and private or parts thereof which are wholly or partially within, flow through, or border upon the State.

Convention on Conventional Weapons: The 1980 Convention on Prohibitions or Restrictions on the use of Certain Conventional Weapons which may Be Deemed to be Excessively Injurious or to have indiscriminate effects, commonly referred to as the Convention on Conventional Weapons (CCW); aims to place prohibitions or restrictions on the use of Conventional Weapons about which there is widespread concern. It includes Protocol V on Explosive Remnants of War.

APPENDIX II

MINE RISK EDUCATION (MRE)
Those who live in mined areas before the mines are removed undergo mine security training aimed at reducing the risk of detonating a mine or an Unexploded Ordnance (UXO). The training is aimed at both children and grown-ups, and can substantially reduce the number of mine accidents. Drama, cartoons, posters and the likes are used in raising awareness among the population.

INFORMATION MANAGEMENT (IM)
In order to gain an over-view of the mine problem in a given area, all available information related to the suspected and confirmed mine fields is collected, systematized and may be couple with Geographic Information Systems. A complete survey (Non-Technical Survey and /or Technical Survey) of the mine problem in a given area, the nature of the places which have been mined, their locality and their effect, eases the prioritizing of resource use, the measurements of possible results and the devising of realistic plans for clearance.

TASK IMPACT ASSESSEMENT (TIA)
TIA is a tool used actively by NPA before, during and after clearance activities, this in order to determine and measure the impact of clearance. TIA is a crucial tool for PA in determining the socio economic effect NPA's work has on people who live in, and the environment of, mine and cluster contaminated areas.

MANUAL DEMINING
This method id used worldwide. Domineers systematically search an area with metal detectors and prodders in order to locate possible mines. When a suspicious object is dictated, the surrounding soil is carefully removed and the mines are defused or detonated. Manual demining is work and time consuming, but very reliable to the defined depth, and has the advantage of not requiring large investments to get started. Manpower is recruited and trained locally, and therefore manual demining has the additional advantage of creating employment.

LAND RELEASE
Historically, inconsistent and inefficient methods of identifying and clearing mines and ERW have wasted precious demining resources and left affected areas contaminated. Past efforts to improve and optimize mine and ERW clearance have revealed that clearance and survey assets are often used too frequently, commanding significant resources to clear and with little or no actual contamination. Limited demining resources are made available and, despite an acknowledge need, this does not seem likely to change. Norwegian People's Aid has worked intensively in cooperation with other

demining stakeholders, towards the creation and implementation of a Land Release policy. The Land release method emphasizes the se of non-technical and technical survey for the release of land, a method now widely recognized by stakeholders. The Land Release method frees expensive and time consuming demining resources for the clearance of factual mined areas and more rapidly frees land for the population for housing, infrastructure projects, and agricultural purposes of other development activities.

Partnership and Community Development
Landmines and UXO contribute to keeping people poor by stopping them from using land. In turn this prevents them from growing extra food they could sell, or building infrastructure that would benefit them. In such a setting it is therefore vital that landmine and UXO clearance is linked with wider development efforts.

Mine Detection Dog (MDD) Teams
MDD teams provide an additional clearance and survey capacity and can achieve faster and more cost-effective clearance than manual demining alone in certain circumstances and when deployed correctly. Dogs can detect mines with a low metal content and mines buried in areas of high metal contamination, because they're able to sniff out the explosive vapour. MDD teams are supported by ground preparation mechanical assets and teams that are able to cut and remove the vegetation from contaminated land enabling access.

Research and Development
Research and Development is an important part of the programme's activities, trialing and evaluating new and different mechanical means of supporting clearance operations and new detector technologies.

Explosive Ordnance Disposal (EOD)
EOD teams clear remnants of armed conflict through reactive (community requests) and pro-active (searching) responses. MAG has further strengthened the reporting system by introducing 'EOD calling cards', so that community leaders can contact teams at any time of the day to request assistance.

Baseline Survey
The development of the national Baseline Survey methodology will provide updated information of the level and scope of remaining contamination, helping to better inform planning and prioritization and enable more accurate long term planning and forecasting in any war affected country.

APPENDIX III

COMMUNITY COURT OF JUSTICE, ECOWAS

SUPPLEMENTARY PROTOCOL (A/SP.1/01/05) Amending the Protocol (A/P1/7/91) Relating to the ECONOMIC COMMUNITY OF WEST AFRICAN STATES

CONTENTS
The High Contracting Parties   5

ARTICLE 1:   6
Reference in the Protocol to the Treaty of 28th May, 1975 reconciled with references in the Revised Treaty of 1993

ARTICLE 2   7
Amendment of Article 4(1) of English version of the Protocol of the Court reconciled with the French version

ARTICLE 3:   8
Article 9 of Protocol on Community Court of Justice substituted

ARTICLE 4:   10
Insertion of a new Article 10 in the Protocol of the Community Court of justice

ARTICLE 5:   11
Renumbering of the Former Articles 10 to 22

ARTICLE 6:   11
Insertion of a new provision which becomes Article 24 of the Protocol of the Court of Justice

ARTICLE 7:   12
Renumbering of the Former Articles 23 to 33

ARTICLE 8:   12
Substitution of Articles 30 of the Protocol of the Community Court of Justice

ARTICLE 9:   13
Substitution of Articles 31 of the Protocol of the Court

ARTICLE 10:   13
ARTICLE 11:   13
Entry into force
ARTICLE 12:   14

Depository Authority

SUPPLEMENTARY PROTOCOL A/S.1/01/05 AMENDING THE PREAMBLE AND ARTICLES 1, 2, 9, 22 AND 30 OF PROTOCOL A/P.1.7/91 RELATING TO THE COMMUNITY COURT OF JUSTICE AND ARTICLE 4 PARAGRAPH 1 OF THE ENGLISH VERSION OF THE SAID PROTOCOL

THE HIGH CONTRACTING PARTIES,
MINDFUL of Articles 7, 8, 9 of the Treaty establishing the Authority of Heads of State and Government and defining its composition and functions;
MINDFUL of Articles 33 of Protocol A/P.1/7/91 relating to amendment to the Protocol on the Community Court of Justice;
MINDFUL of the Rules of Procedure of the Community Court of Justice;
MINDFUL of Regulation C/REG. 15/01/03 dated 23rd January, 2003 as amended by Regulation C/REG.5/6/03 of 27th June, 2003 establishing an ad hoc Ministerial Committee on the harmonization of Community Legislative texts, particularly Article 2 thereof, which defines the terms of reference of the Committee;
CONSIDERING that the Articles of the Treaty referred to in the Protocol relating to the Community Court of Justice are Articles of the Treaty of 28th May, 1975 and that it is therefore necessary to harmonize such reference with Articles of the revised Treaty adopted on 24th July, 1993;
CONSIDERING the need to align English version of Articles 4 paragraph 1 of the Protocol relating to the Community Court of Justice with the French version of the text so as to ensure consistency;
CONSCIOUS of the role the Court of Justice can play in eliminating obstacles to the realization of Community objectives and accelerating the integration process;
CONVINCED of the need to empower the Community Court of Justice to play their part in effectively ensuring that Member States fulfil their obligations;
DESIRING to facilitate the task of the Court in this regard expanding its competence and powers;
DESIRING ALSO to take all necessary measures to ensure smooth operations of the Court and guarantee effective implementation of its decisions;
CONSIDERING the report of the fifty-second Session of the Council of Ministers held in Abuja on 16th and 17th July 2004, on the draft Protocol amending the Preamble and Articles 1, 2, 9, 22 and 30 of Protocol A/P.1/91 relating to the Community Court of Justice and Articles 4 paragraph 1 of the English version of the Protocol;
HEREBY AGREE AS FOLLOWS:

Article 1:
Reference in the Protocol to the treaty of 28th May 1975 reconciled with references in the Revised Treaty of 1993.

All references to the Article of the Treaty of 28th May 1975 in the Protocol relating to the Community Court of Justice are hereby deleted and replaced by references to the revised ECOWAS Treaty adopted on 24th July 1993 as follows:

a) In the preamble, references to Articles 4(1), 5, 11 and 56 of the Treaty are replaced by Articles 6, 7, 15, and 76(2) of the revised Treaty respectively;

b) In Article 1, references to Articles 1, 5, 6, 8(1), 8(2), and 11 of the Treaty are replaced by Articles 2, 7, 10, 17(1), 17(2) and 15 of the revised Treaty respectively.

c) In Articles 2, the reference to Article 11 of the Treaty is replaced by Article 15 of the revised Treaty; and

d) In Article 9, the reference to Article 56 of the Treaty is replaced by Article 76(2) of the revised Treaty.

Article 2:
Amendment of Article 4 (1) of English version of the Protocol of the court reconciled with the French version.

Article 4 paragraph 1 of the English version of the Protocol relating to the Community Court of Justice is amended as follows:

"**Article 4:   Terms of Office of Members of the Court.**

Members of the Court shall be appointed for a period of five (5) years. Their term of office may be renewed for another term of five (5) years only, except that for members of the Court appointed for the first time, the terms of office of three (3) members shall expire at the end of three (3) years and the term of the other four (4) members shall expire at the end of five (5) years".

Article 3:
Article 9 of protocol on Community Court of Justice Substituted.

Article 9 of the Protocol relating to the Community Court of Justice is hereby detected and substituted by the following new provisions:

"**Article 9: Jurisdiction of the Court**

1. The Court has competence to adjudication on any dispute relating to the following:

a) The interpretation and application of the Treaty, Conventions and Protocols of the Community;

b) The interpretation and application of the regulations, directives, decisions and other subsidiary legal instruments adopted by ECOWAS;

c) The legality of regulations, directives, decisions and other subsidiary legal instruments adopted by ECOWAS;

d) The failure by Member States to honour their obligations under the Treaty, Conventions and Protocols, regulations, directives, or decisions of ECOWAS;

e) The provisions of the Treaty, Conventions and Protocols, regulations, directives or decisions of ECOWAS Member States;
f) The Community and its officials; and
g) The action for damages against a Community institution or an official of the Community for any action or omission in the exercise of official functions.

2. The Court shall have the power to determine any non-contractual liability of the Community and may order the Community to pay damages or make reparation for official acts or omissions of any Community institution or Community officials in the performance of official duties or functions.
3. Any action by or against a Community Institution or any Member of the Community shall be statute barred after three (3) years from the date when the right of action arose
4. The Court has jurisdiction to determine cases of violation of human rights that occur in any Member State.
5. Pending the establishment of the Arbitration Tribunal provided for under Article 16 of the Treaty, the Court shall have power to act as arbitrator for the purpose of Article 16 of the Treaty.
6 The Court shall have Jurisdiction over any matter provided for in an agreement where the parties provide that the court shall settle dispute arising from the agreement.
7. The Court shall have al powers conferred upon it by the provisions of this Protocol as well as any other powers that may be conferred by subsequent Protocols and Decisions of the Community.
8. The Authority of Heads of State and Government shall have the power to grant the Court the power to adjudicate on any specific dispute that it may refer to the Court other than those specified in this Article.

Article 4:
Insertion of a new Article 10 in the Protocol of the Community Court of Justice.
The Protocol on the Community Court of Justice is amended by the insertion of the following new Article as follows:
Article 10: Access to the Court.
Access to the Court is open to the following:
a) Member States, and unless otherwise provided in a Protocol, the Executive Secretary, where action is brought for failure by a Member State to fulfil an obligation;
b) Member State, the Council of Ministers and the Executive Secretary in proceeding for the determination of the legality of an action in relation to any Community text;
c) Individual and corporate bodies in proceedings for the determination of an act or inaction of a Community official which violates the rights of

the individuals or corporate bodies;
d) Individuals on application for relief for violation of their human rights; the submission of application for which shall:
i) Not be anonymous; nor
ii) Be made whilst the same matter has been instituted before another International Court for Adjudication;
e) Staff any Community institution, after the Staff Member has exhausted all appeal processes available to the officer under the ECOWAS Staff Rules and Regulations;
f) Wherein any action before a court of Member State, an issue arises as to the interpretation of a provision of the Treaty, or the other Protocols or Regulations, the national court may on its own or at the request of any of the parties to the action refer the issue to the Court for interpretation."

Article 5:
Renumbering of the former Articles 10 to 22
The former articles 10, 11, 12, 13, 14, 15, 16, 17, 18, 19, 20, 21 and 22 are hereby renumbered to read 11, 12, 13, 14, 15, 16, 17, 18, 19, 20, 21, 22 and 23 respectively.

APPENDIX IV

INSTRUCTIONS TO THE CHIEF REGISTRAR
ARTICLE 12 OF THE RULES OF PROCEDURE
SECTION ONE
THE REGISTRAR

The Registrar of the Court shall be open to the public from Monday through Friday between 9am and 5pm, except on ECOWAS holidays, and days declared as official holiday by the authority of the country where the Court has its seat.

Article 2

1. The Chief Registrar shall be responsible for the proper organization of cases.
2. The Chief Registrar shall promptly execute task assigned to him by the Judge Rapporteur.
3. Once the Written Procedure is enclosed and the date for hearing of the oral procedure is fixed, the Chief Registrar shall notify the parties within fifteen days.

Article 3

1. The Chief Registrar shall ensure that service, notifications and communications are carried out, pursuant to Article 74 of the Rules of Procedure of the Court. Post office shall include any registered courier service at the place where the Court has its seat.
2. If highly voluminous documents are lodged in single copy at the Registry, the Chief Registrar, after consultation with the Judge Rapporteur, shall inform the parties through the most appropriate means, to access the documents at the Registrar.

Article 4

Before each public hearing of the Court, the Chief Registrar shall draw up and sign the language of the case, a cause list. This cause list shall contain:
- The date, time and venue of the hearing;
- The nature of the cases to be called;
- The names of the parties
- The names and status of the agents, advisors and lawyers of the parties.

The cause list shall be posted at the entrance of the Court room.

Article 6

The Chief Registrar shall, on the instructions of the President of the Court, draw up a list of experts.

SECTION TWO
TRANSLATION OF DOCUMENTS BY THE LANGUAGE SERVICES DIVISION OF THE COURT

Article 7

As soon as applications and other documents that require translation are received, the Chief Registrar shall submit them to the Language Service Division of the Court for translation within one week.

Article 8
In order to ensure the accuracy of the translation of Court processes, the translating service of the Court may translate documents to be used in Court proceedings at a prescribed fee to be paid to the Court.

Article 9
When an institution fails to provide the translation of its pleadings as required by Article 32(2) of the Rules, the translation may be done by the translating service of the Court but at a fee to be paid by the institution concerned before the translation is done.

Article 10
1. Where one of the parties has full partial translation of its own pleadings or of those of the other party in the language of the case, this translation should as a matter of course be transmitted to the Registry of the Court. The same applies to the annexures.
2. These translations will be examined and certified by the translation service of the Court and will then be communicated to the other party. If is not certified, it will be rejected and the Chief Registrar will notify the party and thereafter Article 8 or 9 will apply. As the case may be.

SECTION THREE
FILING FEES AND LEGAL COST

1. Only the fees mentioned in the Rules of Procedure, or in the present document shall be charged.
2. The payment of Registry fees shall be done in cash to the Court at the Court cash office or by payment into the special account of the Court, at the bank indicated on the payment notice.

Article 12
The cost for translation to be shall as stipulated hereunder or as may be reviewed by the Court from time to time:
a) Translation of application instituting proceedings, and other documents .... N5000 per page.
b) Translation of annexure .... N600 per page.

Article 13
The lodgment of all applications, pleadings, briefs of arguments and addresses in respect of any proceedings before the Court is free except for copying and certification which shall attract a uniform fee of N200 per page.

Article 14
1. In the event of having to recover amounts due in respect of execution of letters rotatory issued by the Court on its own motion, such amounts shall be claimed by registered mail or any other appropriate means, made and signed by the Claimant and addressed

to the Chief Registrar.

2. Where the letters rogatory are issued on the application of a party, such party shall be liable to pay fully for it and shall be required to pay a deposit to be determined by the Chief Registrar.

SECTION FOUR
PUBLICATIONS
Article 15

1. The Chief Registrar, assisted by the Court Registrars, shall be in charge of the publications of the Court.
2. There shall be published in the Languages stipulated in paragraph 2, Article 87 of the Revised Treaty, a compendium of the case-law of the Court, comprising, except where otherwise stated, judgments of the Court, Rulings, Advisory Opinions and others.

Article 16

The Chief Registrar shall see to the publication in the Official Journal of the Community of the notice of registration of an application initiating proceedings. The notice shall contain:

a. The date of registration of the application,
b. The names and address of the parties,
c. The subject matter of the proceeding,
d. The form of order sought by the applicant,
e. A summary of pleas in law and the main supporting arguments.

PRACTICE DIRECTIONS IN ECOWAS COURT (2014)
ARTICLE 100 OF THE RULES OF PROCEDURE
SECTION ONE
THE USE OF TECHNICAL MEANS OF COMMUNICATION
Article 1

1. A copy of the signed original of any Court process may be transmitted to the Registry in accordance with Article 32(6), 33(3) and 74(3) of the Rules of Procedure either by: Telefax to Fax number ………………………………….. or
As an attachment to an electronic mail: registry@courtecowas.org
2. Where Transmission is by electronic mail, only a scanned copy of the signed original will be accepted. An ordinary file or one bearing an electronic signature or a computer generated fax signature will not fulfil the conditions of Article 32(6) and 33(3) of the Rules of Procedure.
3. The document should be scanned at a resolution of 300 DPL and whenever possible, in PDF format (image and text).

Article 2

1. A document lodged by telex or electronic mail will only be treated as in compliance with the relevant time limit if the signed original

itself reaches the Registry within the time limit specified in Article 32(6) of the Rules of Procedure. The signed original must be sent without delay, immediately after dispatch of the copy, without any corrections or amendments, even of a minor nature. In the event of any discrepancy between the signed original and the copy previous lodged, only the date of lodgment original will be taken into consideration.

2. Where, in accordance with Article 33(3) of the Rules of Procedure, a party agrees to be notified by telex or other technical mean of communication, the statement to that effect must specify the telex number and/or the electronic mail address to which the Registry may send that party documents to be served.

SECTION TWO
PRESENTATION OF APPLICATION
Article 3

1. Cases may be brought before the Court by an application addressed to the Court Registry. This application shall set out the subject matter of the dispute and the parties involved and shall contain a summary of the facts put forward as well as the pleas in law of the plaintiff.
2. An application of the kind referred to in Article 11 of the Protocol shall comply with the provisions of Article 33 of the Rules of Procedure.

Article 4

In drawing up its written pleads, each of the parties is to bear in mind the fact that these pleadings are intended not only to reply to the submissions and arguments of the other party, but also, and above all, clearly present his own submission and arguments.

Article 5

1. Within a month after service on him of the application, the Defendant shall lodge a defence that complies with the provisions of Article 35 of the Rules of Procedure.
2. The time limit laid down in the previous paragraph of this Article may be modified based on a reasoned application by the Defendants.
3. The structure of the legal argument must, so far as it possible, reflect the pleas in law put forward in the application.
4. The factual background is to be recapitulated in the defence only in so far as presentation in the application is disputed or calls for further particulars. If any fact alleged by the other party is contested it must be clearly indicated and the basic on which it is challenged must be stated explicitly.

Article 6

The reply and rejoined must not recapitulate the factual and legal background expect in so far as its presentation in the previous pleadings is disputed or exceptionally, calls for further particulars. Any fact alleged y the other party contested must be clearly indicated and the basic on which it is challenged must be stated explicitly.

Article 7

1. The statement in intervention must not develop new arguments in relation to those put forward by the main parties. It may be confined to mere reference to the other arguments.
2. The statement in intervention must not recapitulate the factual and legal background except in so far as its presentation in the previous pleadings is disputed or calls for further particulars. If any fact alleged by the other party is contested it must be stated explicitly.

Article 8

1. Legal argument submitted to the Court must appear in the legal argument and not in the annexes.
2. Only documents mentioned in the actual text of the application and necessary in order to prove or illustrate its contents may be submitted as annexes.
3. Annexes will be accepted only if they are accompanied by a schedule of annexes (Article 32(4) of the Rules of Procedure).

    That schedule must indicate for each document annexed:
    a) The number of the annexes;
    b) A short description of the document (e.g. 'letter', followed by its date, author and address and its number of pages);
    c) A reference to the page and paragraph number at which the document is mentioned and from which the need to produce it is apparent.
4. Each reference to a document lodged must state the relevant annex number as given in the schedule of annexes in which it appears and indicate the pleading to which it is annexed

Article 9

1. In the interest of rapidity in drafting pleadings, it is advisable that the following points must be taken into consideration:
    a) The application is examined on the basis of the pleadings; in order to facilitate this examination; document must be structured concise and must avoid repetition;
    b) To facilitate translation, it is recommended to make use of short sentences and vocabulary should be simple and precise.
2. The application must not exceed 15 pages, A4 paper, font size 12 or higher except in exceptional circumstances related to the nature or the complexity of the case.

3. The parties should refrain from submitting new document after the closure of the written procedure.
4. A party nevertheless desiring to introduce a new document after the closure of the written procedure shall explain why it considers it necessary to include the document and the reasons preventing the production of the document at the earlier stage.

   In the absence of consent of the other party, the Court will authorize the production of the new document only in exceptional circumstances, if it considers it necessary and if the production of the document at this stage of the proceedings appears justified to the Court.
5. If a new plea in law has been introduced under Article 37 of the Rules of Court, the other party, when answering upon it, shall confine the introduction of any further pleas to what is strictly necessary and relevant to its answer on what is contained in this new plea

Article 10

A party applying by separate document under Article 59(2) of the Rules of Procedure for a case to be decided by the Court by expedited procedure must brief state the reasons for the special urgency of the case. Such application, save in exceptional circumstances, must not exceed 5 pages. A4 paper, font size 12 or higher. As the expedited procedure is largely oral, the pleading of the party requesting it must be confined to a summary of the pleas relied upon.

Article 11

Parties soliciting provisional measures under Article 21 of the Protocol of the Court must comply with Article 79 of the Rules of Procedure and must indicate the fact and/or circumstances for the urgency, the party must equally show that the measure solicited is appropriate to safeguard a part of the case beyond what is strictly necessary for that purpose.

Article 12

1. At the hearing oral argument is limited to 30 minutes maximum for each party. Speaking time exceptionally be extended beyond these limits on oral application to the Presiding Judge.
2. The purpose of oral argument is not to prevent a party's point of view afresh but to clarify any matter which the agent or lawyer deems particularly important, especially those referred to in the application for hearing. Repetition of what has already been stated in the written pleading must be avoided if necessary reference to the pleadings during the course of the oral argument will suffice.
3. Very frequently the Judge Rapporteur will listen to oral argument via simultaneous interpretation. In order to facilitate the interpretation, agents and lawyers should speak at a natural and unforced pace and use short sentences of simple structure.

4. During the oral procedure, the Court may in respect of any issue for determination or question of law direct the parties to lodge and exchange written submissions or addresses and after adoptions by the parties the Court, with the consent of the parties, may decide not to hear oral argument.

SECTION THREE
SERVICE
Article 13

1. Article 33(2) and 35(1) of the Rules of Procedure requires the parties to state an address for service in the place where the Court has its seat while Article 74 of the Rules Procedure is in respect of service of Court Processes. For ease of service, any Court process for service on a Member State or Institution of a Member State may be affected by the bailiff of the Court through the diplomatic representative of that Member State where the Court has its seat, such service shall be deemed valid and proper service upon proof of delivery, or acknowledgement of receipt.
2. If there are difficulties in affecting service of Court processes, pursuant to the provisions of Article 74 of the Rules of procedure of the Court, the Court may, at the request of the party, order substituted service of the process.

DONE AT ABUJA ON THE 4TH DAY OF JUNE, 2012

IN A SINGLE ORIGINAL IN ENGLISH, FRENCH AND PORTUGUESE LANGUAGES, ALL TEXTS BEING EQUALLY AUTHENTIC.

HON. JUSTICE AWA NANA DABOYA
President, **Community Court of Justice, ECOWAS ABUJA-NIGERIA**
COMMUNITY COURT OF JUSTICE, ECOWAS

THE RULES OF THE COMMUNITY COURT OF JUSTICE, (ECOWAS), ECONOMIC COMMUNITY OF WEST AFRICAN STATES (ECOWAS)

Contents	3
Interpretation *(Article 1)*	5

TITLE 1: ORGANIZATION OF THE COURT
Chapter I:	Judges.	7
Chapter II:	Presidency and composition of the court	8
Chapter III:	Registry.	9

Section 1:	The Chief Registrar and the Registrars.	9
Section 2:	Other departments.	12
Chapter IV:	The working of the Court.	13
Chapter V:	Languages.	15
Chapter VI:	Rights and obligations of agents, advisers and lawyers.	17

TITLE II: PROCEDURE

Chapter I:	Written procedure.	19
Chapter II:	Preparatory inquiries and other preparatory measure.	24
Section 1:	Measures of inquiry.	24
Section 2:	The summoning and examination of witnesses and experts.	25
Section 3:	Closure of the preparatory inquiry.	29
Section 4:	Preparatory measures.	29
Chapter III:	Oral procedure.	29
Chapter IV:	Expedited procedures.	31
Chapter V:	Judgments.	32
Chapter VI:	Costs.	34
Chapter VII:	Discontinuance.	37
Chapter VIII:	Service.	37
Chapter IX:	Time-limits.	38
Chapter X:	Stay of proceedings	40

TITLE III: SPECIAL FORMS OF PROCEDURE

Chapter I:	Suspension of operation or enforcement and other Interim Measures.	41
Chapter II:	Preliminary procedure.	43
Chapter III:	Intervention.	44
Chapter IV:	Judgments by default and applications to set the aside.	46
Chapter V:	Exceptional review procedures.	47
Section 1:	Third-party proceedings.	47
Section 2:	Revision.	48
Chapter VI:	Interpretation of Judgments.	49
Chapter VII:	Opinions.	50

TITLE IV: MISCELLANEOUS PROVISIONS   52

INTERPRETATION

Article 1

In these Rules:

"Treaty" means the Revised Treaty of the Economic Community of West African States and includes protocol and conventions and annexure;

"Authority" means the Authority of Heads of State and Government of the Community established by Article 7(1) of the Treaty.

"Chairman of the Authority" means the current Chairman of the Authority of Heads of State and Government of the Community, elected in accordance with the provisions of Article 8.2 of the Treaty;

"Community" means the Economic Community of West African States (ECOWAS) referred to under Article 2 of the Treaty;

"Court of Justice" means the Court of Justice of the Community established under Article 15(1) of the Treaty;

"Member State or Member States" means Member State or Member States of the Community;

"Council" means the Council of Ministers of the Community established by Article 10(1) of the Treaty;

"Parliament" means the community parliament established under Article 13(1) of the Treaty;

"Executive Secretariat" means the Executive Secretariat established under Article 17 of the Treaty;

"Executive Secretary" means the Executive Secretary of the Community appointment under Article 17.1 of the Treaty;

"Protocol" means the Protocol relating to the Court of Justice of the community;

"Court" means the Community Court of Justice (C.C.J) established by Article 15(1) of the Treaty;

"President" means the President of the Court elected by the members of the Court in accordance with Article 3(2) of the Protocol;

"Vice President" means the member of the Court elected as such by the member of the Court in accordance with Article 3(2) of the Protocols;

"Member of the Court" or **"Members of the Court"** means a person or persons appointed as judge or judges in accordance with the provisions of Article 3(2) of the Protocol"

"Judge" or **"Judges"** or **"Justice"** means Members of the Community Court of Justice;

"Judge – Rapporteur" means a Judge nominated by the President to summarize or give a report on a case or issue.

"Staff Regulations" means ECOWAS Staff Regulations.

TITLE I
ORGANIZATION OF THE COURT
CHAPTER I
JUDGES
Article 2

The term of office of a Judge shall begin on the date laid down in his instrument of appointment. In the absence of any provisions regarding the date, the term shall begin on the date of the instrument.

Article 3

1. Before taking up his duties, a judge shall before assuming his appointment take the following oath before the chairman of the Authority:

   "I... Solemnly swear (declare) that I will perform my duties and exercise my powers as member of the Court honorably, faithfully, impartially and conscientiously"

2. Immediately after taking the oath, a Judge shall sign the declaration.

Article 4

1. When the Court is called upon to decide whether a member no longer fulfils the requisite conditions or no longer meets the obligations arising from his office, the President shall invite the Judge in the presence of the other Judges to make representations to the Court, in closed session and in the absence of the Chief Registrar. Article 4.7 of the Protocol shall apply.

2. Where it involves the President, the Vice President shall preside.

Article 5

Judge shall rank equally in precedence according to their seniority in the Court. Where there is equal seniority in office, precedence shall be determined by age. Retiring Judges who are reappointed shall retain their former precedence.

Chapter II
PRESIDENCY AND COMPOSITION OF THE COURT

Article 6

1. The Member of the Court shall be appointed by the Authority and selected from the list of persons nominated by Member State; no Member State shall nominate more than two persons. The President and the Vice President of the Court shall take precedence before all other Members.

2. If the office of the President of the Court falls vacant before the normal date of expiry thereof, the Court shall elect by consensus a successor for the reminder of the term.

3. Failure to reach a consensus the election shall be by secret ballot. If a judge obtains an absolute majority ha shall be elected. If no Judge obtains an absolute majority, a second ballot shall be held and the Judge obtaining the most votes shall be elected. Where two or more Judges obtain an equal number of votes, the oldest serving Judge shall be deemed elected.

Article 7

The President is responsible for the administration of the Court and he presides at hearing and deliberations.

Article 8

1. When the President of the Court is absent or prevented from attending or when the office of the President is vacant, the functions of the President shall be exercised by the Vice President according to the order of procedure laid down in Article 5 of these Rules.
2. If the President and Vice President are prevented from attending or their posts are vacant at the same time, the functions of the President and Vice President shall be exercised by one of the other Judges according to the order of precedence laid down in Article 5 of these Rules.

Chapter III
REGISTRAR
Section 1: The Chief Registrar and the Registrars
Article 9

1. The Court shall appoint the Chief Registrar. Two weeks before the date fixed for making the appointment, the President shall inform the Members of the Court of the applications which have been made for the post.
2. An application shall be accompanied by full details of the candidate's age, Nationality, University degrees, Knowledge of any languages, present and past occupations and experience, if any, in judicial and international fields.
3. The Chief Registrar shall be appointed for a term of six years. He may be reappointed for a further term.
4. The Chief Registrar shall take the oath in accordance with Article 17(2) of these Rules before the President of the Court.
5. The Chief Registrar may be deprived of his office only if he no longer fulfils the requisite conditions or no longer meets the obligations arising from his office; the Court shall take its decision after giving the Registrar an opportunity to make representations.
6. If the office of Chief Registrar falls vacant before the normal date of expiry of the term thereof, the Court shall appoint a new Chief Registrar for a term of six years.

Article 10

The Court may, following the procedure laid down in respect of the Chief Registrar, appoint one or more Registrars to assist the Chief Registrar and to take his place in so far as the Instructions to the Chief Registrar referred to in Article 14 of these Rules allow.

Article 11

Where the Chief Registrar and Registrars are absent or prevented from attending or their posts are vacant, the President shall designate an official or other servant to carry out temporarily the duties of the Chief Registrar and Registrars.

Article 12

The Court acting on a proposal from the President shall adopt instructions to the Chief Registrar.

Article 13

1. There shall be kept in the Registry, under the control of the Chief Registrar, a register initialed by the President, in which all pleadings and supporting documents shall be entered in the order in which they are lodged.
2. When a document has been registered, the Chief Registrar shall make a nota to that effect on the original and, if a party or requests, on any copy submitted for the purpose.
3. Entries in the register and the notes provided for in the preceding paragraph shall be authentic.
4. Rules for keeping the register shall be prescribed by the Instructions of the Chief Registrar referred to in Article 14 of the Rules.
5. Persons having an interest may consult the Chief Registrar at the Registry and may obtain copies or extracts on payment of a charge on a scale fixed by the Court on a proposal from the Chief Registrar.

    The parties to a case may on payment of the appropriate charge also obtain copies of pleadings and authenticated copies of judgments and orders.
6. Notice shall be given in the official journal of the community of the date registration of an application initiating proceedings, the names and addresses of the parties, the subject-matter of the proceedings, the form of order sought by the applicant and a summary of the pleas in law and of the main supporting argument.

Article 14

1. The Chief Registrar shall be responsible, under the authority of the president, for the acceptance, transmission and custody of documents and for effecting service as provided for by these Rules.
2. The Chief Registrar shall assist the Court, the President and the Judges in all their official function.

Article 15

The Chief Registrar shall have custody of the seals. He responsible for the records and be in charge of the publications of the Court.

Article 16

Except as otherwise provided in these Rules, the Chief Registrar shall attend the sittings of the Court.

Section 2: Other Department

Article 17

1. The officials and other servants of the Court shall be appointed in

accordance with the provisions of the Staff Regulations.

2. Before taking up his duties, an official shall take the following oath before the Court:
"I swear (declare) that will perform loyally, discreetly and conscientiously the duties assigned to me by the Court of Justice of the Economic Community of West African States"

Article 18
The organization of the departments of the Court shall be laid down, and may be modified, by the Court on a proposal from the Chief Registrar.

Article 19
The Court shall set up a translating service staffed by experts with adequate legal training and a thorough knowledge of several official languages of the Court in accordance with Article 87(2) of the Treaty.

Article 20
1. The Chief Registrar shall be responsible, under the Authority of the President, for the administration of the Court.
2. The financial and Accounts management of the Court shall be carried out by the Management Accountant under the Authority of the President.

Chapter IV
THE WORKING OF THE COURT

Article 21
1. The dates and times of the sessions of the Court shall be fixed by the President in accordance with Article 27 of the Protocol.
2. The Court may choose to hold one or more session in a place other than that in which the Court has its seat in accordance with Article 26(2) of the Protocol.

Article 22
1. Where, by reason of a judge absent or prevented from attending, there is an even number of Judges, the most junior Judge within the meaning of Article 5 of these Rules shall obtain from taking part in the deliberations, unless he is the Judge – Rapporteur. In that case the Judge immediately senior to him shall abstain from taking part in the deliberation.
2. If after the Court has been convened it is found that the quorum referred to in Article 14(2) of the Protocol has not been attained, the President shall adjourn the sitting until there is a quorum.
3. The setting of the Court shall comprise of an uneven number of its members.
4. The sitting of the Court shall be public. The Court may however sit in camera at the request of one of the parties or for reasons, which only the Court may determine.

Article 23
1. The Court shall deliberate in closed session.

2. Only those Judges who were present at the oral proceedings shall take part in the deliberation.
3. Where one of its member who was present at the oral proceedings is absent, the Court nevertheless shall continue its hearing provided that its parties to disputes so agree in accordance with Article 27(4) (b) of the Protocol.
4. Every Judge taking part in the deliberations shall state his opinion and the reasons for it.
5. Any Judge may require that any questions be formulated in the language of his choice and communicated in writing in the Court before being put to the vote.
6. The conclusions reached by the majority of the Judges after final discussion shall determine the decision of the Court. Votes shall be cast in reverse order to the order of procedure laid down in Article 5 of these Rules.
7. In case of divergent opinions on the subject or on the question of interpretation the Court shall decide by votes.
8. Where the deliberation of the Court concern questions of its own administration, it shall be put to vote. The Chief Registrar shall be present, unless the Court decides to the contrary.

Article 24

1. Subject to any special decision of the Court, its vacations shall be as follows:
a) From 18 December to 10 January,
b) 4 days before Easter to 4 days after Easter,
c) From 15 July to 15 September,
2. The Holidays of the Court shall include Sallah holidays, public holidays and ECOWAS public holiday.
3. During the vacations, the functions of the President shall be exercised at the place where the Court has its seat by the President himself or the Vice President or any other Judge designated in that respect.
4. Where necessary, the President may convene the Judges during the vacations.
5. The Court shall observe the official holidays of the place where it has its seat.
6. The Court may, in proper circumstances, grant leave of absence to any Judge.

Chapter V
LANGUAGES
Article 25

1. The official languages of the Court shall be languages of the Community in accordance with Article 87(2) of the Treaty.

2. The language of a case shall be chosen by the applicant, except that:
a) Where the defendants is a Member State the language of the case shall be the official language of that State;
b) Where that State has more than one official language, the applicant may choose between them.
3. The language of the case shall in particular be used in the written and oral pleadings of the parties and in supporting documents, and also in the minutes and decisions of the Court. Any supporting documents expressed in another language of the case.
4. In the case of lengthy documents, translations may be confined to extracts. However, the Court may, of its own motion or at the request of a party, at any time call for a complete or fuller translation.
5. Where a witness or expert states that he is unable adequately to express himself in one of the languages referred to in paragraph (1) of this Article, the Court may authorize him to give his evidence in another language.
6. The Court may in conducting oral proceedings, use one of the languages referred to in paragraph (1) of this Article other than the language of the case

Article 26
1. The Chief Registrar shall, at the request of any Judge, or of a party, arrange for anything said or written in the course of the proceedings before the Court to be translated into the languages in Article 25(1).
2. Publications of the Court shall be issued in the languages referred to in Article 25(1) of these Rules.

Article 27
The texts of documents drawn up in the language of the Court or in any other language authorized by the Court pursuant to Article 25(1) of these Rules shall be authentic.

Chapter VI
RIGHTS AND OBLIGATIONS OF AGENTS, ADVISERS AND LAWYERS
Article 28
1. Agents, advisers and lawyers appearing before the Court or before any judicial authority to which the Court has addressed letters rogatory, shall enjoy immunity in respect of words spoken or written by them concerning the case or the parties.
2. Agents, advisers and lawyers shall enjoy the following privileges and facilities:
a) Papers and documents relating to the proceedings shall be exempt from both search and seizure; in the event of a dispute the customs officials or police may seal these papers and documents; they shall then be immediately forwarded to the Court for inspection in the presence of the

Chief Registrar and of the person concerned;
b) Agents, advisers and lawyers shall be entitled to travel in the course of duty without hindrance.
3. The lawyer acting for a party must lodge at the Registry a certificate that he is authorized to practice before Court of the Member State, which is a party to the Treaty.

Article 29

In order to qualify for the privileges, immunities and facilities specified in Article 28, persons entitled to them should furnish proof of their status as follows:

a) Agents shall produce an official document issued by the party for whom they act, and shall forward without delay a copy thereof to the Chief Registrar.

b) Advisers and lawyers shall produce a certificate signed by the Chief Registrar. The validity of this certificate shall be limited to a specified period, which may be extended or curtailed according to the length of the proceedings.

Article 30

1. The privileges, immunities and facilities specified in Article 28 of these Rules are granted exclusively in the interests of the proper conduct of proceedings.
2. The Court may waive the immunity where it considers that the proper conduct of proceedings will not be hindered thereby.

Article 31

1. Any adviser or layer whose conduct towards the Court or a Judge in incompatible with the dignity of the Court, or who uses his rights for purposes other than those for which they were granted, may at any time be excluded from the proceedings by an order of the Court. The person concerned shall be given an opportunity to defend himself. The order shall have immediate effects.
2. Where an adviser or lawyer is excluded from the proceedings, the proceedings shall be suspended for a period fixed by the President in order to allow the Party concerned to appoint another adviser or lawyer.
3. Decisions taken under this Article may be rescinded.

TITTLE II
PROCEDURE
Chapter I
WRITTEN PROCEDURE
Article 32

1. The original of every pleading must be signed by the party's agent

or lawyer. The original, accompanied by all annexes referred to therein, shall be lodged together with five copies for the Court and a copy for every other party to the proceedings. The Party lodging them in accordance with Article 11 of the Protocol shall certify copies.
2. Institutions shall in addition produce, within time limits laid down by the Court, translators of all pleadings into the other languages provided for by Article 25(1) of these Rules.
3. All pleadings shall bear a date. In the reckoning of time limits for taking steps in proceedings, only the date of lodgment at the Registry shall be taken into account.
4. To every pleading there shall be annexed a file containing the documents relied on in support of it, together with a schedule listing them.
5. Where in view of the length of a document only extracts from it are annexed to the pleading, the whole document or a full copy of it shall be lodged at the Registry.
6. Without prejudice to the provisions of paragraphs 1 to 5, the date on which a copy of the signed original of a pleading, including the schedule of documents referred to in paragraph 4, is received at the Registry by telefax or other technical means of communication available to the Court shall be deemed to be the date of lodgment for the purpose of compliance with the time-limits for taking steps in proceedings, provided that the signed original of the pleading, accompanied by the annexes and copies referred to in the second subparagraph of paragraph 1 above, is lodged at the Registry no later than ten days thereafter.

Article 33

1. An application of the kind referred to in Article 11 of the Protocol shall state:
a) The name and address of the applicant;
b) The designation of the party against whom the application is made;
c) The subject-matter of the proceedings and a summary of the pleas in law on which the application is based;
d) The form of order sought by the applicant;
e) Where appropriate, the nature of any evidence offered in support.
2. For the purpose of the proceedings, the application shall state an address for service in the place where the Court has its seat and the name of the person who is authorized and has expressed willingness to accept service.
3. In addition to, or instead of, specifying an address for service as referred to in the first subparagraph; the application may state that the lawyer or agent agrees that service is to be affected on him by telefax or other technical means of communication.

4. If the application does not comply with the requirements referred to in the first and second subparagraphs, all services on the party concerned for the purpose of the proceedings shall be effected, for so long as the defect has not been cured, by registered letter addressed to the agent or lawyer of that party. By way of derogation from the Article 77(1), service shall then be deemed to be duly effected by the lodging of the registered letter at the post office of the place where the Court has its seat.
5. The application shall be accompanied, where appropriate, by the documents specified in the first paragraph of Article 15 of the Protocol.
6. If the application does not comply with the requirements set out in paragraphs 1 to 4 of this Article, the Chief Registrar shall prescribe a period not more than thirty days within which the applicant is to comply with them whether by putting the application itself in order or by producing any of the above-mentioned documents. If the applicant fails to put the application in order or to produce the required documents within the time prescribed, the Court shall, after hearing the Judge Rapporteur, decide whether the non-compliance with these conditions renders the application formally inadmissible.

Article 34

The application shall be served on the defendant. In a case where Article 33 (6) applies, service shall be effected as soon as the application has been put in order.

Article 35

1. Within one month after service on him of the application, the defendant shall lodge a defense, stating:
a) The name and address of the defendants;
b) The arguments of fact and law relied on;
c) The form of order sought by the defendant;
d) The nature of any evidence offered by him.

The provisions of Article 32(2)-(6) of these Rules shall apply to the defense.

2. The time limit laid down in paragraph 1 of this Article may be extended by the President on a reasoned application by the defendant.

Article 36

1. The application initiating the proceedings and the defense may be supplemented by a reply to be filed within one month from the date of receipt of the defense and by a rejoined by the defendant within one month from the date of the receipt of the reply by the applicant.
2. The time limits laid down in paragraph 1 of this Article may be extended by the President.

Article 37

1. In reply or rejoinder a party may offer further evidence. The party

must, however, give reasons for the delay in offering it.
2. No new plea in law may be introduced in the course of proceedings unless it is based on matters of law or of fact which come to light in the course of the procedure.
3. If in the course of the procedure one of the parties puts forward a new plea in law which is so based, the President may, even after the expiry of the normal procedural time-limits, acting on a report of the Judge – Rapporteur and after hearing the parties, allow the other party time to answer on that plea.
4. The decision on the admissibility of the plea shall be reserved for the final judgment.

Article 38
1. The Court may, at any time, after hearing the parties order that two or more cases concerning the same subject matter shall, on account of the connection between them, be joined for the purposes of the written or oral procedure or of the final judgment.
2. The Cases may subsequently be disjoined.

Article 39
1. The President shall fix a date on which the Judge Rapporteur is to present his preliminary report to the Court, either
a) After the rejoined has been lodged, or
b) Where no reply or no rejoined has been lodged within the time limit fixed in accordance with Article 36(1) of these Rules, or
c) Where the party concerned has waived his right to lodge a reply or rejoined. Or
d) Where the expedited procedure referred to in Article 59 is to be applied, when the President fixes a date for the hearing.
2. The preliminary report shall contain recommendations as to whether a preparatory inquire or any other preparatory step should be undertaken it shall also contain a relief, if any, as to the possible omission of the oral part of the procedure of provided for in Article 53 of these rules.
3. The Court shall decide, what action to take upon the recommendations of the Judge – Rapporteur.

Article 40
1. Without prejudice to any special provisions laid down in these Rules, the procedure before the Court shall also include an oral pat. However, after the pleadings referred to in Article 32-39 as the case may be, have been lodged, the Court, acting on the application of a party setting out the reasons for which he wishes to be heard, may decide otherwise.
2. The application shall be submitted within a period of one month from notification to the party of the close of the written procedure, the President may extend that period.

Chapter II
PREPARATORY INQUIRIES AND OTHER PREPARATORY MEASURES
Section 1: Measures of Inquiry
Article 41

1. The Court shall decide the measure of inquire that it considers appropriate. Before the Court decides on the measures of inquiry the parties shall be heard. The decision of the Court shall be notified to the parties.
2. Without prejudice to Article 16 of the protocol the following measures of inquiry may be adopted:
a) The personal appearance of the parties;
b) A request for information and production of documents;
c) Oral testimony;
d) The commissioning of an expert's report;
e) An inspection of the place or thing in question.
3. The measures of inquiry that the Court has ordered shall be conducted by the Judge Rapporteur. The Court and parties shall take part in the measures of inquiry.
4. Evidence may be submitted in rebuttal and previous evidence may be amplified.

Article 42
The parties shall be entitled to attend the measures of inquiry.

Section 2: The Summoning and Examination of Witnesses and Experts
Article 43

1. The Court may, either of its own opinion or on application by a party, order that witnessed prove certain facts. The order of the Court shall set out the facts to be established.
2. The Court may summon a witness of its own motion or no application by a party to attend.
3. An application by a party for the examination of a witness shall state precisely about what facts and for what reasons the witness should be examined.
4. The witness shall be summoned by an order of the Court containing the following information:
a) The surname, forenames, description and address of the witness;
b) An indication of the facts about which the witness is to be examined;
c) Where appropriate, particulars of the arrangements made by the Court for reimbursement of expenses incurred by the witness, and of the penalties, which may be impose on defaulting witnesses.
5. The order shall be served on the parties and the witnesses.

6. The Court may make the summoning of the witnesses for whose examination a party has applied conditional upon the deposit with the Registry of the Court of a sum sufficient to cover the taxed costs thereof; the Court shall fix the amount of the payment. The Registry shall advance the funds necessary in connection with the examination of any witness summoned by the Court of its own motion.
7. After the identity of the witness has been established, the President shall inform him that he will be required to vouch the truth of his evidence in the manner laid down in these Rules.
8. The witness shall give his evidence to the Court, the parties having been given his main evidence the President may, at the request of a party or of his own motion, put questions to him.
9. The other Judges may do likewise. Subject to the control of the President, the representatives of the parties may put questions to witnesses.
10. Before giving his evidence his evidence, the witness shall take the following oath:
"I swear or declare that I will speak the truth, the whole truth and nothing but the truth."
11. The Chief Registrar shall draw up minutes in which the evidence of each witness is reproduced.
12. The minutes shall be signed by the President and by the Chief Registrar. Before the minutes are thus signed, witnesses must be given an opportunity to check the content of the minutes and to sign them. The minutes shall constitute an official record of the Court. Proceedings may be recorded by any modern technologies means.

Article 44

1. Witnesses who have been duly summoned shall obey the summons and attend for examination.
2. If a witness who has been duly summoned fails to appear before the Court, the Court may impose upon him a pecuniary penalty not exceeding UA 1 0001 and may order that a further summons be served on the witness at his own expense.
3. The same penalty may be imposed upon a witness who, without good reason, refuses to give evidence or to take the oath or where appropriate to make a solemn affirmation equivalent thereto.
4. If the witness proffers a valid excuse to the Court, the pecuniary penalty imposed on him may be cancelled. The pecuniary penalty imposed may be reduced at the request of the witness where he establishes that it is disproportionate to his income.

Article 45

1. The Court order than an expert's report be obtained. The order appointing the expert shall define his task and set a time limit within

2. The expert shall receive a copy of the order, together with all the documents necessary for carrying out his task. He shall be under the supervision of the Judge – Rapporteur, who may be present during his investigation and who shall be kept informed of his progress in carrying out his task.
3. The Court may request the parties or one of them to lodge security for the costs of the expert's report.
4. At the request of the expert, the Court may order the examination of witnesses. Their examination shall be carried out in accordance with Article 43 of these Rules.
5. The experts may give his opinion only on points, which have been expressly referred to him.
6. After the expert has made his report, the Court may order that he be examined, the parties having been given notice to attend.
7. Subject to control of the President, question may be put to the expert by the representatives of the parties.
8. Before carrying out his task, the expert shall take the following oath in written from or before the Court:
"I swear or declare that I shall conscientiously and impartially carrying out my task".

Article 46

1. If one of the parties objects to a witness or to an expert on the ground that he is not a competent or proper person to act as witness or expert or for any other reason, or if a witness or expert refuses to give evidence or, to take the oath or to make a solemn affirmation equivalent thereto, the matter shall be resolved by the Court.
2. An objections to a witness or to an expert shall be raised within two weeks after service of the order summoning the witness or appointing the expert; the statement of objection must set out the grounds of objection and indicate the nature of any evidence offered.

Article 47

Witnesses and Experts summoned by the Court shall be entitled to reimbursement of their travel and subsistence expenses. The Registry of the Court may make a payment to them towards these expenses in advance.

Article 48

The Court may, on application by a party or of its own motion, issue letters rogatory for the examination of witnesses or experts.

Article 49

1. The Chief Registrar shall draw up minutes of every hearing. The minutes shall be signed by the President and by the Chief Registrar and shall constitute an official record.

2. The parties may inspect the minutes and any expert's report at the Registry and obtain copies at their own expenses.

Section 3: Closure of the Preparatory Inquiry
Article 50
1. Unless the Court prescribes a period within which the parties may lodge written observations, the President shall fix the date for the opening of the oral procedure after the preparatory inquiry has been completed.
2. Where a period had been prescribed for the lodging of written observations, the President shall fix the date for the opening of the oral procedure after that period has expired.

Section 4: Preparatory Measures
Article 51
The Court may request the parties to submit within a specified period all such information relating to the facts, and all such documents or other particulars, as they may consider relevant. The information and/or documents provided shall be communicated to the other parties.

CHAPTER III
ORAL PROCEDURE
Article 52
1. Subject to the priority of decisions provided for in these Rules, the Court shall deal with the cases before it in the order in which the preparatory inquires in them have been completed. Where the preparatory inquires in several cases are completed simultaneously, the order in which they are to be dealt with shall be determined by the dates of entry in the register of the applications initiating them respectively.
2. The President may inn special circumstances order that a case be given priority over others. The President may in special circumstances, after hearing the parties, either on his own initiative or at the request of one of the parties defer a case to be dealt with at a later date. On a joint application by the parties the President may order that a case be deferred.

Article 53
1. The proceedings shall be opened and directed by the President, who shall be responsible for the proper conduct of the hearing.
2. The oral proceedings in cases heard in camera shall not be published.

Article 54
1. The President may in the course of the hearing put questions to the agents, advisers or lawyers of the parties.
2. The other Judges may do likewise.

Article 55

A party may address the Court only through his agent, adviser or lawyer.

Article 56

After the conclusion by the parties, the President shall declare the oral procedure closed.

Article 57

1. The Court may at time, in accordance with these rules, after hearing the parties, order any measure of inquiry to be taken or that a previous inquiry be repeated or expanded.
2. The Court may direct the Judge – Rapporteur to carry out the measures so ordered.

Article 58

The Court may order the reopening of the oral procedure.

Chapter IV
EXPEDITED PROCEDURE

Article 59

1. On application by the applicant or the defendant, the President may exceptionally decide, on the basis of the facts before him after hearing the other party, that a case is to be determined pursuant to an expedited procedure derogation from the provisions of these Rules, where the particular urgency of the case requires the Court shall give its rolling with the minimum of delay.
2. An application for a case to be decided under an expedited procedure shall be made by a separate document lodged at the same time as the application initiating the proceedings or the defense, as the case may be.
3. Under the expedited procedure, the originating application and the defense may be supplemented by a reply and a rejoined only if the President considers this to be necessary.
4. An interview may lodge a statement in intervention only if the President considers this to be necessary.
5. Once the defense has been lodged or, if the decision to adjudicate an expedited procedure is not made until after that pleading has been lodged, once that decision has been taken, the President shall fix a date for the hearing, which shall be communicated forthwith to the parties.
6. He may postpone the date of the hearing where the organization of measures of inquiry or of other preparatory measures so requires.
7. Without prejudice to rules, the parties may supplement their arguments and offer further evidence in the course of the oral procedure. They must, however, give reasons for the delay in offering such further evidence.
8. The Court shall give its ruling after hearing the parties.

Chapter V
JUDGMENTS
Article 60

The judgment contain:
a. A statement that it is the judgment of the Court,
b. The date of its delivery,
c. The names of the President and of the Judges taking part in it,
d. The name of the parties,
e. The name of the Chief Registrar,
f. The description of the parties,
g. The names of the agents, advisers and lawyers of the parties,
h. A statement of the forms of order sought by the parties,
i. A statement that the parties have been heard,
j. A summary of the facts,
k. The grounds for the decision.
l. The operative part of the judgment, including the decision as to costs.

Article 62
1. The judgment shall be delivered in open court.
2. The parties shall be given notice to attend to hear it.
3. The original of the judgment, signed by the President, and by the Judges who took part in the deliberations and by the Chief Registrar, shall be sealed and deposited at the Registry.
4. The parties shall be served with certified copies of the judgment.
5. The Chief Registrar shall record on the original of the judgement the date on which it was delivered.

Article 62
The judgment shall be binding from the date of its delivery.

Article 63
1. Without prejudice to the provisions relating to the interpretation of judgments the Court may, of its own motion or on application by a party made within one month after the delivery of judgement, rectify clerical mistakes, errors in calculation and obvious slips in it.
2. The parties whom the Chief Registrar shall duly notify may lodge written observations within a time prescribed by the President.
3. The original of the rectification order shall be annexed to the original of the rectified judgment. A note of this order shall be made in the margin of the original of the rectified judgment.

Article 64
1. Where the Court omits to give a decision on a special head of claim or on costs, any party may within a month after service of the judgment apply to the Court to supplement its judgment.
2. The application shall be served on the opposite party who has one

month within which to lodge written observations. The time limit laid down in paragraph 1 and 2 of this Article may be extended by the President on a reasoned application by the party.
3. After these observations have been lodged, the Court shall decide both on the admissibility and on the substance of the application.

Article 65
The Chief Registrar shall arrange for the publication of reports of cases before the Court.

Chapter VI
COSTS
Article 65
1. A decision as to costs shall be given in the final judgment or in the order, which closes the proceedings.
2. The unsuccessful party shall be ordered to pay the costs if they have been applied for in the successful party's pleadings.
3. Where there are several unsuccessful parties the Court shall decide how the costs are to be shared.
4. Where each party succeeds on some and fails on other heads, or where the Circumstances are exceptional; the Court may order that the costs be shared or that the parties bear their own costs.
5. The Court may order a party, even if successful, to pay costs which the Court considers that party to have unreasonably or vexaciously caused the opposite party to incur.
6. The Member States and institutions, which intervene in the proceedings, shall bear their own costs.
7. The Court may order an intervener other than those mentioned in the preceding subparagraphs to bear his own costs.
8. A party who discontinues or withdraws from proceedings shall be ordered to pay the costs if they have been applied for it in the other party's observations on the discontinuance.
9. However, upon application by the party who discontinues or withdraws from proceedings, the costs shall be borne by the other party if this appears justified by the conduct of that party.
10. Where the Parties have come to an arrangement on costs, the decision as to costs shall be in accordance with that agreement.
11. If costs are not claimed, the parties shall bear their own costs.
12. Where case does not proceed to judgment the costs shall be in the discretion of the Court.

Article 67
Costs necessarily incurred by a party in executing a judgment or order of the Court shall be refunded by the opposite party on the scale in force in the State where the execution takes place.

Article 68
Proceedings before the Court shall be free of charge, except that:

a) Where a party has caused the Court to incur avoidable costs the Court may, after hearing the parties, order that party to refund them;
b) Where copying or translation work is carried out at the request of a party, the costs shall, in so far as the Chief Registrar considers tit excessive, he paid for by that party on the scale of charges referred to in Article 13(5) of these Rules.

Article 69
Without prejudice to the preceding Article, the following shall be regarding as recoverable costs:
a) Sums payable to witnesses and experts under Article 47 of these Rules.
b) Expenses necessarily incurred by the parties for the purpose of the proceedings, in particular the travel and subsistence expenses and the remuneration of agents, advisers or lawyers.

Article 70
1. If there is a dispute concerning the costs to be recovered, the Court shall, on application by the party concerned and after hearing the opposite party, make an order.
2. The parties may, for the purposes of enforcement, apply for an authenticated copy of the order.

Article 71
1. Sums due from the Registry of the Court shall be paid in the currency of the country where the Court has its seat.
2. At the request of the person entitled to any sum, it shall be paid in the currency of the country where the expenses to be refunded were incurred or where the steps in respect of which payment is due were taken.
3. Other debtors shall make payment in the currency of their country of origin.
4. Conversions of currency shall be made at the official rates of exchange ruling on the day of payment in the country where the Court has its seat.

Chapter VII
DISCONTINUANCE
Article 72
If, before the Court has given its decision, the parties reach a settlement of their dispute and intimate to the Court the abandonment of their claims, the President shall order the case to be removed from the register and shall give a decision as to costs in accordance with Article 66(8), having regard to any proposals made by the parties on the matter.

Article 73
If the applicant informs the Court in writing that he wishes to discontinue the proceedings, the President shall order the case to be removed from the register and shall give a decision as to costs in accordance with Article 66(8)

of these Rules.

Chapter VIII
SERVICE
Article 74

1. Where these Rules require that a document be served on a person, the Chief Registrar shall ensure that service is effected at that person's address for service either by the dispatch of a copy of the document by registered post with a form for acknowledgement of receipt or by personal delivery of a copy against a receipt.
2. The Chief Registrar shall prepare and certify the copies of documents to be served, save where the parties themselves supply the copies in accordance with Article 32(1) of these Rules.
3. Where, in accordance with Article 33(3), of these Rules the addressee has agreed that service is to be effected on him by telefax or other technical means of communication, any procedural document other than a judgment or order of the Court may be served by the transmission of a copy of the document by such means.
4. Where, for technical reasons or on account of the nature or length of the document, such transmission is impossible or impracticable, the document shall be served, if the addressee has failed to state an address for service, at his address in accordance with the procedures laid down in paragraph 1 of this Article.
5. The addressee shall be so advised by the telefax or other technical means of communication.
6. Service shall then be deemed to have been effected on the addressee by registered post on the tenth day following the lodging of the registered letter at the post office of the place where the Court has its seat, unless it is shown by the acknowledgement of receipt that the letter was received on a different date or the addressee informs the Chief Registrar, within three weeks of being advised by telefax or other technical means of communication, that the document to be served has not reached him.

Chapter IX
TIME-LIMITS
Article 75

1. Any period of time prescribed by the Community Treaty or, the Court or these Rules for the taking of any procedural step shall be reckoned as follows:
a) Where a period expressed in days, weeks, months or years is to be calculated from the moment at which an event occurs or an action takes place, the day during which that event occurs or that action

	takes place shall not be counted as falling within the period in question;
b)	A period expressed in weeks, months or in years shall end with the expiry of whichever day in the last week, month or year is the same day of the week, or falls on the same date, as the day during which the event or action from which the period is to be calculated occurred or took place. If, in a period expressed in months or in years, the day on which it should expire does not occur in the last month, the period shall end with the expiry of the last day of that month;
c)	Where a period is expressed in months and days, it shall first be reckoned in whole months, then in days;
d)	Periods shall include official holidays, Sundays and Saturdays;
e)	Periods shall not be suspended during the judicial vacations.
2.	If the period would otherwise end on a Saturdays, Sunday or an official holiday, it shall be extended until the end of the first following working day.

A list of official holidays drawn up by the Court shall be published in the Official Journal of the Community.

Article 76

1. Where the period of time allowed for initiating proceedings against a measure adopted by an institution runs from the publication of that measure, that period shall be calculated, for the purposes of Article 75(1) (a), from the end of the 14th day after publication thereof in the Official Journal of the Community.
2. The prescribed time limits shall be extended on account of distance by a single period of ten days.

Article 77

1. Any time-limit prescribed pursuant to these Rules may be extended by whosoever prescribed it.
2. The President may delegate to the Vice President power of signature for the purpose of fixing time limits which, pursuant to these Rules, it fails to them to prescribe or of extending such time-limit.

Chapter X
STAY OF PROCEDURE
Article 78

1. The proceedings may be stayed:
a) In all cases, by decision of the President adopted after hearing the parties and, save in the case of references for a preliminary ruling.
b) The proceedings may be resumed by order or decision, following the same procedure.
c) The orders or decisions referred to in this paragraph shall be served on the parties.

2. The stay of proceedings shall take effect on the date indicated in the order or decision of stay or, in the absence of such indication, on the date of that order or decision.
3. While proceedings are stayed time shall cease to run for the purposes of prescribed time limits for all parties.
4. Where the order or decision of stay does not fix the length of stay, it shall end the date indicated in the order or decision of resumption or, in the absence of such indication, on the date of the order or decision or resumption.
5. From the date of resumption time shall begin to run afresh for the purposes of the time limits.

TITTLE III
SPECIAL FORMS OF PROCEDURE
Chapter 1
SUSPENSION OF OPERATION OR ENFORCEMENT AND OTHER INTERIM MEASURES
Article 79

1. An application under Article 20 of the Protocol shall state the subject-matter of the proceedings, the circumstances giving rise to urgency and the pleas of fact and law establishing a prima facie case for the interim measures applied for.
2. The application shall be made by a separate document and in accordance with the provisions of Article 32 and 33 of these Rules.

Article 80

1. The application shall be serves on the opposite party, and the President shall prescribe a short period within which that party may submit written or oral observations.
2. The President may order a preparatory inquiry.

Article 81

1. The President shall refer the application to the Court within 48 hours.
2. If the President is absent or prevented from attending, Article 8 of these Rules shall apply. Where the application is referred to it, the Court shall postpone all other cases, and shall give a decision after hearing the parties. Article 80 shall apply.

Article 82

1. The decision on the application shall take the form of a reasoned order. The order shall be served on the parties forthwith.
2. The execution of the order may be made conditional on the lodging by the Applicant of security, of an amount and nature to be fixed in the light of the circumstances.
3. Unless the order fixes the date on which the interim measure is to

lapse, the measure shall lapse when final judgement is delivered.
4. The order shall have only an interim effect, and shall be without prejudice to the decision of the Court on the substance of the case.

Article 83
On application by a party, the order may at any time be varied or cancelled on account of a change in circumstances.

Article 84
Rejection of an application for an interim measure shall not bar the party who made it from making a further application on the basis of new facts.

Article 85
The provisions of this Chapter shall apply to applications to suspend the execution of a decision of the Court or of any measure adopted by another institution, submitted pursuant to these rules. The order granting the application shall fix, where appropriate, a date on which the interim measure is to lapse.

Article 86
1. The President shall give his decision in the form of an order. Article 82 of these Rules shall apply.
2. If the President is absent or prevented from attending, Article 8 of these Rules shall apply.

Chapter II
PRELIMINARY PROCEDURE
Article 87
1. A party applying to the Court for a decision on a preliminary objection or other preliminary plea not going to the substance of the case shall make the application by a separate document.
2. The application must state the plea of fact and law relied on and the form of order sought by the applicant and any supporting documents must be annexed to it.
3. As soon as the application has been lodged, the President shall prescribe a period within which the opposite party may lodge a document containing a statement of the form of order sought by that party and its pleas in law.
4. Unless the Court decides otherwise, the reminder of the proceedings shall be oral.
5. The Court shall, after hearing the parties decides on the application or reserve its decision for the final judgment. If the Court refuses the application or reserves its decision, the President shall prescribe new time limits for the further steps in the proceedings.

Article 88
1. Where it is clear that the Court has no jurisdiction to take

cognizance of an action or where the action is manifestly inadmissible, the Court may, by reasoned order, after hearing the parties and without taking further steps in the proceedings, give a decision.

2. The Court mat at any time of its own motion consider whether there exists any absolute bar to proceeding with a case or declare, after hearing the parties, that the action has become devoid of purpose and that there is no need to adjudicate on it; it shall give its decision in accordance with Article 87(4) and (5) of these Rules.

Chapter III
INTERVENTION
Article 89

1. An application to intervene must be made within six weeks of the publication of the notice referred to in Article 13(6) of these Rules.

The application shall contain:
a) The description of the case;
b) The description of the parties;
c) The name and address of the intervener;
d) The intervener's address for service at the place where the Court has its seat;
e) The form of order sought, by one or more of the parties, in support of which the intervener is applying foe leave to intervene;
f) A statement of the circumstances establishing the right to intervene, where the application is submitted pursuant to Article 21 of the protocol. The intervener shall be represented in accordance with Article 12 protocol. Articles 32 and 33 of these Rules shall apply

2. The application shall be served on the parties. The President shall give the parties an opportunity to submit their written or oral observations before deciding on the application. The President shall refer the application to the Court.

3. If the Court allows the intervention, the intervener shall receive a copy of every document served on the parties. The Court may, however, on application by one of the parties, omit secret or confidential documents.

4. The intervener must accept the case as he finds it at the time of his intervention.

5. The President shall prescribe a period within which the intervener may submit a statement in intervention. The statement in intervention shall contain:

a) A statement of the form of order sought by the intervener in support of or opposing, in whole or in part, the form of order sought by one of the parties;

b) The pleas in law and arguments relied on by the intervener;

c) Where appropriate, the nature of any evidence offered.
6. After the statement in intervention has been lodged, the President shall, where necessary, prescribe a time limit within which the parties may reply to that statement.
7. Consideration may be given to an application to intervene, which is made after the expiry of the period prescribed in paragraph 1 but before the decision to open the oral procedure provided for in Article 40(1). In that event, if the President allows the intervention, the intervener may, on the basis of the Report for the Hearing communicated to him, submit his observation during the oral procedure, if that procedure takes place.

Chapter V
EXCEPTIONAL REVIEW PROCEDURE
Section 1: Third-party proceedings
Article 91

1. Articles 32 and 33 of these Rules shall apply to an application initiating third-party proceedings. In addition such an application shall:
a) Specify the judgment contested;
b) State how that judgment is prejudiced to the rights of the third party;
c) Indicate the reasons for which the third party was unable to take part in the original case.
2. The application must be made against all parties to the original case.
3. Where the judgement has been published in the *Official Journal of the Community,* the application must be lodged within two months of the publication.
4. The Court may, on application by the third party, order a stay of execution of the judgment.
5. The provisions of Title III, Chapter I, of these Rules shall apply.
6. The contested judgment shall be varied on the points on which the submissions of the third party are upheld.
7. The original of the judgment in the third-party proceedings shall be annexed to the original of the contested judgment. A note of the judgment in the third-party proceedings shall be made in the margin of the original of the contested judgment.

Section 2: REVISION
Article 92

An application for revision of the judgment shall be made within three months of the date on which the application is based came to the applicant's knowledge.

Article 93

1. Articles 32 and 33 of these Rules shall apply to an application for revision.
2. In addition such an application shall:
a) Specify the judgment contested;
b) Indicate the points on which the judgment is contested;
c) Set out the facts on which the application is based;
d) Indicate the nature of the evidence to show that there are facts justifying revision of the judgement, and that the time laid down in Article 92 has been observed.
3. The application must be made against all parties to the case in which the contested judgment was given.

Article 94

1. Without prejudice to its decision on the substance, the Court in closed session, shall, after hearing the parties and having regard to the written observations of the parties, give in the form of ta judgment its decision on the admissibility of the application.
2. If the Court finds the application admissible, it shall proceed to consider the substance of the application and shall give its decision in the form of a judgment in accordance with these Rules.
3. The original of the revising judgment shall be annexed to the original of the Judgment revised. A note of the revising judgment shall be made in the margin of the original of the judgement revised.

Chapter VI
INTERPRETATION OF JUDGMENT
Article 95

1. An application for interpretation of a judgment under Article 23 of the Protocol shall be made accordance with Article 32 and 33 of these Rules. In addition it shall specify:
a) The judgment in question;
b) The passages of which interpretation is sought.
2. The application must be made against all the parties to the case I which the judgment was given.
3. The Court shall give its decision in the form of a judgment after having given the parties an opportunity to submit their observations and after hearing the parties.
4. The original of the interpreting judgment shall be annexed to the original of the judgment interpreted.
5. A note of the interpreting judgment shall be made in the margin of the original judgment interpreted.

Chapter VII
OPINIONS
Article 96

1. Any request by any of the institutions of the Community, for an opinion pursuant to Articles 10 of the Protocol shall be served on the Chief Registrar, who shall immediately inform member states, notifying them of the time limit fixed by the President for receipt of their written observations or for hearing their oral declarations.
2. The request for advisory opinion as contained in paragraph 1 of Article 10 shall be made in writing.
3. The request shall contain a statement of the question upon which the advisory opinion is required.
4. The stamen shall be accompanied by all relevant documents likely to throw light upon the question.
5. The Court shall give the advisory opinion in public.
6. In the exercise of the advisory function, the Court shall be governed by the Protocol, which applied in continuous cases where the Court recognizes them to be applicable.

Article 97

1. As soon as the request for an Advisory Opinion has been lodged, the President shall designate a judge to act as Rapporteur.
2. The Court sitting in closed session shall, after hearing the Judge give its decision.
3. The Opinion shall be delivered in accordance with the provisions of Article 10 of the Protocol.
4. The Opinion, signed by the President, by the Judges who took part in the Deliberations and by the Chief Registrar, shall be served on the Institution concerned.

TITLE IV
MISCELLANEOUS PROVISIONS
Article 98

The President shall instruct any person who is requires to take an oath before the Court, as witness or expert, to tell the truth or to carry out his task conscientiously and impartially, as the case may be, and shall warn him of the criminal liability provided for I his national law in the event of any breach of this duty.

Article 99

Subject to the provisions of the Protocol and after consultation, the Court shall adopt supplementary rules concerning its practice in relation to:
a) Letters rogatory;
b) Reports of perjury by witnesses or experts.

Article 100
The Court may issue practice directions relating in particular to the preparation and conduct of the hearings before it and to the lodging of written statements of case or written observations

Article 101
These Rules, which are authentic in the languages mentioned in Article 87 of the Treaty shall be published in the Official Journal of the Community and shall become valid soon after their publication.

REFERENCES
Baljit Singh (1989): Definition and prevention of terrorism
Bintliff, Russel L., (2010) Preparing and Responding to Bomb threats and letter Bombs Manual
Blacks Law Dictionary 5th Edition 1979; Page 479
Cartegena Action Plan 2010 – 2014 (Ending the sufferings caused by anti-personnel Mines).
Collin King, (2010) Publication Title: Jane's mines and mine clearance
Community Court of Justice (2010) Law Report Ccjelr; 221 – 229.
Community Court Of Justice, Ecowas Law Report (2010) CCJELR
Constitution Of Federal Republic Of Nigeria 1999 (as amended)
Court Of Justice, Ecowas Law Report (2004-2009) CCJELR
Dappa Sogbere Ph.D: A Hand Book of imstructions on Explosive Ordnance Disposal (EOD) In The Nigerian Police Published 2012 by Keny & Brothers Enterprises, Asata Enugu, Nigeria
Evidence Act 2011
Hollman B., (1999): "Inside terrorism", Columbia University Press,
Leon Friedman, The Law of War; A Documentary History
Oladele Akadiri: Diplomacy World peace and security
Samuel J. Hooper, (1941 – 1980): The History of U.S. Army Bomb Disposal and Explosive Ordnance Disposal
Theodore Okonkwo – Ph.D: The Law Enforcement Liability 2nd Edition
Theodore Okonkwo. International Protection of the Environment: Law and Practice
Udenwa Achike: Nigeria/Biafra Civil War: My Experience
Wikipedia – The Online Encyclopaedia

JOURNALS
Health Organization, 2003: Article
Kenneth R. Rutherford (Rutherford), Peer-to-peer Support Vital to
Landmines Monitor 2008. 2011 (Glossary)
Newspoint Newspaper Vol. 8; No. 71 June 4 – 5, 2012
Nicholas E. Walsh and Wendy S. Walsh, The Bulletin of the World
Programme of Event for the Stockpile Destruction Ceremony of Unexploded Ordnance and Explosive Remnants of War (ERW) dated 15th September, 2011.
Programme of Events for the Official Blast off Ceremony of Demining Project in the Civil War Affected Parts of Nigeria dated 29th June, 2009.
Seminal Paper: The Role of International Donors in Assisting Mine Victims in Nigeria by Bala B. Yakubu dated 8th September, 2011
The Journal Of Erw And Mine Action: Issue 14.2/Summer 2010

PERIODICALS
Abia Daniel, Living With Bombs – Insider Weekly; Aug 31, 2009
Communique of Stakeholders in Owerri; dated 25th January, 2012.
The Nationa on Sunday September 14, 2014; Page 3

INDEX

178,000 sq. kilometers of land	-	69
178000 Sq. Kilo. Of Lands	-	32
50, 000 Bombs	-	77
656 Locations containing Landmines	-	69, 70
A Military Tribunal	-	52
A.E. Udofia Chief	-	4
Aba	-	15
Abakaliki Ebonyi State	-	73
Abandoned Bombs	-	31
Abandoned Explosive Ordnance	-	54
Abba	-	22
ABBA	-	22
Abubakar Tafawa Balewa	-	10
Aburi	-	11
Achike Udenwa	-	52, 58
Action Group	-	10
Ada Ugorji Nwauwa	-	16
Adamawa	-	33
Adebayo Brigedier	-	11
Adekunle Fajuyi (Col.)	-	11
Adetokunbo Kayode (SAN)	-	116
Afikpo	-	12
Agwu	-	17
Ahiara Mbaise	-	25
Akokwa	-	22
Alex N.N Williams	-	112, 114
Alhaji Shehu Shagari	-	32
Aloysius Mefor	-	18
Amadi Bello	-	10, 11
Amakohia Ubi	-	18
Ambassador Maria O. Laose	-	109
Angola	-	78
Aniebo I.N.C	-	52
Anti-Handling device	-	37
Anti-Personnel Mine	-	37
Anti-Personnel Mines	-	31
Anti-Tank Mine	-	55
Anti-Vehicle Land Mines	-	31
Aquinas Sec. School Osu Mbano	-	73
AXO's	-	33

Awgu	-	12
Awo-Mmama	-	29
AXO's	-	31
Ayozie Njoku	-	26
B.O.G Awuzie	-	24
Bakassi Peninsular	-	77
Bala Yakubu	-	70, 112, 123
Bama	-	33
Battle Area Clearance	-	62
Bende	-	73
Benny Chabki	-	123
Biafra Army	-	58
Biafra Note	-	25
Biafra shore-Battery	-	58
Biafran Army	-	29
Biafran Mines	-	58
Biafrian Army	-	13
Boko Haram	-	32, 33
Bomb Detection	-	151, 155
Bomb	-	31, 53, 76, 152
Bon Okereafor	-	74
Boniface Akanwa	-	74
Boniface Onwuliri	-	74
Bosnia Herzegovina	-	79
Brusels Declaration of 27 June, 1997	-	36
C. I Nebo	-	122
C.A. Nwawoo Brig	-	4
Calabar	-	12
Cambodia	-	79
Canada	-	34
Carl E. Case: Mine Free Central Africa	-	71
Cartegena (Colombia)	-	78
Cartagena Action Plan	-	123
Charles H.T Uhegbu	-	118, 123
Mine Fields	-	103
Chief A.E. Bassey	-	2
Uzoma Onyeike, Barr.	-	113
Chief P.I. Okeke	-	4
China	-	78
Chukwu Dolue	-	17
Chukwuemeka Odumegwu Ojukwu Lt. Col.	-	1, 5, 7, 11

Chukwukadibia Agwuocha Noel	-	113, 123
Clementina Chinyere Chikezie	-	74
Cletus Akpan Ogbonna	-	74
Contaminated Areas	-	32
Convention on Certain Conventional Weapons	-	67
Croatia	-	80
Dappa Sogbere	-	163, 164, 165, 170, 171
David Ejoor Lt. Col.	-	11
David Ogunewe Lt. Col.	-	4
De-mining	-	59
Dennis Osadebe	-	10
Department of State Security Service	-	123
Diobu	-	14
Dodan Barracks	-	4
Donatus Obilor	-	74
Dr. Emeka Uhegbu	-	118, 123
E. Aguma	-	3
East Central State	-	5
Eastern Nigeria	-	11
Eastern Region	-	11, 33
ECOWAS Court	-	94, 95, 96, 98, 99, 101, 112, 113, 122, 123, 124
ECOWAS	-	72
Eddie Opara	-	74
Edwin Ukachukwu	-	23
Egbema	-	18, 19, 23
Egbu	-	19, 26, 28
Egwe Oguta	-	23
Ejemekuru	-	18
Ekeocha	-	26
Emetom	-	21
Emii	-	29
Emmanuel Mjiole Onwuka	-	18
Emmanuel Opara	-	23
End of War Speech	-	59
Eni Njoku Prof.	-	4
Environment	-	149
Ernest Ihejirika	-	21
ERW's	-	31
Etiti	-	20
Etuk John Essien	-	123
Evil Forest	-	53
Existing Explosive Remnant of War	-	54

Explosive Ordnance Disposal (EOD)	-	57, 62
Explosive Ordnance	-	54
Explosive Remnants of War	-	31, 33
Eze Richard	-	74
Ezi Orsu	-	23
Eziama Ikeduru	-	19
Femi Falana	-	123
Festus Okotiebo	-	10, 11
Francis Njoku	-	74
Francis Obi	-	16
Fulani Hides men	-	32
G.U. Nneji	-	15
Gabriel Kamalu	-	18, 23
Gabriesl Ugwuoha	-	18
Gaza Strip	-	87
General Gowon	-	3, 4, 12
Geoffrey Okorie	-	18, 20
Georgia	-	78, 80
Ghana	-	11
Godwin Nwaneri Rev.	-	29
Gombe	-	33
Gwoza	-	33
Harold Hongju Koh	-	100
Hassan Kastina Lt. Col.	-	11
Helen Opara	-	26
Humanitarian demining	-	56
I. Eke Dr.	-	4
Ibeme	-	19
Ibeme	-	19
Igbos	-	11
Ike C. Ibe	-	113
Ike C. Ibe	-	123
Ikot Ekpene Sector	-	27
Ikot Ekpene	-	15
Ikwere	-	13
Imo State Govt. House	-	73
Improvised Explosive Device (IED)	-	155
Information Management (IM)	-	61
Injury to Citizens	-	31
International Campaign to Ban Land Mines	-	36
International Court of Justice	-	135
International Court	-	97

International Humanitarian Law	-	37, 53
International Red Cross	-	36
Iran	-	86
Irete	-	15
Irete	-	28
Izombe	-	16
J. E Nyambi	-	25
J.E. Nyambi	-	20
J.I. Emembolu	-	4
J.I. Ezeilo Wing Commander	-	4
J.M. Echeruo Chief	-	4
J.P Iyang	-	27
J.P. Iyang	-	15
J.T. Aguiyi Ironsi Major Gen.	-	11
Jams Okenwa	-	26
Jordan	-	81
Joseph Egbujuo Dike Ukwu	-	74
Joseph Ngozi Okere	-	74
Jude Ujunwa Egbe	-	74
Justice Nlemibe	-	17
Kano Uprisings	-	32
Kenneth R. Rutherford	-	71
Kidnaping	-	32
Kidnapping	-	63
Konduga Battle	-	33
Kosovo	-	85
L.N. Akparanta	-	24
Land Mines	-	30, 53, 54, 58, 89
Lebanon	-	87
Lao PDR	-	81
Live Bombs	-	77
Livinus Eke Nnadi	-	74
Louis Mbanefo	-	3
Madagali	-	33
Maiduguri	-	33
R. Ogbonna (Major-Gen.) Rtd	-	27
Malawi	-	86
Manual Demining	-	61
Maria Okorie	-	74
Mark 47 SMC Riffles	-	58
Massacre of Ibos	-	11
Matthew Ozuzu	-	26

Mbaise	-	24, 25
Mechanical Mine Clearance (MMC)	-	62
Meeting of State Parties	-	47
Mgbele Refugee Camp	-	17
Michael Okpara	-	10
Military Demining	-	59
Min Ban Treaty	-	60
Mine Action Center	-	122
Mine Areas	-	31
Mine Awareness Campaign	-	116
Mine Ban Treaty	-	35, 90
Mine Detection Dog (MOD)	-	62
Mine Fields	-	31
Mine Risk Education (MRE)	-	61
Mine Risk Education	-	103
Mine Victims	-	72
Mine	-	37
Ministry of Defence	-	110
Ministry of Environment	-	110
Ministry OF Foreign Affairs	-	110
Moldova	-	82
Moses Emeanuru	-	123
Mozambique	-	84
Myanmar	-	78
Nairobi Action Plan	-	102
Nathaniel Chimezie	-	18
National Red Cross	-	40
NATO	-	83
Naze	-	26
Ndegwu	-	18
Ngor Okpala LGA	-	74
Ngwaland	-	63
Nicholas E. Walsh & Wendy S. Walsh	-	60
Nig. Defence Academy	-	35
Nigeria Civil War	-	30
Nigeria Police Force	-	110
Nigeria Soldiers	-	28
Nigeria	-	88
Nigerian Biafran War	-	30
Nkechi Osuji	-	74
Nkwesi	-	17

Nnamdi Azikiwe	-	10
Northern Iraq	-	86
Northern People's Congress	-	10
Northern Region	-	11
Nsukka	-	12
Nwogu	-	74
O.A.U	-	3, 8
Obinikpa	-	23
Obinze	-	15
Obolo	-	19
Obudi Agwu	-	16
Odi	-	32
Odua People's Congress (OPC)	-	32
Ogbaku	-	15
Ogbunigwe	-	12, 58
Ogwa	-	20
Ohaji Farm Settlement	-	17
Ohiafia	-	73
Ohoba in Ohaji/Egbema LGA	-	73
Ojukwu Bucket	-	12, 58
Okigwe	-	20
Olusegun Obasanjo Gen. (Rt.)	-	69
Onitsha	-	13
Onukaogu	-	21
Onyeami Cyriacus Chukwuma	-	74
Organization of African States	-	71
Orie Amaraku	-	22
Orlu	-	20
Orlu	-	22
Orogwe	-	15
Osina	-	22
Oslo Norway	-	49
Ottawa Convention	-	32, 65, 66
Ottawa Declaration of Oct. 1996	-	36
Owerri	-	15, 20, 22
P.C. Amadi	-	3
Pakistan	-	78
Patrick Amadi	-	5
Patrick Anwuna Lt. Col.	-	5
Patrick Okeke	-	5
Pauline Ijeoma Ufom	-	123
Philip Effiong (Maj. Gen)	-	3, 4
Port Harcourt	-	13, 14
Prince Charles Ozuzu	-	123

Prince Chukwuemeka Charles Ozuzu	-	30
R.M.S Shittu	-	122
Radio Biafra	-	58
Refugee Camp	-	16
Reginald Odunze	-	14
Republic of Biafra	-	12
Republic of Biafra	-	103
Red Crescent	-	36
Rising Sun of Biafra	-	5
Rules of ECOWAS Court	-	133
Russia	-	78
Rwanda	-	86
S.L Maduagwu	-	26
Sambisa Forest	-	33
Samuel Ladoke Akintola	-	10, 11
Serbia	-	82
Shedrack Njoku	-	18
Shores of Otaba	-	58
South Iraq	-	81
South-East Zone	-	31
South-East, South-South	-	32
Sri Lanka	-	86
St. Patrick's Sec. School Ogbe Ahiazu Mbaise	-	73
St. Peter Clever Seminary Okpuala	-	73
State House Enugu (Etiti)	-	21
Stock Pilling	-	54
Sudan	-	82
Sylvester Mbakwe	-	16
Sylvester Ezeukwu	-	14
Taiwo Abidogun	-	122
Tajikistan	-	87
Task Impact Assessment TIA)	-	61
Terrorism	-	152, 153
Thailand	-	83
The Charities International	-	12
The International Red Cross Society	-	12
Theodore Okoronkwo	-	135, 151
Transfer	-	37
Types of Explosives	-	156, 157
U. Thant	-	8
U.N	-	58, 73

U.N	-	73
Ubakala	-	25
Uganda	-	83
Ugiri Mbano	-	22
Uguta	-	14
Ukpabi Asika	-	72
Ulakwo Obube	-	29
Umuahia	-	11, 63
Umudum Mbano	-	20
Umuguma	-	15, 17
Umuna	-	21
UN Headquarters in New York	-	49
Unexploded Ordnance	-	54
UNITA	-	78
United Nations Voluntary Trust fund	-	40
United Nations	-	8, 32
United Progressive Grand Alliance	-	10
Uratta County Council	-	26
Urualla Orlu	-	21
USA	-	60
USO's	-	33
UXO's	-	31
Uzoagba Ikeduru	-	19
Uzoakoli	-	73
Victim Assistance	-	90, 91
Victims Assistance Commission	-	76
Victims	-	32, 88
Vietnam	-	84
Vincent Agu	-	74
Vivian Kelechi Obasi	-	74
W.A. Anuku Capt.	-	4
Western House of Assembly	-	10
Western Sahara	-	85
World Council of Church (WCC)	-	12
Yakubu Gowon	-	11, 52, 59
Yar'adua Musa	-	69
Yobe	-	33
Zakibiam	-	32
Zambia	-	84

www.ingramcontent.com/pod-product-compliance
Lightning Source LLC
Chambersburg PA
CBHW051638170526
45167CB00001B/247